A New Song

From the backstreets of Liverpool to a
global House Fellowship movement

Gill Silver

O&U
Onwards & Upwards

Onwards and Upwards Publishers

4 The Old Smithy
London Road
Rockbeare
EX5 2EA
United Kingdom

www.onwardsandupwards.org

First edition, published in the United Kingdom by Onwards and Upwards Publishers Ltd. (2024).

ISBN: 978-1-78815-961-6
Typeface: Sabon LT

"He hath put a new song in my mouth –
Praise to our God;
Many will see it and fear,
And will trust in the LORD."

Psalm 40:3

Acknowledgements

The Fellowships who have shared their history and testimonies in this book are not exhaustive, as some of the original groups no longer exist. Others continue to meet but are not mentioned, whilst others meet under a slightly different umbrella.

Some of the original groups include those that were in Ripon, Leamington Spa, Otley, Grimsby, Whitley Bay, Nottingham, Newton Abbot, Tiverton and Broadstone in Dorset.

Others include Leeds, Walsall, Leominster, Lampeter and Bracknell. From the original Liverpool Fellowships, we now have off-shoots such as Sefton, Prescott, The City Church, New Beginnings and Warrington. One of the off-shoots, Day Spring, has now closed.

We would like to extend our gratitude to the staff at Cliff College, Derbyshire, for providing a photograph of one of their original Nissen huts that were used for accommodation during our conference days with them as well as allowing us to use their photograph of the conference centre shown from their main college, as seen on their website.

Another sincere 'thank you' goes to Sue Heathcote for kindly sharing her photos of her parents, Bob and Norah Love, which have been included in tributes to them.

We do apologise for needing to edit some of the testimonies, but we were required to remain within the editorial limits.

We are particularly grateful, too, to Roger Jacobs, an elder of the Longcroft church, who has tirelessly helped with editing and proof-reading, as well as Julian Cliff and Barbara Llendup, and Peter Elks, also an elder of The Longcroft, who has been so supportive in many ways.

Not least, we are more than grateful to all of you who have given your time and thoughts in sharing with us and contributing to this amazing story, which, as you will know, is still ongoing. We have all been so encouraged by how God has worked; the miracles that He has wrought and the love and grace He has poured out into countless lives, not only throughout the UK but globally.

Contents

Foreword by Ron Bailey iii

Introduction v

1. The End of an Era 1

2. Early Preparations 10

3. Queens Road, Liverpool 21

4. Jenny's Story 41

5. Devonshire Road..51

6. The Longcroft 71

7. Expansion and Growth 88
    Birmingham; Victoria Park Christian Fellowship, Manchester; further outreach, Manchester

8. Further Growth and Expansion in the South East 100
    Crystal Palace; Hotton Kirby; Topsham, Eltham Green, London; Winchmore Hill Christian Fellowship, London; Earley Christian Fellowship, Reading; Worthing Christian Fellowship, Sussex; Beaconsfield Christian Fellowship, Broadstairs

9. Exeter 114

10. "Give Me This Valley" 131

11. Epsom Christian Fellowship 139

12. Auchenheath House 161

13. Conferences 172

14. Special Features of the Fellowships 189

Conclusion 215

Appendix 1: Additional Testimonies 217

Appendix 2: What About Head Covering? 237

Appendix 3: Tributes 244

Appendix 4: UK Fellowships..275

Appendix 5: Missionary Outreach Abroad..........................279

A New Song

Foreword by Ron Bailey

For over 40 years Ron Bailey has been engaged in pastoral care and Bible teaching in a variety of settings at home in the UK and in many parts of the world. This has included home groups, churches, Bible schools and conferences, local radio and TV. He also hosts 'The Biblebase' – a teaching resource for Bible students to be found at biblebase.com.

Luke's Gospel begins with a claim that he had included those *"who from the beginning were eyewitnesses"[1]*. While not claiming the same degree of inspiration, Gill Silver has done us the service of providing a warm and affectionate collection of persons and events that illuminate the events and experiences of 'things from the beginning'; the beginning, that is, of a remarkable movement of the Spirit of God.

She was well-placed to observe and relate the touch of God on a variety of people and places. These records have filled in a lot of gaps for me and warmed my heart to hear of the early days of many whom I have since come to love and know as friends and colleagues. Many of them have already gone on to greater service, but the Song lives on in various expressions throughout the world.

As I read, I marvel at the united and unique ministry of three men in particular: G.W. North, Norman Meeten and Dave Wetherly. Mr North, as he preferred to be called, was born in 1913 and his style and poise were almost the exact opposite of Dave Wetherly, who was a whirlwind of abandoned love and service. Norman Meeten, an ex-Anglican curate, was often referred to by Mr North as "the father of the Fellowships", and his long-term pastoral care of younger leaders was fundamental to the early growth of the Fellowships. If Norman Meeten was the father of the Fellowships, then Mr North was a spreading flame of life and truth. His life and teaching opened up hearts and minds to a fresh expression of the gospel. His teaching on the new covenant and its implications for everyday life became my own 'key' to the Bible. The new covenant is not a development of the old covenant but an authentic paradigm shift in which *"old things have passed away [and] all things have become new"[2].*

[1] Luke 1:2
[2] 2 Corinthians 5:17

These men set before us an example of abandonment to the person and will of Jesus Christ. They were 'all or nothing' men. They lived their lives recklessly and it was infectious. The spirit of 'all for Jesus' is present in so many of these accounts. Great grace was given and great sacrifices were made, but the harvest continues until the Day makes all things plain.

Reading between the lines of Gill Silver's accounts, we trace the thread of Hudson Taylor's comment that "There are three stages to every great work of God; first it is impossible, then it is difficult, then it is done." God's works are always 'originals'; we are, according to Hebrews 6, to imitate their faith. Not their works, or their style, but their 'all their eggs in one basket' faith.

May the great Originating God use these simple records to encourage us to imitate their faith and to press on into an ever greater enjoyment of a Better Covenant based on Better Promises made good by a Better Mediator... and to share what we have received.

> O might my lot be cast with these,
> The least of Jesus' witnesses:
> O that my Lord would count me meet
> To wash His dear disciples' feet!
>
> This only thing do I require:
> Thou knowest 'tis all my heart's desire,
> Freely what I receive to give,
> The servant of Thy church to live.[3]

---

[3] *Hymns of Eternal Truth* 68 part 2; Charles Wesley

Introduction

When a dear senior elder of a Fellowship abroad was asked if he would be willing to share a little of his testimony of 'the early days' for this book in just a couple of paragraphs, his response was, "You must be kidding! Mission impossible!"

Of course, he was right! How can any major, miraculous, lasting work of God ever be confined to just a few sentences? Needless to say, many of the responses were of a similar nature, and so, when possible, licence has been given to share a little more fully, even though still inadequately. Not a few people have ventured forth and confessed, "I could write a book…!"

When talking to people in so many of the Fellowships over many years, each one has said the same thing: "I always felt that there must be more to the Christian life, but did not know what it was, until I heard Mr North, Norman Meeten, Dave Wetherly (or whoever). Then I realised – and God met me and changed my life!"

Mr North, whose parents were committed Salvation Army Officers living in the heart of the East End of London, was born in 1913 and, having accepted Christ into his life at the early age of three, lived for a further eighty-seven years.

As he sought the Lord, he was clearly directed into pastoral positions in a variety of denominations, finally embracing the Holiness movement, which led him into an exceptional itinerant ministry not only throughout the UK but worldwide.

A tribute given by a close friend of his at his memorial service is recorded in Appendix 3. A full account of his life can be read in a biography written by one of his daughters, Judith Raistrick, under the title *The Story of G.W. North – A 20th Century Preacher,* published by Ambassador International.

Norman Meeten, initially a curate within the Anglican Church and affectionately known as "the father of the House Fellowships", lived on Merseyside with his wife Jenny on the rare occasions when he was not travelling and ministering, primarily in Nepal and India, but also in Cyprus, France, Sicily and many other countries as opportunity was given.

Dave Wetherly, as a young man and a qualified carpenter, presented himself one day at the door of Norman's derelict house in the backstreets of Liverpool with his bag of tools, announcing unabashed that he had come to live with him and offering any help that was needed! His godly life and leadership skills were soon made apparent, and he spent many years as an elder with Norman and others, which then extended to a very fruitful ministry abroad in various countries as well as putting his practical abilities into much valued use.

Dave's own testimony has been included on page 218 in Appendix 1, and a tribute by Fred Tomlinson, now with the Lord, who pastored his own Fellowship in Canada, has been recorded in Appendix 3.

This story of how God so wonderfully birthed these Fellowships into being, forming the very first house church, as far as we are aware, in the early 1960s, is surely miraculous. Countless lives have been touched, brought from death to life, delivered and set free, and now know the living reality of Christ living within them and through them in a way that they never believed would be possible.

There will be two parts to this story.

Part one (this book) will cover the origins and development of the Fellowships from very small beginnings in Merseyside to their spreading throughout the UK. The life of God is never static; it must increase and be shared with others.

Part two (a future book) will continue the amazing extension and spread of what God has been doing, right across the globe, to seventy-four different countries and nations – a wonderful fulfilment of the vision that God first gave to Norman fifty years ago. He was shown a picture of a golden-leaved tree like a maple in autumn. As he looked at these leaves, they began to drop down, not haphazardly but into a large heap, and began to burn together but were not extinguished. After a time, the wind blew and caught them up, blowing and scattering them across the globe. This was linked to the vision described in Revelation 22:2b: *"The leaves of the tree were for the healing of the nations."*

Norman believed that God was showing him how Fellowship people would be used, after a time of "burning together in love", to reach out to all the nations of the world with these wonderful scriptural truths that would bring healing and restoration to so many.

Within these pages is an ex-Anglican curate's testimony to the faithfulness of God in every aspect of not only his own life and ministry, but also the lives of countless others who were brought across his path.

Together with others, under the direction, power and authority of the Holy Spirit, he has had the privilege of *"bringing many sons to glory"*[4].

---

[4]   Hebrews 2:10

A New Song

1

The End of an Era

"Norman, for God's sake, stop trying and let Me live!"

Such was the cry from God's heart to a young Anglican curate, as he sat on a cushion in the corner of a room in 'The Longcroft' on the Wirral (a large family home where God's people began to meet) attending a trustee meeting. Possibly not the sort of thing one would normally hear in such a meeting! But God knew His man, and He knew that here was a chosen vessel through whom He would be able to be poured out; initially into the context of the local church, and then spreading out to not only the rest of the UK, but ultimately to seventy-four countries worldwide.

In Norman's own words, "I had been trying to live for the Lord and He suddenly revealed to me that He didn't expect me to live for Him; He was wanting to live His life in me and live His life out through me."

This same revelation had come to the apostle Paul when God called him through His grace. *"But when it pleased God, who separated me from my mother's womb and called me through His grace, to reveal His Son in me, that I may preach Him among the Gentiles,"[5]* he could then testify, *"It is no longer I who live, but Christ lives in me, and the life which I now live in the flesh I live by faith in the Son of God..."[6]*

As far as Norman knew, no-one else in the room was aware of what was happening, but he did discover later on that they had sensed the presence of God in a very special way on that particular occasion. It had been a pivotal moment. Following the conclusion of the trustee meeting, he had to take a youth meeting at Barnstondale – a short walk away along the lane from The Longcroft.

66 I had never been aware of the Lord in such a remarkable way. So many of those young people responded to the Lord. I had had a

[5] Galatians 1:15,16
[6] Galatians 2:20

most infernal migraine which had been my constant companion since I was a small boy, but shortly after that, it left me and has never returned. I knew that in a remarkable way, the Lord had come. It was only later that I was able to understand biblically and theologically what it was that the Lord had done, and in retrospect I realised that I had not only been baptised in the Spirit, but I had been born again of His Spirit, and now had the ability to live the life which the Scriptures describe as normal Christian living!

It needs to be said that what God had been doing in Merseyside was something that He was also doing around the world, although at the time, they had not been aware of this. God was pouring out His Spirit, and there was a deep quickening within hearts to know Him in a way that they had not known before.

The central teaching within the Fellowships has been the cross. For this to be outworked in our lives we first need to receive the *"new heart and ... new spirit"* which Ezekiel speaks about, which so clearly defines the real new birth, thus making it possible to live free from sin.[7]

One sister writes the following in her testimony:

66 Having encountered the Lord sometime in the '60s, the Lord graciously provided me with precious and vital fellowship at the local Evangelical church I was attending. However, I increasingly sought Him for something much more than I'd known so far. I began to visit every kind of church in the city, but remained unsatisfied. An invitation came to spend a weekend in Exeter at the Exeter Christian Fellowship. There, in the working kitchen of the community, I recognised the life of God poured out along with His unconditional love. It so happened that the preaching on that Sunday, being given by a visiting brother, proved to be slightly other than their norm; but I'd seen the life in that place and knew the truth was there. Later I was to realise that the basis of the preaching of the Fellowships was the work of the cross in one's life, the so-far missing factor in my experience. I once heard it said that there was nothing else in that place other than the cross: no extras, no frills. Those days of the moving of the Holy Spirit cannot be easily put aside. Wherever else we may move to, as time moves on, the inward personal experience of His workings

---

7 See Ezekiel 36:26-27

remains at the core of our being. The privilege of having known these things is inestimable, but comes with great responsibility.

What do we understand by the cross? Certainly, this would include that by Christ's sacrificial death on the cross and His rising again, we can know complete cleansing and forgiveness of all sin, by which we are, in God's sight, *"justified"[8]*. He took upon Himself all of our sin; became sin, so that we could be saved from sin and the power of sin.[9] However, there is so much more, as those whose testimonies are shared within this book portray. There can be a true outworking of His resurrection life in us and through us as we continually choose to lay down all that we are – our lives, our wills – and reckon ourselves dead to sin so that Christ can live in us and through us.[10] It is a deliberate choice. As we receive our new hearts, we find His life and His Spirit rising up from deep within us, and it is His life that overcomes sin. Our old nature and old life has been crucified with Christ,[11] and as we embrace this fact and allow the power of the cross to work within us, Christ will be increasingly seen and heard.

The Brethren assemblies

It was not only within the Anglican community that God was working, but within the Brethren movement as well. Many who had been with the Brethren will testify how grateful they were for the very thorough grounding they had received in the study of the Scriptures. This was certainly their strength. However, they could not accept that the baptism in the Spirit or the receiving of the gifts of the Spirit were for today. They would see this as heresy, and so sadly, when those in their assemblies began to seek God and experience this, they were either asked to leave or chose to do so. Somebody once said, "We pray for revival, we pray for God to work and to pour out His Spirit amongst us; and then when He does, we run away!" They had put God in a box, and because He began to work outside of the box and sovereignly move in a way that was not in the way that they felt He should or would work, then it had to be wrong! Possibly many of us have been guilty of this.

It would be true to say that most of us who are in the Fellowships today, and particularly those who were part of their origins in the 1960s,

---

[8]   Romans 5:1
[9]   See 2 Corinthians 5:21
[10] See Romans 6:10-12
[11] See Galatians 2:20

are so grateful for all that we have heard; the life that we have seen lived out and personally experienced for ourselves; the ministry under which we have had the privilege to sit and be a part of; and for every aspect of church life. We will be eternally indebted to God for the men whom He raised up to see this amazing movement truly 'birthed' and who have so faithfully shared the heights and depths, the breadth and lengths of the riches of Christ, and to expound the whole counsel of God to our hearts. These men, with a hunger and thirst for God that knew no bounds, sacrificially laid down their lives in ceaselessly waiting upon God day and night in prayer, in studying the Scriptures and "mastering it until it mastered me" as Mr North once testified, enabling the Holy Spirit to reveal to each of them the deep and hidden treasures in His word. It was from this, and because of this, that they have then been able to pass on these wonderful and life-changing revelations from God's word to so many over the years. It is one thing to have a theoretical understanding of Scripture, but that alone will not bring us into the life of God. The letter will kill.[12] It is only the Holy Spirit who can bring life, and that can only come as we allow Him to reveal the things of God to our hearts.

A new beginning

66 Having been brought up amongst the Brethren, my wife and I were involved in a very closed circle of Christian fellowship for most of our lives. Despite several major doubts, we still clung to what we felt was 'the truth' until we were forced out in 1994 by the marriage of our youngest daughter to a Christian outside of the church which we attended. We then had to look for other fellowships and wanted a church where true body ministry was experienced. Although we knew of the Devonshire Road Christian Fellowship in Liverpool, we initially decided to join a smaller group where we would not feel too overwhelmed. However, in 1998 we had the privilege of staying at 'Devy Road' for several months and were able to attend some of the meetings there. Early in 1999, we felt the Lord was clearly leading us to join the Fellowship, and have truly enjoyed being a part of it ever since.

It should be said that those who had been a part of the Brethren Assemblies were never critical. They benefited and appreciated their

---

[12] See 2 Corinthians 3:6

biblical foundations upon which their Christian lives had been founded. An elder in the early days of the Devonshire Road Christian Fellowship shares this:

66 I am truly grateful for my heritage in the Brethren Assemblies and I benefited greatly from that. We had wonderful people who were completely sincere and very scholarly in their approach to the Scriptures. They were experts in their presentation, *"rightly dividing the word of truth"* as Paul writes in 2 Timothy 2:15, yet something was missing. They had the words of the gospel but they lacked the power of the gospel. I can't speak for anybody else, but I know with certainty, that that was my experience. Once I had been exposed to the ministry within this Fellowship here in Liverpool, I knew I had to leave all that had been so rich and so much a part of my life in terms of what had gone before, because I had come under the influence of the Holy Spirit – the Spirit of life, the Spirit of Jesus. We had had the words before, but here we were in the presence of His life – the vitality of God, the life of the Holy Spirit – and I recognised it immediately. It was as though someone had just turned on the light in the room, and understanding came. Something was illuminated in my heart that I had not known before.

God heard my cry
Peter Coates

66 Back in the late 1960s to the early 1970s, a small group of us used to meet in a little terraced house in Stafford. We had been introduced, by a young couple who had been in contact with Fellowship folk, to some of the great Wesley hymns. They had a guitar and we sang these hymns from a hymn book called *Hymns of Eternal Truth*. We were astonished that additional verses, which we had never come across before, seemed to add a real potency and life. We truly enjoyed singing these hymns as they whetted our appetites for what we later discovered was the deep work of the baptism with the Holy Ghost, and the deliverance from the power of sin was one of Wesley's key messages that really struck us.

For a couple of years, I struggled with myself. I attended conferences where we heard Mr North and others minister this truth, but I couldn't understand why I couldn't, or wouldn't, respond to the life-changing messages, even when there was an invitation to do so. In the end I reached rock bottom. This drove me to cry out to the Lord out of my deep sin, weeping and groaning for the mercy of God.

I was staying in someone's bedsit in Liverpool, attending a long Easter weekend conference held in a Fellowship house in Devonshire Road where Norman Meeten was to preach. After we had sung the first hymn, I immediately prayed a prayer for the first time from my heart. I cried to the Lord, "Lord, You are all around me, above me, underneath me, in front of me, behind me, but not in my heart!" I had prayed publicly before, but my prayers were not from my heart. Up until this time, the Holy Spirit had been showing me that everything I did, even what I thought were the best things, came from a sneaky, evil motive that was in my heart. That was what brought me to desperation – but God delivered me! However, at the time, I was just relieved that at last there was hope for my deliverance, because I knew that this was God's only remedy for indwelling sin.

For the next few days, I joyfully told those around me that God had spoken to me and that I knew He was going to set me free. At the end of the very last meeting, there was a request for a driver to take a young man home to a place some distance out of Liverpool. I put my hand up straight away and said, "I will." At that moment, I knew that I had said yes to God. I approached this man, who wanted to leave there and then so we went out and got into my car. Just then, a big chap whom I 'sort of' recognised got into the back seat, and said, "Peter, you don't know your way back here from this man's home. I'll come with you." I knew this was God, and immediately the Holy Ghost flooded my being; the fire of God burnt up all my sin and I knew that I was thoroughly purified and set free! My heart was full of rejoicing and I testified to them of what God had just done.

Another lady, on her first visit to Devonshire Road, affectionately called 'The House', writes this:

66 From the moment I entered the meeting, my initial feelings of trepidation left, and I became aware of an atmosphere of love, joy and absolute unity between those assembled and the God they had

come to worship. I also became aware of my own unworthiness and of the sacredness of events which I was witnessing as an outsider.

God was working powerfully, and it was not easy to remain in 'neutral'. Either people found their hearts irresistibly drawn to all that God was doing, to the end that they wholeheartedly embraced Him and allowed Him to plumb the depths of their hearts and be completely changed, or, as was occasionally known to happen, they would walk out and slam the door behind them – not an uncommon occurrence! This did not unduly concern the elders and those in leadership. They understood that when God was at work, the Holy Spirit would move and stir people to respond... in a variety of ways! Scripture teaches clearly that the Holy Spirit has come to convict *"of sin, and of righteousness, and of judgement"*[13] – not always a comfortable experience, not always welcomed, but always needful. Surely it must be better that we find ourselves being stirred and convicted of our need than to remain untouched and unmoved, asleep and indifferent to the moving of God around us.

❞ I entered the room to be greeted by a joyful singing of one of John Wesley's hymns. I did not join in or take part in any of the service, because the faith which these people possessed was one of which I had never personally experienced. Instead I observed the people throughout the meeting. Some, as they sang, lifted up their arms in adoration of a Saviour who was very much alive and whose presence filled that room; others, with children on their laps, sat and sang; still others went freely in and out to greet people as they arrived; but each person had an expression of joy and a radiance of character which I believe can come through no earthly means.

Everybody's testimony will be different in so many ways because we are all so different! We all have a unique story to tell, but there are similarities too. We find a hunger and thirst within us that causes us to reach out for more. We may find ourselves dissatisfied with our Christian walk, knowing somehow that there must be more that we need to enter into. There may be problems of ongoing sin which we know we should not have but freedom from it is not a reality. Gradually we will find ourselves being brought to the end of ourselves, until we cry out to God to meet with us and to change us. For some, this may take but a short

---

[13] John 16:8

time; for others, much longer, even years; yet He is always so faithful, and He will love us to the end as He gently leads us on.

  ❝ For the first time in my so-called 'Christian life', after a period of about seven years of sheer hypocrisy, I had been brought to the end of myself and, more importantly, was able to admit it. I had made a commitment to Christ, in that I had accepted that I was a sinner, asked God to forgive me and asked Him to come into my heart. Apparently, I was now a Christian and 'born again'. ... It took seven years to realise otherwise.

    Outwardly, I had been supposedly an active, committed Christian; a member of a Baptist church where I was baptised, involved in outreach, helping with the Girl Covenanter group, running the Nurses' Christian Fellowship during my general training, and even spent two years at a Bible college where, towards the end of the second year, I produced a special study on 'The Believer's Union with Christ' from 1 Peter.

    In reality, it was a completely different story. I was a hypocrite of the first order. I had simply been carried along by what other people thought of me and what I had been told – a sure recipe for disaster. Gradually the Lord began to show me my real heart state. At one point, I got carried away with the Charismatic movement, being told that I needed to be baptised in the Spirit, but that didn't happen either.

    It was in Scotland that I first heard, saw and tasted what it really meant to receive a new heart and new spirit. Mr North was there at the time; and under his ministry, how wonderful were those meetings that we were so privileged to be a part of! It was heaven upon earth. I had been so blind, so deaf and so dead, but now, with God's Holy Spirit within me, I was truly 'born' – and a part of His body and His kingdom. It was revolutionary. The miracle had happened, and from then onwards, God was able to really deal with me – from the inside – and He has never stopped.

Terry Watson – an elder, at one point responsible for a Fellowship in Eltham, London – in his introduction to his book *The Pastoral Ministry*, describes so honestly how both he and his wife Fran struggled increasingly, before God graciously met with them – which was to prove life-changing and a completely new beginning.

" The last three years had probably been the most traumatic of our lives together in marriage. We both realised that in our Christian experience, although we had been very faithful in our church life, we lacked the reality of the power of God. Our lives were empty and fruitless. This awareness of a real lack of the Lord had created in us a desperate hunger and thirst for God, whose presence and reality I could not find, although I prayed earnestly. As a friend and I chatted together about these things, he passed me a small card inviting me to some meetings in Crystal Palace in the home of Peter and Joy Palmer. The speaker was to be a Mr G.W. North, and we agreed that we would attend.

Terry goes on to describe his first impressions.

" As they prayed, a sense of real love for the Lord emanated from their hearts, and I began to be attentive. I remember leaving the meeting that night with the knowledge that I had found what I had been looking for and that all I needed to do was to ask God to implant this in my heart. I must have agonised and searched for about three months, praying and seeking God without success, until one week I determined to arise very early each day until this blessing of reality was bestowed on me. The first two days, I prayed without anything happening, but on the third day, the Lord Himself came and flooded my heart, and I knew I had received the life of the living God. I had in fact been born again of His Spirit and been introduced into the life of God, which I have never lost or doubted.

Norman had no idea, as he sat on the floor in the corner of the lounge in The Longcroft all those years ago, when God spoke so clearly to him to stop trying to live the Christian life and to allow Him to live His life in him, what the outcome would be. All he knew was that he was desperate. He knew that all his strivings and aspirations weren't bearing fruit. His ministry within the Anglican church had meant everything to him, but in it all, he felt a complete failure, having to admit that he couldn't live that which he preached. God had shown him the impossibility of anybody being able to live the Christian life. Galatians 1:16 took on a whole new meaning as the Holy Spirit revealed the indwelling Christ within him, who alone could live the life of God. His old life ceased from that moment. It was the end of an era!

2

Early Preparations

Called of God

Before I formed you in the womb, I knew you. Before you were born, I sanctified you; I ordained you a prophet to the nations.[14]

Norman was born in West Sussex, in the south of England, and spent his childhood in a small village called Washington, in the district of Horsham. His father had been a demolition contractor, with particular responsibilities for the demolition of war defences. The family were poor, not educated but honest and hard-working.

The only church in the village was Anglican. There was a Methodist church in the neighbouring village, but as he had been informed that "very strange, funny people" went there, it was out of bounds! His grandmother's home happened to be facing immediately opposite to it, so he had a very privileged vantage point from which to observe these dear people. In his childhood obedience, he never darkened their door!

He has happy memories of cycling around the local country lanes, singing and enjoying the beautiful countryside around him.

There had been some evangelical input in the village, to which he had responded when he was just four years old. This is how he recalls it:

66 I believe that God first spoke to me when I was just four years old, sitting under a sycamore tree in a gap in the hedge. Three dear people came to our village year by year to preach the gospel to us: one man and two ladies. The man's name was Mr Compton. The ladies were affectionately known as Aunty May and Aunty Vi. They were quite elderly. I can't remember anything that they said, but I believe that they were instrumental in the hands of God to

[14] Jeremiah 1:50

speak His initial word into my heart. Since then, I have had one great desire and that is to live for Him, to serve Him, and above all to please Him. Glory to God! I will never forget that time.

Many years later, I saw Mr Compton. One of the ladies had gone to be with the Lord and the other was in a residential home. Mr Compton was still living in his own home. I went up to him and said, "I remember you! You came to our village many years ago and preached the gospel. I can't remember what you said, but I believe that as a result of you coming, I am where I am today."

It is wonderful how God uses simple, ordinary people. Mr Compton had formerly been an alcoholic. He had been delivered, born again, baptised in the Spirit, and had lived from that day onwards for the glory of God. Praise God for those who have been instrumental in the hands of God to minister some facet or aspect of the truth that has lodged deep into our hearts and then developed.

Norman attended St Mary's C. of E. Primary School, although as the second world war broke out, much of his time was spent in bunkers. From St Mary's, he went to a secondary modern school for three years, followed by five years at Horsham Technical College, from the ages of thirteen to seventeen. His parents had high ambitions for him to train as an architect because of his exceptional artistic abilities. At one point, he was required to write an essay on his choice of career, but when it was revealed that he wanted to be a minister of the gospel, his parents insisted he tore it up.

Following college, he entered the Royal Marines for two years and was stationed in Lympstone in Devon, with the marine commandos. From here, he was posted to Eastleigh, Hampshire, working with the naval gunnery.

The deep desire that God had obviously and indelibly laid on his heart to be a minister of the gospel always remained, and so it was that he decided to leave the Royal Marines and to train for the Anglican ministry; a calling that he embarked upon with characteristic fervour, zeal and a true and total heart commitment, qualities that have never diminished. Such were his aspirations to totally abandon himself to the will of God, that he recounts an amusing story during this time, when he approached his bishop for some serious advice concerning his desire to possibly enter a religious order. This man knew Norman well. They were on good terms. He sat there very pensively, with his one glass eye staring blankly ahead of him and his good eye concentrating astutely on his much-valued curate and vicar-to-be. He took his time before answering. Then, with a deliberate and kindly response, he simply said, "Norman, my boy, I would suggest that any order that you would join would soon become *dis*-order!" Even bishops can get it right sometimes! Norman had his answer. He humbly accepted the verdict.

During his early ministry as a curate, he first worked for three years in the parish of St Helen's in Lancashire, and then was thrust into the heart of Liverpool 8 for a further three years, in the parish of St Saviour's, Faulkner Square. There, every known gross manifestation of sin as a regular pattern of daily life was the norm. Such were the dire needs confronting him, that increasingly his awareness of his inadequate experience of God brought depression and despair to his heart.

❝ I was supposed to be God's answer to these people's needs, but I did not have the answer myself. I was unable to fulfill that for which I knew I was ordained – that is, an authoritative minister who could say that Jesus Christ is God's answer to sin and human need.

There was much heart searching. He reasoned within himself that if the written word of God was indeed true, then it must work or God was a liar. He challenged God concerning this, asking Him for a specific answer within a given time. God was not slow, and it was the following day – a pivotal moment, sitting on the floor in the corner of the lounge at The Longcroft – that God spoke to him.

❝ God literally rent heaven open and avalanched into my life, saying, "Norman, for God's sake, stop trying and let Me live!" For the first time, I knew that Jesus was alive and now I could say without a doubt, *"I have been crucified with Christ; it is no longer I who live, but Christ lives in me; and the life which I now live in the flesh I live by faith in the Son of God, who loved me and gave Himself for me."*[15]

At the time I could not define what had happened, but three months later, in conversation with the Rev. Martin Peppiatt, I was told that the baptism in the Spirit had taken place in me. I was

[15] Galatians 2:20

caused to realise that this experience of Christ was a living reality, and I felt the evidence of a true new birth.

On moving from St Helen's in Lancashire to Liverpool 8, the whole issue of infant baptism became a real crisis for him. The very last infant baptism which he had administered was indescribable. All the godparents had been drunk, one had urinated on the floor during the course of the baptism, and when he took the certificate of baptism to the parents' home the following morning, where the child was supposedly living, they denied all knowledge of him. This was Liverpool 8!

He continued on for a further eighteen months after God had met with him, after which he knew that he could no longer be a part of the Anglican community, primarily because the Lord had now brought him to this crisis on water baptism.

66 I had been baptised as a baby, as most Anglicans are, but the Lord had been speaking to me about water baptism for years, even when I was at college. In fact, the principal called me an Anabaptist. If he had been wise, he would have put me out of the college at that point! But I struggled on. In my first parish in Lancashire, I was able to cope because the minister, Roy Barker, was so efficient. He was a tremendous inspiration to me. From St Helen's, Roy Barker moved to St Mary's Upton on the Wirral, where on arrival he found only a handful of parishioners, but within only a matter of months they had to duplicate the services because of his tremendous ability to pastorally care for the people within his charge.

Norman knew that on resigning his post he would be without a home, without a job and penniless, but his heart and conscience told him that he could not stay. God was calling him out. He was walking away from everything that had totally occupied his whole life and into which he had invested everything, but he knew that he could no longer be a part of it. It was a sacrifice that needed to be made if he was to remain obedient to the call of God upon his life.

The final challenge had come when he heard Mr North preaching on the need to "lengthen the cords of the tent and strengthen the stays". The question was asked, "What tent peg are you holding on to?" Immediately God spoke into Norman's heart: "Baptism." He had already had discussions about this with his bishop, who had simply glossed over the issues, saying, "Oh, we all have these problems as young men; you'll get over it," and suggesting that he wait another six months before doing anything. However, God had now spoken to him clearly that morning, and he knew what he had to do. He spoke to Mr North immediately after the meeting, asking him if he would baptise him after lunch. "I will!" was his reply.

❝ I think that was the most traumatic hour I have ever spent, wrestling, because I knew that for me it wasn't just the end of everything that I had lived for, prayed for, believed for, studied for and longed for. I didn't know anything outside of the Anglican Church.

Before he was baptised, he wrote a letter to the bishop and told him that by the time he received this letter, he would have been baptised as a believer and if that equated to his resignation from the Anglican Church, please would he accept it. He had been told that if ever he was baptised as a believer, he would have to leave, so he knew what he was wrestling with. He was literally relinquishing everything that had been dear to him up until that moment, and everything, according to his understanding and knowledge, which he had believed for – and obeyed.

The response from the bishop, which arrived just a few days later, was not as expected and left him in a somewhat difficult position. The letter said that his actions had not equated with his resignation. The bishop had made a complete U-turn!

Norman remained within the Anglican Church for a further few months, until he became not only an embarrassment to himself but to other Anglicans throughout Merseyside. He decided to relinquish his legal right to function as an Anglican minister. If he ever wanted to go back to the Anglican Church, all that would be required of him would be for him to write a letter to the Archbishop of York to assure him that he would obey the *Thirty-Nine Articles*, which are the doctrinal statement of the Anglican Church, and to be a good boy in the future! Needless to say, this was never to take place, for, as Norman testifies, "The longer I am away, the further I am away. I could never go back on what the Lord said to me on that occasion."

Not many of us have been in such an extreme situation as when he finally made the break. The security of a home had gone, he had no job or income, and he was utterly penniless. It was not only the material and physical issues that confronted him but, possibly more acutely, the emotional wrench and pain. He walked away with his dog Scampy, whom he had 'acquired', and a few articles of clothing in a small bag. All else had been either stolen from him, borrowed but not returned, or had simply disappeared. These had been his ongoing 'blessings' and rewards for living in Liverpool 8! "If you had anything," said Norman, "and you had a heart anything other than stone, you had to share it or give it away."

He went home for two weeks, but then returned north at the invitation of the other trustees of The Longcroft (of which he was one), who asked him to come and live there for a while, to assess its potential for future use.

The Longcroft belonged to the Milner family. They were God-fearing and had a heart to care for those in need. Within Mrs Milner's own family, there were serious mental issues that were troubling and difficult. As a result of seeing God miraculously heal her sister following a failed leucotomy, she wanted her home to be used for "the freeing of the captives". She became increasingly convinced that not all those dear souls who had been relegated to a mental hospital or institution were necessarily suffering from a mental disorder, but possibly had underlying spiritual problems.

One particular Christian book had impacted both her daughter Mary and her. This was titled *Life on the Higher Plane*, by Ruth Paxson, and Mary had read it whilst away at Bible college. She enthusiastically shared this with her mother upon her return, and the Lord used this to bring her into a very deep and personal relationship with Himself.

Norman stayed at The Longcroft for approximately two months, but he soon realised the impracticalities of this when all of his contacts and meetings with which he was involved were on the other side of the Mersey. It just didn't make sense. He began to pray that the Lord would direct him to a suitable house in Liverpool.

A friend of Mrs Milner's house companion, Mrs Dorothy Roberts, who was a secretary to an estate agent in Liverpool, heard about Norman's need and gave him details of a property in Queens Road, Anfield that was available. It was in very poor condition. The rent was £3.50 per week, which was not very much – but a fortune if you didn't have anything. However, God was clearly speaking to him and leading him. All he needed to do was to remain obedient and to trust Him. In the meantime, he continued to travel over to Liverpool several times a week.

God does not despise the day of small things.

Small beginnings

Moreover, the word of the LORD came unto me, saying:

"The hands of Zerubbabel have laid the foundation of this
*   temple;*
His hands shall also finish it.
Then you will know that the LORD of hosts has sent Me to
*   you.*
For who has despised the day of small things?
For these seven rejoice to see
The plumb line in the hand of Zerubbabel.
They are the eyes of the LORD,
Which scan to and fro throughout the whole earth."[16]

A few youngsters, mainly in their mid-teens, who had also left the Anglican church, met with Norman to pray and really seek the Lord. They needed direction and to know what was in His heart for them.

Various venues were used for this, but each with its own problems. The owners of Gordon Hall in Blackburn Place in Liverpool decided after just two weeks that they were heretics, and they were asked to go. The Methodists complained that their meetings were too long, so again they were shown the door. From there they were given permission to use the Friends' Meeting House in Hunter Street, which was home to the Quakers. They were totally indifferent to what they believed or how long the meetings were, so they were able to continue there for a few months.

The meetings were hair-raising! Extraordinary things happened, partly because God was moving and partly because of their inexperience and possible ignorance; their exuberance and youthful gusto and enthusiasm could become somewhat misguided. However, God saw their hearts and their deep desire to know Him. They were challenging times – for Norman in particular, who needed to remain very sensitive to the leading of the Holy Spirit, to learn how to handle each situation as it presented itself and to minister the word of God aright. This was a new beginning indeed, but refreshing and vibrant.

It was during this time that they were first introduced to Mr North, of whom they had previously heard from a brother called Percy Gutteridge, at that time a pastor of a church in Stockport. Mr North, who had moved from Kent to Bradford, was pastoring a Christian

[16] Zechariah 4:8-10

holiness church, where God was moving in true revival amongst a people who 'just wanted God'. Lives were being transformed, the Holy Spirit was being poured out, healing and miracles were almost an everyday reality, and there was a hunger and thirst for God that knew no bounds. Mr North never claimed to possess any of the spiritual gifts as listed in 1 Corinthians 12, but he did testify that during his ongoing ministry he had seen all the gifts in operation. His one heart-cry that underpinned all of his preaching was the very crucial and radical need for men to truly know and to receive new birth, which the Lord had so clearly and powerfully revealed and opened up to him as he had pored over and studied the Scriptures over many prayerful years. It was this that has revolutionised thousands upon thousands of lives all over the globe from the Day of Pentecost and ever since. This true new birth was seen as synonymous with the one baptism, or 'baptism in the Spirit' – that would enable a person to embrace the working of the cross in his life. It was this, and this alone, that could deal with inbred sin and enable men and women to experience a holiness and righteousness that was not their own. It was the fulfilment of what Ezekiel prophesied – that we could receive *"a new heart"* and *"a new spirit"* in exchange for our old hearts of stone.

> *I will give you a new heart and put a new spirit within you; I will take the heart of stone out of your flesh and give you a heart of flesh. I will put My Spirit within you and cause you to walk in My statutes, and you will keep My judgements and do them.*[17]

It was these same truths that God had shown to Norman too, as well as countless others, and as these two men were introduced to each other, it soon became apparent to both of them that God had surely brought them together for His purposes and for the extended ministry of the gospel and to His church.

To record all that God was doing during this time would surely be impossible. As they met for prayer and Bible study, the group grew from about six to over eighty in a matter of weeks. People came from near and far because of what the Lord was doing and because they were spiritually hungry.

Dick Hussey, one of the early elders in Liverpool, says, "I can only describe these meetings as a baptism of love and holiness. The fire of God came."

[17] Ezekiel 36:26,27

One person who joined them was a lady called Mrs Joan Porter, whose husband was the assistant director of the local Criminal Mental Hospital, notorious for having in their custody and care the most hardened of criminals with deep psychiatric disorders, both men and women. Permission was given to visit them twice a week. They asked for a room in which they could hold some meetings.

"You're wasting your time," replied the senior medical officer. "They won't even come to a social event, let alone to a Christian meeting." They were shown to the smallest room in the hospital, just big enough to hold about five people. Within a very short time they were using the largest room in the hospital!

Norman approached the senior medical officer on one occasion and said, "Dr McDougall, what answer have you got for your patients?" He replied, "None," to which Norman commented, "You are one of the most qualified psychiatrists in the country. How is it that you say that you have no answer?" He sadly admitted, "Because I have no answer for myself." Both he and his family had serious addiction problems and major mental disorders. They were in a mess. Norman knew that there had been a time in his curacy days that he too had had to admit that he had not known an answer to his deep needs. Wonderfully, God had since met with him.

Joan Porter was desperate. She had seen what God was doing. She was witnessing first-hand the transformed lives around her. She knew that she needed to receive this baptism in the Spirit; to be truly born of God and know the reality of His life within her. In her desperation, she bought a ticket that would take her around the world to visit all her Christian friends and ask them to pray for her – America, Australia, Hong Kong, wherever these friends were to be found!

Norman takes up her story:

❝ Her plan was to come back to England via Hong Kong, but she remained so desperate because nothing had happened that she turned around and went all the way back to San Francisco, to her Pentecostal friends. They prayed over her again, they shook her, they talked to her, they did everything that they believed they ought to do, but all to no avail. She came back as desperate as when she went.

She owned a caravan in North Wales, so she set off and spent a week fasting and praying. Still nothing, so she said to the Lord,

"Lord, what do I do now?" He spoke to her and said, "In the midst of the battle you will be anointed." Then she remembered this gathering of people over in Bradford. Straight away, she packed up, jumped into her car and drove over.

She arrived half an hour late at the meeting. It was being held in a room above a car show room in Westgate. She quietly went up the stairs and gently pushed the door open, not wanting to cause any disturbance. As she pulled the door open, there was a man halfway down the congregation who was prophesying, and at that precise moment he said, "In the midst of the battle you will be anointed," and the Spirit of God fell upon her! She crept into the back of the meeting, and after it was over, she went to Mr North, who was the pastor, introduced herself and told him a little of what was happening in Liverpool. Because she was the wife of the Assistant Superintendent of the Criminal Mental Hospital, she invited him to come over and speak at one of the meetings – which he did! God's timings are always perfect, and there is always a far bigger picture than our very limited perspectives often recognise.

Mr North soon realised that God was moving amongst them, but also discerned that their understanding of things was very limited and "in embryo". However, the all-important thing was that they had had a genuine encounter with the Lord, which He Himself had initiated, and they praised Him for the day when Mr North was introduced into their midst. It was from then onwards that he began to come over on a more regular basis.

What is a church?

Whilst Norman was living at The Longcroft, the Lord was speaking to him about "the church" – what did he understand by this?

He answered, "Life."

Then the Lord said, "Well, where do you live? Do you live in a church building?"

Norman soon realised that it was not a church building. God lives in homes.

By this time, he was deeply involved with many young people in the City, many of whom were in poverty and homeless, with major needs of all description and living on the street.

66 I had one great desire, and that was that there should be at least one home in Liverpool which they could call their home, where they would be welcome and never turned away and never be refused a meal.

It wasn't going to be too long before this God-given vision was to unfold and become a reality.

3

Queens Road, Liverpool

The miracle begins

*But seek first the kingdom of God and His righteousness,
and all these things shall be added to you.*[18]

As we have seen, Norman left the Anglican Church with nothing, but the Lord had spoken to him and promised that if he was faithful in seeking first His kingdom and His righteousness, He would take care of everything else; and from that moment onwards, He has done just that. He has miraculously and overwhelmingly provided for him so wonderfully, often on a moment by moment basis, without him ever making any of his needs known or having been involved in any form of fundraising. He was obeying the Lord's command to him that he was never to disclose to any other human being what his needs were, or the needs of his family, or the needs of any work with which he was involved.

137 Queens Road

Queens Road was in one of the neediest areas in the city, with the highest delinquency rate. Norman and a friend, Mrs Porter, visited this eleven-roomed property one wet November afternoon.

66 Despite the filth, gloom, holes in the roof and water in the basement, I felt before the Lord that I should take it. I didn't have enough money to pay for one week's rent, never mind renovations or furnishings, but the Lord had spoken to me on an earlier occasion concerning material matters, from Matthew 6:31-34. I trusted God to fulfill His promise.

[18] Matthew 6:33

The general overall structure of the building appeared to be satisfactory, but the inside was a completely different story. It had not been attended to for a long time, and as a result it was completely derelict. The estate agent agreed to fix the roof if they took responsibility for the inside.

Norman moved in with Scampy, his 'inherited' dog, and some of the neediest of the young people whom he had come to know and love. Someone kindly gave him a mattress. He possessed one mug, a bucket and a few bowls. For the first six weeks, they cooked their food in the bucket on an open fire which was hanging off the wall! Their 'fuel' was the ten layers of linoleum which covered the basement floor. They tore it up, strip by strip! They had the same meal for breakfast, dinner and tea, apart from one delightful day when Mrs Porter arrived on the scene with some delicious cream doughnuts. Sheer luxury!

Within the first six weeks, with the help of a wonderful team of young people, the whole house was transformed from top to bottom. It is amazing what happens when water, cleaning materials and paint are put to good use. It was hard-going and physically demanded every ounce of strength – and more – but this was more than compensated by the close fellowship and unity that they knew between them, and the Lord's blessing flooded their hearts. One purpose, one vision: that God should be glorified and move in their midst.

Memories
Margaret Jones

66 I had given my heart to Jesus one evening in a youth meeting in Kendal and, a year later, was invited to an Easter conference by a school friend. There were five 'Kendal girls' who travelled to Liverpool together and we stayed in a house in Queens Road. Memories of that place are of many young people sleeping on floors; people busying themselves in the kitchen; people smiling and calling each other "brother" and "sister". At that time, I was full of fear and self-consciousness and just wanted to go home, but what I have remembered all my life (and can still see the scene today) is a man called Norman Meeten who spoke to us on our last morning and asked us if God would be sufficient for us if we were completely alone, stranded on a desert island. He then went on to tell us that we could have "all of God" in us through the Holy Ghost. I thought, "This is what I want" – and God heard.

From the very beginning, the spiritual side of the work took priority. They prayed much and spent time waiting on the Lord and seeking Him for all the very diverse needs that confronted them day by day – and night by night! Many people sought ministry, and the Lord moved and met them. They were also much blessed by the volunteers who just turned up offering to help in whichever way they could. A dear brother, Dave Wetherly, known to many, arrived one day with some clothes in one hand and a toolbox in the other and simply announced, "I've come to live with you. Please go down to Kent and tell my mother that I have been ordained. She'll understand because she's an Anglican!" Norman dutifully obeyed and travelled to Kent to meet Mrs Wetherly and to explain to her about her son. She remembered Norman from a previous occasion and was quite amicable. Dave, as a qualified carpenter, was certainly a timely and wonderful provision, as well as having a vibrant ministry, and was such a help and support to Norman.

Norman's initial vision for The House was to see it being available as a support to the local churches and to share the light and revelation of the gospel that God had shown to them, which had been so transforming. The home was also purposed to be a rest home for the Lord's people and any others in spiritual or physical need. There was a continual flow of people from all walks of life and from all parts of the world. Many who came regularly had deep needs resulting from alcohol abuse and narcotic addictions. No-one was turned away.

Once The House was renovated, they held meetings on a Tuesday, Thursday and Sunday, with Monday being kept free for a day of prayer and fasting. Mr North began to come on a regular basis.

After a few months of moving into The House in Queens Road, there was a request from many people for Norman to produce a prayer letter so that there could be an intelligent understanding of the particular needs for which to pray. In response to this, here is the exact copy of Norman's reply, together with 'The Principles of the House' which he knew to be central to the work, an overview of how the work began, the ministry of the Spirit and points for praise and prayer.

My dear Friends,

Let everything that hath breath Praise the Lord.

For a long time now, people have been pressing me to write a prayer letter. This has also been the desire of my heart, but demands for ministry have excluded it. But I can delay no longer. Your prayers are vital and if you are to pray intelligently and effectively, you must have information.

Praise the Lord for all that HE has accomplished during the past nine months. As one seeks to assess what has been done, one is convinced again that our God is the God of the impossible. He is all that He claims to be in the Scriptures and means exactly what He says.

There is so much to say about the work to put you in the picture that I have decided to write separate articles on each section of the work.

Can I say before I go any further how tremendously grateful we all are for your faithfulness towards us in prayer and other ways. *'The Lord who sees in secret will reward you openly.'*[19] We do value your continued prayers above everything else.

May the Lord bless each one of you abundantly.

Your servant in Christ,

Norman Meeten

THE PRINCIPLES OF THE HOUSE

1. The House should first be a REAL home to which any Christian can feel free to come and bring any in need.

2. It should be a place where the Body of Christ is free to operate according to the New Testament pattern.

3. It should be a place from which we move out to present the Full Gospel of Jesus Christ, as a Body, by the power of the Holy Spirit, to those right outside the church.

   a) Forgiveness of sin by the cleansing of the precious blood of Jesus and His finished work at Calvary.
   b) The Fullness of the Holy Spirit – by the New Birth and Baptism in the Holy Spirit, to enable men to live the 'Christ-Life' – blameless before God and Man.
   c) The operation of all the Gifts of the Holy Ghost as revealed in the New Testament.

---

[19] Matthew 6:4 (paraphrase)

24

Those sharing in this ministry should be prepared to accept New Testament simplicity and sacrificial living – so that the maximum amount of time, money and energy can be devoted to the Lord Jesus.

We must trust the Lord ONLY for all our needs, both spiritual and material.

These are no more than a bare outline. Our desire is, that we should be elastic in the hands of the Lord – to move as the Spirit leads. We have no desire to become an organisation, denomination or 'church'. We believe that if we did, we would defeat the object for which the Lord has allowed us to come into being. Probably one of the greatest temptations is to be secure – to be organised and to have absolute control.

Our chief desire is to honour the Lord Jesus and uplift Him and to be the handmaid to anybody that desires to do the same.

From the very first day, the spiritual side of the work has had priority. Much praying was done amidst the painting and cleaning. Numbers of people sought for ministry in those days and were blessed.

The first room to be completed was the largest room in the house – the front room on the first floor – which was the fellowship room. Here we meet regularly for worship and fellowship, and twice a week we have a Bible Study, when Mr North, spiritual Overseer of the Longcroft, usually ministers.

The House seems to be very much like an Inn between earth and heaven. There is a continual flow of people from all walks of life and more and more from all parts of the world.

My prayer is that it may continually be a Bethel – a place where men and God meet.

THE MINISTRY OF THE SPIRIT

'God also hath made us able ministers of the New Testament; not of the letter, but of the Spirit; for the letter killeth, but the Spirit giveth life.' (II Corinthians Ch.3:6)[20]

No doubt many of you are asking the question where and how do we minister? The fields of service and doors of opportunity seem to be almost unlimited. There is need on every hand.

Here are some of the spheres and ways in which we work:

First of all, the house is open twenty-four hours a day. Many people come with all manner of problems. There is always someone available to counsel and minister. Some come for just an hour or so; others have stayed as long as four months – according to the need.

Then there is the regular ministry of the Word of God here Tuesday evenings at 7.30 pm, Sunday afternoons at 3.00 pm. and on Thursday evenings at 7.30 pm.

Those who feel particularly called and anointed unto the work amongst the outsider, go to the City Centre in the evening to do personal work.

We also have many openings into Christian Unions. Every week I go into the Liverpool Collegiate Grammar School for boys; three times a week into the Art College. Almost every Teacher Training College in the area has sent invitations to minister. Every Sunday there are opportunities to minister two or three times a week in all denominations. Frequently we are asked to send teams of people to take Young People's meetings. We have been asked to assist in three different coffee bars, evangelism at Speke, Halewood and Maghull. Twice a week a team is able to go to the Criminal Mental Hospital at Maghull and recently I have been given an invitation to go into Walton Prison every week for at least the next six months. To give you just an idea; during the last eight days I have spoken at some twenty different meetings apart from anything else. Other avenues include letter writing to such people as men in

[20] Based on KJV

prison and Borstal and the writing of articles for magazines and newspapers.

Praise the Lord of the harvest that He will send forth labourers into the harvest. A harvest not reaped is a harvest lost. God forbid that through our slothfulness the harvest of men's souls should be lost.

Our vision is 'THE WHOLE WORLD SHOULD HEAR THE GOSPEL IN OUR GENERATION'.

So let it be, Lord Jesus.

'Seek ye first the Kingdom of God and all these things will be added unto you.'[21]

You will have noticed in the Principles of the work that 'we must trust the Lord only for all our needs both spiritual and material'.

For a very long time the Lord has been speaking to me and leading me into a life of utter dependence upon Him alone. When I left Falkner Square, He gave me the promise above, three times in two weeks. He has kept His word unto this day and will keep it unto eternity. Hallelujah.

When the Lord led me into this work, I believed that He would have us adopt the same principles. We did. Again, we find HIM faithful who has promised, who also will do it. He has ministered to us above all that we could ask or think out of His riches in glory by Christ Jesus.

The day I signed the agreement to take the house, I hadn't the money to pay for the first week's rent, let alone the £1,000 that would be needed to renovate the house. Within a few days, I was given a cheque for over £700 to establish the work. This was a tremendous encouragement.

I have to say that there have been times when my faith has been greatly exercised, but the Lord has never failed.

---

[21] Based on Matthew 6:33 (KJV)

One of the things that I said to the Lord when we began this work was, "Stop the money if we go out of Your will or if Your purpose is fulfilled."

During the summer I was away at a conference. While I was there a person came to me and told me that over the next three years a sum of £600 a year would be paid into my bank account for the work of the Lord. To me this is a tremendous seal of the Lord's approval of what we are doing.

May we be found faithful stewards of all His precious gifts.

PRAISE AND PRAYER

'Let everything that hath breath praise the Lord'[22]

1. Praise the Lord for bringing this work into being

2. Praise the Lord for providing the house and for the help of Miss D Roberts

3. Praise the Lord for providing all our needs

4. Praise the Lord for each member of the team

5. Praise the Lord for the numerous openings for ministry

6. Praise the Lord for those who have been Born Again and set free

7. Praise the Lord for all that He is going to do in the future

God said: *'Where two or three are agreed as touching any matter I will do it.'*[23]

1. Pray that the Lord Jesus might always have the pre-eminence

2. Pray that we might know His will in all things

3. Pray that the Lord invest us with power to fulfil all the desire of HIS heart

4. Pray that the Lord will revive His church

[22] Based on Psalm 150:6 (KJV)
[23] Based on Matthew 18:19 (KJV)

5. Pray for the team

6. Pray for the 'outreach' amongst the young people in the City, in the Criminal Mental Hospital, in Walton Prison, at the Art College Christian Union, at the Liverpool Collegiate Grammar School Christian Union, in the Teacher Training Colleges, in the Hospitals, the Personal contacts in the house, by correspondence, in the coffee bar evangelism

7. Pray for the future plans a) Bible School b) Extended property in the City

Challenged

John and Celia Valentine

66 In St Leonard's, Bootle, a church that I attended, there was a Church Army captain who was also chaplain at Walton Prison, a large gaol not far from where I lived. He invited me, along with others, to preach and speak to the prisoners. Among those who went to testify in the prison was the Rev. Norman Meeten, and I was placed with him to preach.

One night the prisoners challenged us. The next Friday they brought a prisoner who was very educated (he already had a couple of university degrees and was writing a book on psychology) and he would try to convince us that there was no God. The Friday came and Peter, the prisoner, was there. He was very cultured and spoke with a public school accent. I do not remember a word that he said but will always remember Norman's challenge to him: "I want to ask you one question, and if you can answer it, we will sit and listen to you. If not, you will sit and listen to us." It was agreed and the question was this: "Do you have the answer to the sin in your life?" Peter looked non-plussed, bowed his head and then, looking at us, said, "If I had the answer to sin in my life, I would not have spent half of my life in prison." He sat down.

I found myself going to prison to hear what Norman was saying and found myself convinced that this man had had a far greater experience of God than anything I knew. He brought others along, including Dave Wetherly, who spoke with the same conviction. They were having meetings in a house in Queens

Road, Everton, and so I began to attend. People were coming from many denominations and there was a tangible presence of God. Mr G.W. North would come from The Longcroft on the Wirral and minister to us. My heart would respond to the messages, and I heard that I could be filled with the Holy Spirit and have power to be a witness for Him. One evening I went forward, got down on my knees and asked God to take over my life. He answered and I got up a different man. I knew that God had come and I knew that I could now live for Him. I was filled with joy. I received the gift of tongues.

John and Celia are now in Zimbabwe, responsible for Ameva Farm Bible School and a primary and secondary school amongst other things, seeing God work miraculously over many, many years amongst the Africans and bearing much fruit in so many lives.

Where there is life, there is growth, and there was certainly phenomenal growth within this eleven-roomed house in Queens Road. The meeting room was on the first floor, being the largest of all. Soon doors needed to be removed, as people overflowed onto the landing, up the stairs, down the stairs and wherever there was a space. Sometimes the floor would literally rock, and Norman lived in dread of it actually collapsing, causing everybody to cascade down into the cellar! It was a real miracle that this never happened.

One morning there was a knock on the door and one of the local lads in deep distress said, "Vic," – he was not their vicar, but this was their affectionate nickname for him – "our house is falling down!"

"Go and tell it to the marines," was Norman's reply.

"But you *are* a marine, or were a marine!"

Norman looked out of the door and the whole gable at the side of their house had collapsed, with a bed and contents hanging out, suspended in mid-air!

This was the context in which they began. So many of the houses in the road had been ear-marked for demolition and were completely derelict.

Full to capacity and overflowing
Marian Williams (née Marian North)

❝ My earliest recollections of the Fellowships concern meetings at a house in Queens Road, Liverpool. I believe that this was during

1966. At this time, I was a member of the New Covenant Fellowship in Bradford, where my father had been pastor up until he moved to The Longcroft, situated on the Wirral peninsular, to minister there. I regularly visited my parents on my days off and somehow became involved in the meetings which I attended in the Queens Road Fellowship.

I remember one meeting distinctly. The room was so packed out, as well as the stairs and landing, that I found myself sitting on the front row, a couple of feet away from Norman Meeten's nose during the hymn-singing! ... It was bursting at the seams...

Marian, with her husband Martin, has also worked out in Africa for many years and they have seen the Lord work in wonderful ways.

'137' was an open home. The door remained the entrance to a home for so many who had never known a home, never known parental love or security; whose life existed of roaming the cold and dangerous streets of Liverpool, of hunger and deprivation that had made and left deep emotional, mental as well as physical scars.

It was not unusual for Norman to be woken up in the middle of the night with a youngster at the door saying, "Vic, we're starving!" They would go down the road to the 'People's Café', which remained open all night, and tuck in to some chicken and chips, or egg and chips, or whatever was available. It was not the most salubrious of places. A large notice on one wall read, "Please do not molest the customers!" Not particularly inspiring or endearing, but it was somewhere that provided some basic food that was just about edible!

"Vic, this doesn't much look like a chicken's leg!" was this lad's remark on one of these three o'clock in the morning visits.

"Don't look at it; just eat it!" was Norman's reply.

It was probably best that the source of their food supplies was not known. These lads were hungry and needed to consume the contents on their plates without asking too many questions!

Keeping company with these street kids and the marginalised from society, coupled with forms of worship and Christian ministry that may be far removed from the norm and expected respectability found in most of the denominational churches, can be a difficult pill to swallow for those unacquainted with such lifestyles. These youngsters loved it. It was a reality that they had rarely if ever seen or known. They had come to love and trust Norman implicitly, and were drawn to the life and love of

God within him, even though they may not have realised what it was initially. Others struggled!

Misgivings
Fred Tomlinson

❝ One unforgettable evening in August 1966, I taxied my brother and my wife Sheila's sister to The House. It was the venue of meetings which they had begun to attend. Everything I had heard about that place made me very uncomfortable. I argued that their doctrines were erroneous and the leaders were leading people astray.

Temporarily parked at the door, with no intention of getting out of my vehicle, I was coerced with such remarks as "You're a policeman. What are you afraid of?" Minutes later, I was sipping tea with a man whom I had never cared to meet – Norman Meeten! I studied him as we chatted. I had to admit that this bearded ex-curate with his purple sweater, jeans and sandals was very likeable. A crack had appeared in my concrete wall of resistance. When I arrived home, I reported to Sheila that I had never seen love like that before.

Days later the unthinkable happened. Sheila and I were sitting in a meeting at The House! Sheila described the atmosphere as "electric". It was certainly unlike the Brethren meetings which we were accustomed to. A Mr G.W. North was the speaker. While neither of us can recall the content of the message, we both experienced God reaching into formerly unfathomed depths of our hearts.

That night the Holy Spirit began a work in Sheila and me that would radically transform virtually every aspect of our lives. We left the meeting echoing the words of two disciples in Emmaus:

"Did not our heart burn within us while He talked with us on the road, and while He opened the Scriptures to us?"[24]

All who were a part of that move of God at 137 Queens Road, Liverpool will remember three very remarkable men: G.W. North, Norman Meeten and Dave Wetherly. Their unique and powerful ministries were equalled only by the Christ-likeness of their lovely lives.

[24] Luke 24:32

Little did any of us realise that something was being birthed in that dilapidated old property, that would spread like fire around the globe.

The need of the human heart will always remain the same, no matter what our backgrounds or who we are. *"All our righteousness is as filthy rags,"*[25] says Isaiah, the Old Testament prophet. We all need to know God's love so personally and powerfully that it will enable us to let go of all that we are for all that He is.

Here is one schoolgirl's testimony and her introduction to 137 Queens Road:

Made clean – born again!
Lynda Cheung (née Hutchinson)

66 In the spring of 1965, I met the first Christian who really impacted my thinking. I was in the sixth form at Kendal High School in the Lake District and went fairly regularly to both Quaker meetings on a Sunday morning and the local evangelical Anglican church in the evening.

When I met Jenny at a friend's home, I knew that here was a person in direct contact with a living God and I wanted to know the same.

I needed God desperately. I had a dream in which I was in a school play and someone handed me my script – which was the Bible! Knowing nothing about the plan of salvation, I just told God that if He wanted me, He could have me.

Returning to the upper sixth year at school, I then threw myself into Christian Union activities and read the New Testament avidly, assuming that the new birth that was described in it had happened to me, because I knew *something* had happened and the direction of my life had changed radically. I became increasingly aware though of a deep emptiness inside of me.

I was invited by a friend to a meeting at the recently acquired house on Queens Road, to which she was now going. It was a Sunday afternoon in February 1966. The place was packed and we were sitting on the stairs looking into a crowded meeting

[25] Isaiah 64:6 (paraphrase)

room. I remember nothing of the preaching but wept through the repeated singing of:

> *His blood can make the foulest clean,*
> *His blood avails for me.*

I had no idea what a prophecy was, but when one was given, the Lord spoke to me very clearly through it, that He knew how filthy I was but would clean me up.

I began my course at Liverpool University in October 1966 and immediately started going regularly to the meetings at the Queens Road house, held on Sunday afternoons and Tuesday evenings. It was a bad area of the City, and I had a long bus ride to it from the more affluent area in the south where my hall of residence was. The journey included a long walk in Anfield between the bus stop and The House, which was probably quite dangerous on dark winter nights but I normally felt very safe and protected. I loved the meetings but became increasingly aware that I was like someone looking in from the outside at a party. Despite all my efforts and longing, I had no assurance of salvation, no direct inward relationship with God and certainly no Holy Spirit. There was only an increasing sense of condemnation, rejection and an inability to trust God.

In the first few months of 1967, I went through a period of great turmoil and at times wasn't sure that I would come out of it sane. At one point, when being prayed for, the Lord clearly showed me the root of my sense of rejection and delivered me from an unclean spirit. I found it very difficult to explain to anyone what was going on inside of me, so most of what happened was what the Lord showed me on my own: about how to trust Him in spite of feelings, the sin of unbelief and so on. By the Easter conference in 1967, I was able to respond fully and wholeheartedly to the call of God through Mr North's preaching, and especially to three separate words: "Come", "Live" and "I love you". This last was what the Lord kept on saying to me for the next three months or so, whoever was preaching and whatever the message. This was all I heard! It was as if I was a baby being fed very tenderly with the *"pure milk of the word"*[26], and having my whole being remade.

[26] 1 Peter 2:2

As far as we know, Queens Road was the very first house church in the UK. The Holy Spirit was certainly working in many other areas of the country, but people tended to keep within their own denominational structures. Within the Liverpool area, many began to hear about what God was doing in Queens Road and, in their hunger for more of God, went along to see for themselves, despite the alarming rumours that were being spread around in an attempt to keep people away. It didn't take too long before they knew that this was where they wanted to be.

It is often quite difficult to describe coherently what happens when God comes to us in such personal ways. This is how one lady, Lesley Cobil, describes it:

Liquid love
Leslie Cobil

66 With a longstanding prayer in my heart to be baptised in the Spirit and to really know God intimately and personally, in the late '60s I was introduced with much trepidation to what seemed to me the strangest of meetings I had ever attended. There, in 137 Queens Road, Liverpool, was a white-headed gentleman speaking to a motley group of people crowded onto benches, singing and praying in the most unconventional way, but with a passion and love for Jesus that I had been looking for. By the end of the meeting, I was crying with longing to have what they had, and to my amazement, this white-headed gentleman, introduced to me as Mr North, was willing to pray for me. He very gently, with absolutely no judgement, identified what was wrong in my heart and then prayed. All I can liken the experience to, as he prayed, was the pouring of liquid love right through me. Whilst I was being washed and filled again and again, which felt just like the purest of golden love, I found myself singing in tongues, pouring my heart out in an ecstasy of worship to God. The Lord Jesus was now the inner reality I had been longing for, and the depth of relationship I had been seeking with Him had begun.

1965-66, a life-changing year
Pat Clague

66 I was introduced to what was to become the Fellowship in 1965 by Jenny Roberts, as she was then. We had done a year's training together and had become friends, a lifelong blessing. She took me

to The Longcroft where I heard Mr North preach, and then to Queen's Road, where there was a work going on led by Norman Meeten, and meetings which I began to attend, at first warily, but soon eagerly.

I had never heard anything like this teaching. We packed in like sardines, and whether Norman or Mr North preached, we could have listened all night. They spoke from the heart as the Lord led them. Mr North, now in middle age, had a prophetic authority, and Norman was brimming over with a new kind of life that had recently come to him. It was all new to me and beyond my grasp, but I knew God was speaking to us. It was riveting. We were tramping the hills of Galilee! New heart, new birth, the cross, love, baptism in the Spirit, death of the old man, the kingdom, the body – if these were astonishing challenges, they were words of eternal life and we were hungry. Besides, we were seeing people set free, transformed; we were hearing prophecy and worshipping in new ways. We were in the presence of a great light.

We were also in the presence of men and women who were living proof of the life that was being preached. They had a quality of life that was not their attainment of a standard but a life that came from within, whose nature was to love, and to which they gave place day by day, minute by minute. I could see it cost – too much for my liking. And yet they had joy. It raised the question that not only was it possible for people to be Christlike, but that this was the meaning of salvation – a very disturbing thought.

Sometimes I felt that I stayed in this light at my peril, but to leave was a greater peril. I tried 'keeping things in balance'. The Lord ignored this and proceeded to draw attention to aspects of my life that were not pleasing to Him. In a way, I was relieved to be given the incentive to get these things sorted, despite having to cause offence, and felt I had got off fairly lightly.

Prior to all this, what I had been sure of was that the Lord is alive, and that He had met me and told me I should go to foreign countries. I knew too that God is truly my Father. As things stood, my life seemed to be on course. I felt I had been obedient to the call and was now due to go to Africa and to be married – a happy prospect in fact. Yet I had never been quite at peace about this, and now the Lord made it very clear that this was not His plan and that I should go back to the point where it had begun. The decision and its outworking had to be faced. So now I was without a clear future but felt safe in the Lord's hands. I had only to wait, be useful if I could, and keep listening.

Not long after this, the Lord held up a mirror to my real self. He did it with a dream. I woke in a horror of knowing that there was no-one I would not betray to save my own skin. I went to the evening meeting heartbroken. People were rejoicing and I thought, "They're acting. I will not leave this room till I find out if this new life is real, or I will leave feet first," so I stayed put.

It was quite late. However, Norman listened patiently to my tale of woe. His answer was, "You've got to die." I longed for this horrible self not to be, but had a horror too of being snuffed out. Again, kindly, Norman said, "You have to die. There is no other way." The desire to *be* someone was absurdly strong and the thought that this was all I amounted to was the last straw. Norman prayed, and I laboured, asking the Lord to show me how I could die.

Suddenly I was aware of Norman saying, "It is finished. It is done," and at that moment it was as if I heard Jesus calling to me across two thousand years from the cross, "It is done!"[27] I saw that He took me into Himself, and when He died, I died too. I saw what He had come to do. The terrible burden was clean gone and I was free.

I jumped up, saying, "I can see it. I *am* dead. I see it!" I flew home, and when I woke up next morning, I found myself a stranger to the pictures on my wall, my books and clothes – and a puzzle to my family. I was a new person. Every leaf seemed new.

Soon after this came baptism, with the solemn words, "I baptise you in the name of the Father, and of the Son, and of the Holy Ghost." Then the quiet words, "Keep your back straight and rock on your heels." I remember the moment of being out of sight under the water and thinking, "Good!" Friends were singing, "Up from the grave He arose," and Mrs North was there with towel and hair dryer and a hot drink. It was sealed – a treasured memory.

Eventually I was relocated to North Sudan and, in June 1966, was waved off at Lime Street Station by my parents and friends on the first leg of the journey. They sang, "Jesus shall reign

[27] See John 19:30

where'er the sun" as the train pulled out, taking me, new-born, bearing precious seed, to learn to work out in practice this new life and share it.

Sixty years later I am still learning! But I had been given a very sure foundation, and despite my slowness and stumbling it has proved sure. The Lord has kept me on His path and led me on, and I am forever bonded with my Fellowship brothers and sisters.

What *was* this foundation? I think what the Holy Spirit was teaching us in so many ways and from so many parts of Scripture, over and over again, was the truth of Galatians 2:18-21. It is all there: the life, the way, the warnings. *"Not I but Christ."[28]* To me this is the hallmark of the Fellowship teaching. It was embedded in us, to be revealed to our understanding, perhaps by degrees, perhaps over time, as the Lord judged best.

Thank you, those who have led us and taught us and been our examples. The cost for you has been high – too high, and we have added to it. But see the harvest. God be glorified!

My testimony
Pat Teal

❝ In 1965, at twenty-five, I had reached the end of hope from my natural self and the world, and was in crisis. As I got to the cliff edge, God began to let me see who He really is, through Norman and Jenny Meeten and through His word.

Pat Clague introduced me to Jenny and gave me a *Daily Light*. Using the March 3rd evening passage, God suddenly called me: *"I am your shield, your exceedingly great reward."[29]* I'd told Jenny I felt like the Dead Sea and she wrote to me, *"[Your life] shall be like a watered garden, and like a spring of water, whose waters do not fail."[30]*

This has turned out to be true ever since, for fifty-four years.

Jenny invited me to a conference at The Longcroft and Barnston Dale Camp. As Norman began to announce a hymn, 'My goal is God Himself, not joy or peace', the Spirit revealed to me a *crucified, resurrected* man. I saw the beauty of holiness, as

---

[28] Galatians 2:20 (paraphrase)
[29] Genesis 15:1
[30] Isaiah 58:11

compared with my own selfish cravings and 'punctured tyre' heart. I wept on and off till the Sunday morning (the third day).

I was sitting on the window seat at The Longcroft when I said to God, "Change me, because I can't go on." Wow! We were in business. He and I saw a baby turning somersaults in a green field and a voice said, "That's you. You're *born*." Then I saw a white bird flying across a blue sky and a voice said, "That's your soul. You're *free*." It was an inner power shower. I was filled with the love of God and joy.

I went to Nigeria within ten days as a missionary, and at Easter 1966 God gave me two prophecies: Isaiah 54 (*"Sing, O barren..."*[31]); and Psalm 45 (*"Forget your own people and your father's house ... Instead of your fathers shall be your children, whom You shall make princes in all the earth."*[32]) These two were a job description.

Jenny showed me the Spirit at work and Norman showed me the cross at work. I am forever deeply indebted to them.

In the arms of Jesus
Ruth Brereton

❝ It is a delight to give testimony to the new covenant and its reality in one's own life.

I am greatly blessed as I look back to the tapestry of my life, understanding that it has been woven by God Himself from the beginning, with the wonderful privilege of having had godly parents.

In my teenage years, I was privileged to have a friendship with Judith North, who was G.W. North's eldest daughter. She was studying at Liverpool University, and we attended the same church. I learnt first-hand about the character of her father, which was most impressive. So when, on return from the 'wilderness' many years later, I was invited to hear him preach, I went willingly. On hearing him, I chose to respond, and while weeping on his shoulder, my experience was that of being in the arms of God. The words He spoke were, "I know." From that moment onwards, I knew I was loved and that God was my Father and I was His child.

[31] verse 1
[32] verses 10,16

The tapestry also included another privilege. I first met Norman Meeten, wearing a black clerical attire, at the maternity hospital where I was working. Later I saw him in various Christian venues with a group of young men always in tow! His decision to leave the Anglican ministry was known by many Christians, and numbers followed him with expectation. I now realise this was God moving mightily in the lives of many. The first house church was formed very near to my parents' home, in Liverpool.

Words fail me to portray the impact of this man of God. He has been in our lives as a family at just the right moments, including the death of my husband, when he allowed Jenny his wife to be with us as he died. I am sure I speak for all who know Norman and Jenny when I say that through their lives, we understand the nature of Jesus, the Word made flesh, and aspiration rises in us to follow Jesus willingly.

One of the young ladies who came to live and help with the work and ministry at Queens Road was a precious young, inexperienced saint called Jenny Roberts (now Jenny Meeten). She had previously been thrown out of a missionary training college because water baptism to them was unacceptable – even more so than being baptised in the Spirit!

It is wonderful how the Lord brings us through so many varied circumstances. Many of these are far from easy, if not sometimes confusing and so difficult to understand. His ways are far above ours, and He always sees a far bigger and more complete picture than we will ever see this side of eternity. It is surely the only way that He is able to gently mould us and to prepare us in fitting and equipping us for what He has called us to, and for each of us that will be different.

Such was dear Jenny's story, which we have recalled in some detail in the following chapter, as in her quiet but exceptional way, she has always been such an integral part of this amazing work of God. Her future life with Norman was going to be so challenging; very demanding and far from normal married life (if there is such a thing!) They both know that their marriage was made in heaven, yet it certainly needed to be outworked down here on the earth!

4

Jenny's Story

Separated unto Him

Trust in Him at all times, you people; pour out your heart before Him; God is a refuge for us.[33]

❝ Firstly, may I say loudly and clearly this is *His story* of amazing grace lavished upon me.

I was not from a Christian home and was unaware of God's call, without interest in Him and with no sense of need. I was not seeking Him *but God* was seeking me.

Having come from India, my mother thought she should send my sister Ann and me to church, but then decided to come with us to the Anglican church at the end of our

Norman and Jenny Meeten

road. Sunday by Sunday, week after week, we confessed in prayer that as miserable sinners we hereafter intended to lead a new life. Whether before or after Confirmation, I do not know, but one Sunday I thought, "I have been 'hereafter intending' for a very long time and nothing has happened; the flipside being that something *could* happen."

Later, at a gospel service at the Methodist church, there was an appeal to which I wanted to respond – but could not. Partly, being an Anglican, I wasn't sure about the Methodists. Also, I didn't want to cause difficulties in our close and loving family. On

---

[33] Psalm 62:8

the way home with friends, I found myself reacting in a somewhat belligerent and unfamiliar manner.

The story had begun – the *conscious* story. Little did I know then that it had begun before the foundation of the world. ·

Looking back, having been born in India, I realised I had been 'saved' twice – once from an appendicectomy at eighteen months and later from a landslide in the mountains.

Isaiah 41:9 is so meaningful to me; to be called from afar, in the beginning geographically, but later to realise the depth of inward 'afar-ness', meaning my distance from Jesus.

I was born in India to loving parents, Robbie and Doris. Many people ask me, "Were they missionaries?" No, they were not even Christians. Dad was with the *Times of India* and worked there for twenty-five years. We returned to the UK in 1945, living two years with my mother's father in London. Then I spent four years in boarding school with Ann – my big sister, who was three and a half years older than me and with whom I felt very loved and secure – so that my parents could return to India. When my parents returned permanently to the UK, we settled in Crosby, North Liverpool at 48 Eshe Road North, and I attended Merchant Taylors' Girls' School. After I had left school, I applied to the teacher training college in Roehampton, London and trained for three years.

As I mentioned above, my reaction after the Methodist service troubled me, and I knew I needed to consider the appeal that had been given and seek some answers, so I began to search for God. When I was asked to be a representative for the Christian Union, I realised I didn't know what I was representing, so I knew I had to resign. It was a difficult time, as I genuinely wanted to help my friend, the president; but I knew I had to be honest and real. I then began to attend an Evangelical church, where the gospel was preached and I responded to the scripture in Revelation 3:20, opening the door of my life.

At a college Bible study, Libby said it was a long time after she had been confirmed that she became a Christian. My friend Sheila and I wanted to ask Libby what she meant, but we took a long time to gain courage to knock and ask her. She was a second-year student and we were freshers! Libby spoke to us concerning the significance of the gospel – that Jesus died personally for us – so we both gave ourselves to the Lord. Apparently, I prayed and Sheila just said, "Me too, Lord." It was a very real beginning and with it came a commitment to attend Bible studies and prayer meetings.

After college I taught in a primary school in London for three years, attending a lively Evangelical church. The minister, John Collinson, had been a missionary in Rwanda, and they were the first godly family and church group that I had known. It was wonderful.

John surprised me one day by asking, "When are you going to offer as a missionary?" I was somewhat annoyed, as he preached, "The need is not the call," and I hadn't been called! I was unsettled and disturbed, realising I was saying no to the Lord, when I felt I should intuitively have been saying yes.

It was an amazing time as I sought the Lord and He unearthed the natural desire to be married. That was a surprise to me, as I enjoyed people, teaching, sport and was not concerned about marriage anyway. I thought, "Who would there be there to marry in the African bush if I did go?" I began to know that I needed a deeper fulfilment as a woman and asked the Lord to meet me.

There was a Chinese friend, Kiat, not a Christian, with whom I had some measure of friendship. I used to pray for him to know Jesus. I found I was getting somewhat emotionally fond, but the Lord kept saying no, which seemed a little hard, until I discovered he was already married with a child of four in Asia. How grateful I was for the Lord's repeated no.

Having clarity from the Lord of His promise of fulfilment, I offered to the Rwanda Mission, which was the only one I knew, asking the Lord to redirect my steps as He chose. The training was under the Church Missionary Society (CMS), which at that time was somewhat liberal, causing me some apprehension. But if I couldn't stand in a liberal setting in the UK, how would I survive in Africa? So I committed the matter to the Lord, writing in my copy of *IF* by Amy Carmichael, "Lord, save me from any heresies," which He did – and to quote St Paul, *"Not only that"[34]*... but more!

Everything was challenged. I was called naïve and immature, and probably was! There were students at the Men's College

[34] e.g. Romans 5:3

speaking about the baptism in the Spirit. My college staff objected, saying it was wrong and heretical. They said my gift was teaching.

I was Chapel Student, which involved practical duties. One morning, as I was cleaning the chapel floor, I felt as if the floor was giving way. I knew I had to leave, go to my room and pray. I closed my door, praying, "Lord, keep people out, keep the devil out and reveal Yourself to me." The room was filled with His presence and I knew He had met with me, later showing me to live by the faith of the Son of God in me and not reach for the unreachable, but let Him live His life of faith in me.

The other issue was speaking in tongues. I was uncertain. It was definitely heresy from the college staff perspective and I also didn't want to be drawn into irrelevances. But I was increasingly frustrated with lack of freedom and expression in worship. So I read all the books the college had banned. Some suggested, just kneel and begin to make utterances, which I tried but thought it unworthy of the Lord. So I said, "Lord, do You mind if I leave it, but when it comes, may it be worthy of the King of Kings?" And it was!

We had quiet days which were silent times in order to seek the Lord. Having been in the garden enjoying the Lord, I came into my room and was reading *Daily Light* for June 17th, which was all about praise. I just started speaking freely in tongues, as if praise to the Lord were continually flowing. I experienced three different languages in sound and delivery.

Although I cannot fully explain, something within was purged and made new. Wonderfully, the responsibility of my parents and sister for whom I had prayed and been burdened since I first became a Christian was lifted; the Lord was saying clearly in my heart, "Where they are not My people they shall be the people of God." I later discovered similar words quoted in Hosea 2:23; Romans 9:25 and 1 Peter 2:10. It was remarkable: to be no longer burdened with responsibility. In time they all responded and now are all in heaven with Jesus, for which I am so grateful and happy.

Now I will share something very personal which was unknown to the college staff. I went to see friends from the men's college – a married family with children. Sadly, on one visit the husband talked with me and said he had fallen in love with me. I was devastated but calmly said I was not in love with him and, besides, he was married with children, and that we should pray and then have no further relationship.

Back in my room I was so distressed, asking the Lord about it, expecting some comforting words, but all I read in Jeremiah and Isaiah indicated that my relationship with the Lord was comparable to being an adulteress. This I resisted regarding my relationship with my friend, as I knew that I had only loved them all as Christian friends. However, God used this event to reveal that I *was* an adulteress – not physically, but *spiritually*, and that I needed to be 'spiritually married' to Him. So one of the hardest words from the Lord transpired to be such a blessing, as I knew then His deep love for me and His desire that I should be His alone. I realised that He had answered my concerns regarding marriage and fulfilment and that, by His grace, I could live single.

There was quite a move at the college related to the baptism in the Spirit, with resulting pressures. I was called to the principal and required to sign a form, which read as follows: 1. I would not join a Pentecostal church (which was not what I would have wanted anyway). 2. I would not speak in tongues in public, to which I said, "I only spoke in tongues last week. I cannot foresee next week." 3. I was not to speak to anyone else about tongues, to which I said, "It is not priority, but if someone asks, I would share as it is in the Bible."

I declined to sign, and the possibility of being asked to leave was increasing. During my time at the college, we were sent to a multicultural church in Liverpool for mission. The opening service was somewhat high Anglican in style, with a procession down the aisle, and I saw a dark-haired clergyman in clerical attire leading with a cross. I thought, "Oh, it is a united service with a Greek Orthodox Church!" The next morning this same curate, Norman Meeten, was with us to explain the mission and our involvement. It was a meaningful week.

Later I returned to this World Friendship House to give practical service somewhere, as required by college. While cleaning in the dingy basement, wondering what a mistake it was to be here, I saw Norman leave the adjoining house and my heart raced. Later I met him packing a suitcase, saying he was leaving the parish and going. He was actually leaving the Anglican community for good. I said, "Oh, I will be packing soon and leaving for east Africa." Inwardly I was thinking we would be packing to go somewhere together... but dismissed it as a 'wrong thought'.

One evening meeting where the Holy Spirit was present, the preaching was from John's Gospel, chapter 4 – the woman at the well. There was a prayer that someone should be a minister of the gospel, at which point everything within me responded but, thinking in Anglican terms, considered it to be a man's role, with a dog collar! I was also a little embarrassed by people with their hands in the air, while I was as if in a protective bubble. However, on the bus home I felt so free I could have hugged everyone. During the night I kept sitting up in bed, hands raised, worshipping the Lord naturally and spontaneously. I was ecstatic. I didn't know it was in the Bible. Then, in my heart, came the strong impression that "This is the man you will marry." I was excited, wary – and not too happy with the beard! I felt Norman was special and I too ordinary.

In the morning I was serious in praying. "If this is Your will, Lord, I must receive it. If it is not, I must renounce it." My reading that day was 1 Samuel 16:12: *"Arise, anoint him; this is the one."* I marked it with the date. Amusingly I had read earlier in verse 7 of the same chapter, *"But the LORD said ..., Look not on his countenance ... for the LORD seeth not as man seeth; for the man looketh on the outward appearance, but the LORD looketh on the heart."[35]*

I felt at peace for some days and then became increasingly concerned this was not normal. So I looked for the lovely passages in Daniel where the Lord says, *"Oh Daniel, man greatly beloved"[36]* as I wanted to be reassured of His love, and for the Lord to know that I loved Him and was not looking for marriage. I was comforted as I read, and then, to my utter amazement, Daniel 10:1 was a very detailed and specific answer: *"The message was true, but the appointed time was long..."* I understood what it meant and had to wait – which I did for two years only but it seemed a lifetime. During that waiting time I was taught many

[35] KJV
[36] Daniel 10:11

lessons through reading in Genesis: on faith, holding fast, relinquishing, submitting and trust.

Later at a conference in the south of England, there was ministry on Hebrews 6, where baptism became a focus – water baptism. I knew I didn't want to be a Baptist but that this signified something between me and Jesus – but I didn't know how or where. Then on my return to Liverpool, at a conference in The Longcroft, the Lord moved in amazing ways for me – not least regarding finances, and then by meeting a lady who was to be baptised in water. She mentioned Mr Ritchie, whom I went to see. After talking with and questioning me, he said he would be happy to baptise me. However, I needed to get in touch with the Mission, who said clearly that if I was baptised by immersion they would not send me.

Confusion reigned. Why would Jesus tell me to do something that would negate His previous leading? (I now know my responsibility is to obey Him.) I was in turmoil for two months, without support or guidance, but looking to the Lord. I asked the Lord to make it abundantly clear and, if necessary, to create a storm to sink the ship in which I was soon to sail! At that time, I received a letter containing a prophecy that had been written when Mr North had been told that I had declined baptism in water. (I had in fact not declined but had been in turmoil.) It certainly created a storm.

To quote: "A man must do the will of God irrespective of the results of the action. Ultimately it must be for the good of everybody, though immediately it may appear to be un-strategic or bad policy to do so. It may even seem wrong or prejudicial to a former call from God, but God cannot give a command subsequent to a call that can be contrary to that call. The cross of the call is in the command. A person cannot be said to be fulfilling the call of God if in doing so he has to disobey the command of God. The call is primarily to obedience. To compromise on what may appear to be an unimportant detail may be to contract a habit of disobedience which will render a person ineffectual in the general call. Minor details do not exist in the realm of heart obedience. Major results are effected and affected by minor defects."[37]

[37] Prophecy given in a meeting by G.W. North

This was so significant.

So I contacted the Mission saying that I must be obedient and be baptised by immersion, and they asked me to withdraw. I had to attend the valedictory service with my friends, and as they were commissioned, I had to leave the service alone in London and rejected. *But...* as I walked away, in my heart I received the assurance, *"God has not given us a spirit of fear, but of power and of love and of a sound mind"*[38]. I had been accused of mental instability in college, because of believing I would marry someone with whom I had no relationship.

I returned home to an unknown future. I applied and was accepted to teach at Merchants Primary School in Crosby. Soon after, I received an unexpected letter from the Rwanda Mission, wanting to accept me and find a way to send me out. I apologised profusely to the school, explaining as best I could and withdrew, which was followed by another letter from Rwanda Mission saying they could not bypass the decision of CMS. Once again I was in limbo and looking to the Lord for direction.

Then, out of the blue, I was phoned and asked if I would consider helping at Queens Road. Norman had rented the house and was there with Edith as a helpful housekeeper and Scampy his dog. Would I go to help with the other women? I was interviewed by Norman and accepted.

It was a wonderful time; exciting, with much demanding practical work alongside conversations and prayer. The work also involved helping in established churches for Bible studies and so on, as requested. We held our main meetings on Sunday afternoons so as not to overlap with the morning services of other churches. Yet through all of this, I was coping emotionally with the Lord's word to me concerning Norman. At some point, the Lord released me to go and work at the Moss Side Criminal Mental Hospital, Maghull, to assist the teacher who was under pressure; a valuable experience.

After about two years at Queens Road, not only did we need a larger property but the house at 137 was due to be demolished. For a time, we used both Queens Road and Devonshire Road, our new home which had been amazingly purchased. It was about this time that things clarified about our marriage. The Lord had

---

[38] 2 Timothy 1:7

clearly spoken to me and later to Norman, so we both knew the Lord's direct leading. After speaking together, Mr North announced our engagement the next Sunday. It was November 1966 and we were married on June 17th, 1967.

My parents were not yet Christians, but we both had lots of Christian friends, so the wedding invitation was "all who will may come", and they did – four hundred of them! In the morning I was reading about the feeding of the five thousand in my Bible, which was encouraging, so I knew the Lord could handle the numbers. Though not a lavish, seated meal, all were abundantly fed and blessed. When Norman went to receive the bill, it had already been paid. God is faithful, and so are His people.

Our honeymoon was a camping holiday, spent travelling for a month around Europe in our VW Beetle, nicknamed "the mad mouse". We had time alone to get to know each other, in a measure. As we were returning to Devonshire Road, I was looking forward to a home, albeit one that was being restored; we would at least have a hook on the back of the door for our clothes. Well, there was no door! We slept on lilos. We had a rack for our clothes, and Norman's briefcase was his office. It was community life in the raw. There were many visitors, lots of helpers and lots of hard work.

I was cooking for about twenty each day on two Primus stoves. There was no water in the kitchen, but plenty in the bathroom nearby. We were living under pressure, but it was an experience not to be missed. It was a formative experience in many lives, not least my own, and the Lord established His church among us. I was really struggling, not merely with the work and lack of facilities, but also emotionally, since with so many demands, Norman and I had very little time together. Often when we said grace for a meal, I would withdraw out of sight and cry. Norman often counselled young couples who were planning to get married, and would explain the scripture in Deuteronomy 24:5 concerning the importance of spending the first year to get to know each other, and for the husband to look after his wife in establishing their relationship, to which he added, "But don't tell Jenny!" Although ours was not the norm in establishing marriage, and there was considerable pressure, we knew somehow that it was the foundation on which the Lord was going to build. We did not want to miss the opportunity and privilege.

At some point (I clearly remember the context and details), I was desperate and wanted to leave for some respite. However, I realised I couldn't just leave without sharing with the elders. I was aware that something wasn't right. Was it sin? Self? Was it a temptation of the devil? In the end, having talked with Norman, I asked to see the elders, who at that time were Mr Moffat, David Wetherly and Dick Hussey. They graciously said, "Jenny, there are seasons in life," to which I replied, "This season must end." Mr Moffat was very concerned and apologised, saying, "Jenny, we are really sorry we have left you with too much responsibility and not enough support." Ultimately the Lord allowed it. I was desperate. Then they asked if they could pray for me, which of course I needed. As they prayed, I broke and wept, the Lord saying in my heart that He had taken it all on the cross; He had dealt with sin and self and the devil. I was wonderfully free, lightened and normal again.

I have shared these things because they have been so significant for me, and in me. The Lord does not leave us to perpetually struggle with difficulty upon difficulty with no resolution. There is an answer in Him, as He ministers His word and sufficiency (even if the circumstances do not alter), which is all part of the cross working in our lives, coming to know more of the Lord Jesus as He becomes more evident in our lives.

I am so grateful that after Norman and I married, we had three wonderful sons and fifty-four very fulfilled years of marriage and ministry, before the Lord took Norman to be with Him forever.

Glory to Jesus!

5

Devonshire Road

God's work, done in God's way will never lack God's supply.[39]

From one derelict home to another! Although it had only been two years since they had first moved into 137 Queens Road in Anfield, Liverpool 6, for a weekly rent of £3.50, it was now needful to look for a larger property. God had wonderfully and miraculously provided for all that had been needful whilst at Queens Road, but it was time to seek God afresh for a further outworking of all that was in His heart.

There are no coincidences in God. The timing of Norman's daily readings and Bible study coincided miraculously with his current situation and his need for clarity for the way forward.

> Consider now, for the LORD has chosen you to build a house for the sanctuary; be strong, and do it.[40]

He knew this to be his answer. He now needed the Lord to show him what 'building' His house was to entail. He certainly had not at this point contemplated buying property. His heart was simply to be open to whatever God was saying.

Once again, Dorothy Roberts, the secretary to an estate agent in Liverpool, drew their attention to 14 Devonshire Road, in Toxteth. This was a large four-storey Georgian house in the notorious area of Liverpool 8. It had nothing to commend it. It had had squatters on the ground floor who had virtually torn the place apart – literally. Basic life skills such as the use of toilets had presumably been completely outside of their comprehension. The basement floor was covered in sewage and rotting mattresses. To say it was a mess and uninhabitable would be a complete understatement.

[39] Hudson Taylor
[40] 1 Chronicles 28:10

Not to be deterred, Norman arranged for a viewing. The following week, Mr North, Norman, Dave Wetherly, Dorothy Roberts and Jenny met together to pray. They decided they should separate for a week without having any communication between them and each specifically ask the Lord two things: firstly, was it God's will that they should buy the property; and if so, for how much? Amazingly and wonderfully, when they all reconvened at the end of the week, God had spoken exactly the same things into each of their hearts. Yes, they were to buy the property – for the price of £2,000. Norman returned to the estate agent.

"I am interested in buying the house. I will pay your client £2,000 cash on the completion of the Deeds."

The estate agent stared at him in disbelief. "You're crazy! My client paid £4,500 for it some years ago. His current price is £5,000. He is a Jewish businessman living in London. He won't lower the price; in fact, he may well increase it."

Norman held his ground.

"By the way," the estate agent continued, "I am a chapel man. I come from Wales, and sometimes prayer does work in chapels but never in business!"

Again, Norman stood unmoved and replied, "I don't really mind what your opinion is about prayer and I am not concerned about how much your client paid for the property, or how much he is asking for it. I am simply telling you that I am prepared to pay £2,000 cash on completion of the Deeds."

The estate agent's sceptical response was somewhat probing. "By the way, have you got £2,000?"

Not a difficult question to answer. "No, I haven't even got two thousand halfpennies, but that is not my problem. If the Lord has told me to buy the property, then He will provide. Please will you write to your client?"

Reluctantly he agreed, but holding out no hope for a positive response.

Within one week, Norman received a letter from the owner in London, confirming that the property would be his for the exact amount of £2,000. During that same week, two young men, independently of each other and not knowing anything of Norman's situation, each sent him a cheque; one for £1,500 and the other for £500. Their only 'instruction' was that he should be free to use the money in any way that he felt was appropriate, for the Lord's work. When Norman returned to the estate agent to ask for the bill for the legal fees, he was informed that it had already been paid! The transaction was complete.

Much prayer was now made concerning the resident squatters; they didn't want to appear to be hard and unsympathetic. Wonderfully, the Lord graciously intervened, and within a matter of a few weeks, the Council had rehoused them, and Norman and his team were now able to begin the daunting and challenging task of renovation. Dave Wetherly, who was now an elder in the Fellowship, moved into the house in May 1967 to prevent further damage, as it was now empty apart from one family living on the bottom floor.

First stop – the basement!

Descending down the creaky stairs to the basement was an experience never to be forgotten and, thankfully, never to be repeated, as far as what lay before them. The filth and stench of rotting mattresses and raw sewage permeated the already musty air. How the squatters had allowed their situation to deteriorate to such depths of degradation is hard to understand, but they had, and now came the stoic task of bailing it all out, clearing the debris, cleaning and renovating. The local supermarkets must have been delighted with the amount of bleach, disinfectant and cleaning equipment that they clocked up on their tills!

It was not only the basement that was filled with sewage – the whole of the entire drainage system underground was blocked. Norman well remembers Dave Wetherly taking a firm hold of his feet and ankles as Norman was suspended head-first down a manhole to manually unclog and remove the offending sewage. In fact, this was a needful procedure that had to be repeated weekly after every meeting. It had been voiced that this was one of the required 'qualifications' for those wanting to preach and minister in the meetings!

These extreme lifestyles can come with a cost, but the Lord faithfully kept them through the many extreme and intense demands that were laid upon them; not only physically, but also emotionally and spiritually.

During that year, in June 1967, Norman and Jenny were married, and were able to have a precious four weeks touring the continent 'under canvas'.

John Wood, now in a Fellowship in the Midlands, remembers an incident during the transitional stage from Queens Road to Devonshire Road.

" My memories of the move to Devy Road in 1967 feature a few of the lads trying to get the piano down the stairs at Queens Road. We struggled, until Marian North came along with her supervisory skills and some muscle, at which point *it* carried *us* down the stairs! We managed to put it diagonally into Fred Tomlinson's Bedford van, which staggered off in the direction of Devy Road with an alarming list to one side.

I also remember very vividly the day that we got the huge RSJ[41] which now holds the house up between the front and back halves of the meeting room. We had to get it through the front window. It was very heavy, until Dave Wetherly got hold of the end of it and propelled it through the window with great gusto. When it was finally installed, none of the doors upstairs would open!

Another occasion that Norman recalls demonstrates once again God's miraculous timing and protection in all that they were undertaking. Renovation was well underway, and the house was gradually showing signs of some sort of 'normality'. He had been away in Scotland, and was returning one night to find these 'eager beavers' just about to pull down the main pillar running from the basement to the attic, that kept the whole house together! No supportive scaffolding had been used, and they were intending to extend the meeting room on the ground floor by knocking two rooms into one. Thankfully, Norman had some understanding of construction engineering which he had learnt from his father, and realised the imminent disaster that was just about to unfold! "STOP!" he cried. "STOP!" Had he arrived just five minutes later, there would have been multiple corpses under a pile of rubble of bricks and mortar. As Norman has said, "The Lord's timing is amazing."

Renovating 14 Devonshire Road was exhausting, challenging, frustrating as well as rewarding, but by far the most treasured thing was the close fellowship and unity between all those who were involved. This proved such a blessing, and far outweighed the trials and hardships. God poured out His blessing in immeasurable ways.

Alongside all the work on the house, they were also involved in outside mission work and evangelism, particularly amongst the university students.

They had their problems too! Norman's phone rang one night just before midnight, with a cry for help from the travelling secretary of the

---

[41] Rolled-Steel Joist

Christian Union and Inter-Varsity Fellowship, Clive Charlton. "Brother, I've got a problem!" The story unfolded. "The CU committee is in a mess. They are being bombarded with other people's problems, but have no answers. This has resulted in them convening their first executive prayer meeting tonight where they all said their prayers. Lynda Hutchinson was also with us, and when they had all finished, she prayed... and the heavens opened! They realised then that they hadn't begun – and they were desperate."

Norman was patiently listening. He would have been mindful of the time when he similarly, as an Anglican curate, also had no answers.

Clive continued, "I challenged them and asked them if they wanted what Lynda has got, and they all said yes. So I said, 'Well, are you prepared to go where Lynda got what she got?' 'Where's that?' they asked. 'That cranky house around the corner in Devonshire Road!'"

Norman recounts that they all came around, just after midnight, and by one o'clock in the morning, God had met them all. The wonderful thing was that their various professional trainings would see them remain in the university for many more years, so providing a real opportunity for God to work. The impact was remarkable.

From one degree of glory to another
Mike Cadman

66 The CU at Liverpool held a three-yearly University Christian Mission. I was a second-year dental student, and a friend and I had heard that Norman had been assigned as the missioner to our hall of residence and that he came from Liverpool. "Can any good thing come out of Liverpool?" we asked ourselves. Neither of us had found a church that we felt at home in and we had never heard of Devonshire Road, but little did we know!

I contacted this man, Norman Meeten, and arranged to meet him at what became known as The House. Happily, Devonshire Road was on the 25-bus route, and so easy to get to from Aigburth. The evening before, some of us were praying and the Lord filled me with His Holy Spirit. So although I did not know it, I was 'ready' to meet this man called Norman! We had a blessed time talking and praying together, and I can remember feeling as if I were floating on air when walking back to the 25-bus stop. Everything had changed. God had begun His work.

Later that day, friends and I were taken back to Devonshire Road to listen to Norman. He was to tell us and show to us from the Scriptures what had happened to us and to give us our first lesson – *"Abide in Me"*[42] – which we have never forgotten. In the following days, many others were also filled with the Spirit. They were amazing times, and so much blessing for us all. Jesus was just so real. There was a real love for the Lord and for each other among us.

One memorable evening, Norman ministered for two hours and twenty minutes on Ezekiel 47 – totally unforgettable! It seemed liked ten minutes, and yet the words were not being put into our heads but really written in our hearts, and have become the living word of God by which we have lived now for forty years and, by the grace of God, have got better and better.

We were told by Norman that if we had the Lord, we had to be the best for Him in everything and to expect to be so – no excuses! *"But God"* was his mantra, and so the vision of the possibilities of God in our lives was set, and our hearts responded to such truth. The Lord really had answered prayer for our Mission, that we should be given the best man in the country. He was certainly best for us.

A preparation for mission
Paul Evans

66 The manifest presence of God in the meetings was sometimes awesome, and the freedom through open worship allowed us to express our love for Him and minister in the gifts of the Spirit. The freedom of worship and the ministry in the gifts, that allowed God to manifest His presence, also allowed the Lord to meet needs of healing, grant deliverance from demonic influences, and save and sanctify. Friends who were at the Fellowship in those days say that they remember with joy the purity of fun, fellowship and the presence of God that was enjoyed together. They have also said how the presence of God and the preaching and teaching meant that you could not hide sin or be undecided about Christ. You either yielded to Him or left the church. There was no sitting on the fence of indecision for long.

[42] John 15:4

The open worship granted opportunity and provided the environment to develop a sensitivity to and an instinct for the moving of the Spirit in the meetings, which has remained with us. We also developed the realisation that open worship is not for soulish expression or an opportunity for a free-for-all activity or domination by one or two individuals. We learnt that all members require leadership – even if invisible and inward and not dependent on one person or a worship or music team.

This experience impacted us to the extent that our ministry and teaching has been primarily to lead those who hear and respond to the preaching of Christ into a real New Testament experience and sealing of the Holy Spirit.

The Principles of the House

These were, and continue to be, the same as those shown for Queens Road, detailed in Chapter 3. Their one desire and purpose was to honour the Lord Jesus in all that was done. A genuine and warm welcome was extended to all Christians and to any friends who were in need of help and ministry. However, discernment was needed. Occasionally there were those who would subtly try to weave their way in for all the wrong reasons, causing unrest and division, and would be lovingly but firmly required to leave.

> *If anyone comes to you, and does not bring this doctrine, do not receive him into your house, nor greet him; for he who greets him shares in his evil deeds.*[43]

The responsibility of the eldership was taken very seriously, and their heart and 'commission' was to ensure that the New Testament pattern for every aspect of church life and worship was known and outworked on a daily basis.

It was also seen as imperative that all those involved in the ministry would look to the Lord alone to meet each need as it presented itself, whether that be material or financial. There would be no fundraising, no requests for money. Wonderfully, and true to His word, the Lord was, and has continued to be, utterly faithful to all of His promises. Ongoing needs were met in a way that honoured Him and brought glory to Him in a way that far outweighed anything else.

[43] 2 John :10,11

Outreach

Reaching out to those outside of Christ has always been seen as an important and integral part of any true church. Without this, a church would become insular and inward-looking, and slowly stagnate the life of God within them. Much outreach was done, not only in the day-to-day places of work (in the universities, schools and colleges) but amongst the prisoners, the drug addicts and alcoholics and the homeless. The City of Liverpool was a mission field teeming with dire need and urgent cries for help; some audible and some silent, but all so real. Much prayer was made day and night, that God should equip them and lead them in all that was on His heart to accomplish.

On one occasion, a group of them met together one night in one of the seedy backstreets of the city to pray, at which point they were suddenly confronted by 'the man in blue' wanting to know what they were up to.

"We're praying!"

The policeman's mouth fell open. Not quite the answer that he was expecting or used to! They began to share the gospel with him and were able to give him a copy of *The Cross and the Switchblade* by David Wilkerson, so well-known for the work that God had called him to do in New York City.

Norman was reminded by one of the elders how he had prayed for a girl many years ago who had been suffering from poor eyesight. The following day she forgot to take her glasses to school and has never worn glasses since.

Friday nights were Liverpool Prison nights. A Church Army captain who worked there was kindly disposed towards the Fellowship folk. Norman's frequent companion on these visits was John Valentine (now involved in a wonderful but challenging work on a Christian farm in Zimbabwe). John was a member of an Anglican church at the time. The two of them would be 'shut in' in one of the rooms with about thirty or so men, with no gimmicks, no musical instruments, absolutely nothing, for two hours, simply sharing the gospel with them. As Norman said, you've either got to know that what you are talking about is real or you are in for a very rough ride. It wasn't long before poor John was in for a rough ride, because these hardened men discovered that although he sang in the choir, he propped the bar up in the local pub for the rest of the evening and that didn't wash with them. They couldn't reconcile the two.

However, through this dilemma, God wonderfully met with John in a very real way, as we read in Chapter 3.

Policemen seem to have had a variety of encounters with Devy Road in these early days: witnessing a group of youngsters one evening praying together in one of the notorious night club areas; another being gently coerced to sip coffee with a vibrant and warm-hearted curate sitting sideways on an armchair in a purple polo neck top, jeans and sandals, who later was to become one of the first elders of the Fellowship; and yet another policeman, also a member of an Anglican church, was continually pestered by a member of the Fellowship as she frequently observed him escorting children across a pedestrian crossing. He too was met by God in a new way and later was asked to join the eldership in Devonshire Road.

Not all encounters with former members of the police force proved so positive. Norman recounts a horrendous crisis that arose during his early days in the Fellowship, and one that almost destroyed him. The enemy is never too far removed from a real, ongoing work of God.

Someone came to Devonshire Road from the south of England, who appeared in a most convincing way to have an exceptional gift of discernment. All those in leadership were more than taken in by this man. He would be able to look at anybody and accurately unravel everything about them, regardless of whether they had previously met or not. He had formerly been with the London police and able to tell them exactly where to go in their search for specific criminals needing to be arrested. He proudly, if not arrogantly, boasted to Norman one day that even when he was a small boy in a preparatory school, he would be able to divide the staff right down the middle by his extreme and almost psychotic behaviour; an occurrence that was repeated time and again. Sometimes he was like a raving lion; sometimes he was like a lamb. Satan will try to counterfeit every true gift of God and this was one of these occasions – in the extreme. This man was operating under a very, very powerful demonic spirit that had only one desire, and that was to destroy all that God was doing.

When Norman first met him in London, he experienced a tremendous reaction right deep down in his spirit. Something in him cried, "NO!" He then followed Norman up to Liverpool and eventually shared his room because nobody else would have him live with them. They were all terrified of him, even though they were continuing to be amazed at his so-called 'gifting'.

Everything in Norman rebelled against that which was operating within this man, but because Norman was, in the natural, very inward-looking, melancholic, introspective and negative, he presumed that everyone else must be right and that he was wrong. He spent days examining himself, desperately trying to determine truth from error. In an attempt to try to regain some sort of peace and sanity, he was encouraged to have a two-week break in North Wales with this ex-policeman. This necessitated him cancelling his own holiday. It proved a fortnight of absolute misery. He returned home, but many more months were needed 'convalescing' at The Longcroft, during which time the Lord revealed very clearly to Mr North that this man was operating under a spirit of a serpent. He was instantly excommunicated, not because of demonic possession but on the grounds of being a railer – that is, someone who is constantly spreading negative comments, causing division and unrest within the body. Demonic possession of itself is not ground to ask a person to leave the church. Most of the other Fellowships adhered to this discipline, but one church reinstated him and allowed him to continue his 'ministry' in a very strategic place in the south of England. It is not known at this point in time where this man stands spiritually.

It was during this time that the Lord began to speak to Norman concerning the plurality of eldership. "I realised that this work was impossible for one man. It had grown to a degree that I could not handle on my own." It hadn't been just the issue of baptism that had eventually caused Norman to leave the Anglican church, but that of a 'one-man ministry' that just wasn't reconcilable with the word of God. "I see it more clearly today than I ever did: that nowhere in the Scriptures does it talk of just one elder; it is always in the plural."

Resulting from this, five elders were appointed over a period of time, namely Ken Moffat, Dave Wetherly, Dick Hussey, John Valentine and Fred Tomlinson.

As we have seen with John Valentine, Dick Hussey, Fred Tomlinson and Len Grates, anyone who has a real desire for the things of God and who abandons himself to His call upon their lives will, out of necessity, go through an initial period of deep heart preparation and life-changing circumstances and experiences. Even more importantly, in one sense this is true if, in the purposes of God, he is being prepared and equipped for ultimate leadership within His body, the church. What can be more sobering than being asked to be responsible for shepherding and teaching men, women, young people and children in the things of God and His word? How serious a thing it would be if they get it wrong.

Ken Moffat, or 'Dad Moff' as he was affectionately called, was no exception as an elder. Ken was a school teacher and was married with two children. As a young lad he had joined the Boys' Brigade company in an Anglican church in Liverpool, and continued there for many years until he enrolled in the army with much trepidation, shortly after the beginning of the second world war, in 1940. These were challenging times for him as a Christian, increasingly being confronted with his own shortcomings and failures.

On leaving the army after the war, he was asked to join a team of twelve men who were directing Christian Stewardship campaigns for the Liverpool Diocese, but deep down he felt bored and frustrated. As he himself confessed, "Forty years is a long time to be barren." His two children had by now become involved with the Queens Road Fellowship and frequently talked about being baptised in the Spirit, but up to now, he had not been able to show much interest in what seemed to him to be a "divisive influence in the church". However, being finally persuaded to go to a conference being held in Barnston on the Wirral by his two highly enthusiastic youngsters, he agreed "with some trepidation and a great deal of wariness, preparing to be very critical!"

On entering the meeting, the general excitement, hearty singing and worship overwhelmed him, but then he reasoned that not too far away, at the Anfield football ground, forty thousand men would be equally if not even more excitably and demonstratively supporting their favourite football team! All that Ken observed and listened to somehow resonated within him that this was of God; that it was genuine and could not be ignored. "I realised," said Ken, "that they had something that I had not. If then, these people were real Christians, what was I? I felt out of it. I *was* out of it. I did not belong." He tried hard to reason again that what he had witnessed on that fateful weekend was not true, not authentic, unscriptural and so on, but he couldn't convince himself. In the end, he took himself off to his bedroom one night with his Bible and got down on his knees. It was April 25th, 1966; 10 pm. He began to realise that he could not pick and choose with God. He knew a decision was required. All excuses had gone and he was desperate. "You've got to do it, Lord," he groaned, in agony of spirit.

66 My wife came and got into bed. When she heard me groaning, she thought I was having a fit and wanted to ring for the doctor. I had never groaned in this way before. I knew I was in earnest – desperately so – but I was not hysterical, or anything like it, for I experienced a wonderful joy such as I had never known before. Praises poured out of me to God and to Jesus. ... I knew that I had received a new heart. I knew that I was one person, whole, the same inside and out. I knew I had been born again of the Spirit of God. I cannot describe the utter joy, the ecstasy, the freedom.

For three weeks, sleep, food, nothing mattered. The Bible became a living book, new and exciting. I understood so much that previously had been hidden. I wanted everyone to have what I had received. I wondered who had been cheating me for so long! Why had I not known? ... I was up at about 4.30 am every morning, praying, rejoicing, reading, and the time just flew...

Just four years later, without seeking or expecting it, 'Dad Moff' found himself in a position of eldership at Devy Road, and continued in that role for many more fruitful years, along with John Valentine, Dick Hussey and Fred Tomlinson. By this time, he had come to two very definite conclusions:

1. that the present 'church' is very different from that established by the coming of the Holy Spirit as recorded in the Book of Acts in the New Testament, and will never turn the world upside down as it was testified the early church had done;[44]
2. that there is a threefold ministry of preaching, healing and deliverance, with a life of power and praise in the spiritual realm readily available to all.

It can truly be said that God was turning lives upside-down in Liverpool 8 – or perhaps it should be said 'the right way up'! The Holy Spirit was moving freely and with power through many, as His word was preached with a new clarity and authority. People were truly born again, healed, delivered and set free.

With many, there had been what could be described as a long gestation period, gradually being brought to a place where they not only had become dissatisfied with what they had known but realised that there was a life in God that they had not yet experienced.

[44] See Acts 17:6

Ken Moffat's son Pete was one such person. His story can be traced back to his school days, following the need to change schools at sixteen to study for his 'A' levels. He had been an acceptable 'evangelical', attending church on a Sunday and being 'a good boy'! His problems began when he went along to join a group of Christians at his new school. He was confronted by youngsters who, in his opinion, were "rather peculiar"! Their lively and enthusiastic times of prayer were frequently interjected with outbursts of "Glory!" or "Praise the Lord!" – and, even worse, they attended this strange Fellowship known as The House! However, their lives stood out, and the way they conducted themselves in school was a challenge to all, even though initially Pete was not particularly enamoured. At the same time, he became somewhat miserable as they obviously were experiencing a life that he knew nothing about. Making friends was also a struggle, as most of them had known each other since the age of eleven and were quite settled in their various clubs and friendship groups.

In answer to a cry to God, he was approached by one of the Christian Union members, who encouraged him to join them at their daily prayer meetings. It was there that, at his own confession, he was introduced to "that which was real". They prayed in a way that he had never known. Although still only fourteen or fifteen years old, they were moving in the gifts of the Holy Spirit – things that many Christians take years to reach.

God was also moving in the rest of the family, who independently were all finding themselves being introduced to people who also went to The House. They were being irresistibly drawn.

The next major event, as Pete describes it, was that his Dad was born again, whose testimony has just been shared. This was obviously a great challenge for all of them; and Pete still struggled, whilst realising that God hadn't really been able to meet him as yet "because I hadn't *let* Him move me". He was still clinging on to all that he – Pete – was: his position, his reputation, his likes and dislikes. His sister had by now also been wonderfully born again and had changed so much that their Dad had been truly shaken to the core. It was Lorna, in fact, whom God used to really challenge him, and he began to seek God in earnest.

It took a long time before things changed for him. Up to then, he had continued to attend all the meetings with his family, but "more or less went to sleep"! Then, during one unforgettable meeting, the person preaching spoke with such power and authority that it shook many; and he was one of them. Wonderfully, in God's perfect timing, after he continued seeking, he too was born again and filled with the Holy Spirit; and as he has since testified, "The effects are still being worked out – bless the Lord!"

Pete is now a leading elder at Devy Road, and has seen the Lord faithfully build His church and move in the hearts and lives of many.

The Christian bookshop

Two ongoing ventures initiating from the Fellowship in Devonshire Road were, firstly, the taking over of a Christian bookshop in Liverpool near to the centre and, secondly, the founding of a Christian school, both of which were a source of great blessing.

The Fellowship opened the bookshop on 1st October, 1979, under the name of 'Contact Christian Books', later changed to 'Gladstones Bookshop & Café' and finally to 'Tree of Life'. The first managers were Peter Buckley and John Woods, both from the Fellowship. They set to work in a very run-down building, being confined to the ground floor due to the fact that the building needed a completely new roof before the first floor could be used. In those early days they saw many people browsing through the numerous Christian titles, both new and second-hand, each day – with the added attraction of it doubling up as a coffee shop and, of course, with home-made delights! Not a few regulars darkened its door from time to time in the years to come, knowing that they would always find a welcome and an opportunity to sit and relax over a 'cuppa' and have a chat.

Built in 1820, the building was in desperate need of repair, and towards the end of the 1980s, the Lord provided the manpower from the Fellowships and the finance in abundance to have the whole building renovated including a complete new roof. They were hard but exciting times to be involved in the Lord's work.

The completion of the building work meant changes were needed, so whilst the café continued to operate on the ground floor, the bookshop was moved onto the first floor. Pete Lock from the Fellowship, a manager at the shop for over twenty years, used to sit quietly at his desk in the far corner working laboriously through the paperwork with the help of a computer, whilst Hazel, his wife, continued to bake quiches and fruit cake for the café. Somehow it was a very special place. The presence of the Lord was sometimes very tangible; as one sister once re-marked, "There was such a sense of His peace and blessing in the room

– from the moment I walked through the door, I could have stayed there all day."

Devonshire Road Christian Fellowship today

Over the years, the Fellowship has supplied many of the staff and also many volunteering their time to help, to serve, to bake and to wash up and all that goes with such a venture.

Subsequently, the bookshop and coffee shop were operated together on the ground floor, with bookshelves along one side of the long room stretching from the front to the back of the shop, with a couple of tables at the front reserved for small displays, stationery and various little extras. An area at the back was home to many much-valued second-hand books. The first floor was used for meetings both on a Sunday and as an outreach centre into the City during the week.

Sadly, due to increasing difficulties, it was felt that it was no longer possible or viable to continue, and the premises have now been handed over to the Liverpool City Mission. Both the bookshop and the café are sadly missed by us all, as well as by many regulars who enjoyed a 'cuppa' and a browse!

The Christian Fellowship School

The Christian Fellowship School also saw its beginnings at a similar time at the beginning of the 1980s. God had clearly spoken to Phil Williamson, a brother at the Fellowship, who shared his vision with two of the elders. They instantly sensed the validity of such a work and mission, and committed themselves to supporting him without any reservation. By this time, the property next to the Fellowship house, No. 16, had also been purchased, and work began to transform the basement into a 'school' with around eighteen pupils.

Phil Williamson was the headteacher, with Carol Jerman and Barbara Lord being the two main teachers. Others volunteered to help, including Len Grates, one of the elders, as deputy head and his wife Julie teaching French. Phil continued for many years until ill health took its toll, and eventually he was promoted to Glory, entering into his full reward for all his labours. Barbara Lord took his place, and successfully headed up this precious but demanding work for some years until she too needed to stand aside due to ill health. Richard Worsley, formerly the deputy head then took over the headship of the school until very recently, but has now needed to step down, continuing to teach on a part-time basis, in order to care for his wife. Rachel Boulton, who was his deputy, was appointed headteacher, continuing to maintain the highest of standards as did her predecessors.

The school – now in a permanent purpose-built school in Edge Hill, which they were able to secure in 1991 after an interim period in another small school near to the Fellowship – continues to thrive, with a hundred and fifty 'eager beavers' occupying its many classrooms and specialist areas, with ages ranging from four to sixteen.

They have continued to have very favourable reports from Ofsted, and it would be true to say that the testimonies from the children and staff alike are a real credit to what the Lord has wonderfully accomplished over the years and is still doing today. As any teacher will confess, school life is demanding, exhausting, stretching as well as rewarding. Christian schools may have their benefits, but there is a spiritual dimension that requires a constant vigil. The enemy is never slow to try to thwart that which is on God's heart, but... God is ultimately the victor. Satan will never have the last word.

Reaching out

As somebody once said, "Christianity is a living, workable faith." Where there is life, there will also be growth and fruit. The Devonshire Road Fellowship, who celebrated their fiftieth anniversary in 2017, is strategically positioned, as was Queens Road, near to the City, and central to so many needy areas. Its preaching and personal ministry, with contacts in churches, universities, prisons, hospitals, colleges and schools, continues to be a vibrant source of evangelism, as well as for the building up and edification of the body of Christ. Neither has it been confined to the streets of Liverpool and its suburbs. Many have moved out to other parts of the UK as well as abroad, in fulfilment of the vision that God first gave to Norman many years ago.

Many, many people have already gone, in joy and in obedience, to countless nations worldwide, bearing much fruit. Many others, not able to go, have had and continue to have the privilege of being able to pray and to support them from home. Eternity alone will reveal just how glorious a work this has been and is continuing to be, and what a wonderful and faithful God we have and serve.

Born from above
Andy Hutchins

❝ Who was the man standing at the front, not on the platform but down among us young people that evening at the Elim chapel at Rainhill, Liverpool? Could he really be a curate – in a black, polo-neck pullover, jeans and sandals? Yes, Norman Meeten really was a curate. In fact, everything about him seemed real: relaxed, fervent, warm, twenty-nine years old; a man of the cloth helping the needy in Faulkner Square of all places! Faulkner Square is nice now, but it was not very nice back then.

I was about to begin my final year at the art college in Hope Street, Liverpool. It was 1965. The college lay just a stone's throw from the Square and a few minutes away from my rented flat in Princes Avenue.

Norman visited me in my one-roomer, three floors up, at No. 27. It was the first time I had seen a vicar-to-be sit sideways in an armchair and throw his legs over one of the arms, completely at ease. This artist / curate – he told me he was an artist – became even more real to me at that moment, in my final year at the art college; the sort of person you could listen to. He was so warm as well, and we became firm friends.

Norman began helping the young people, particularly young men, from Liverpool's back streets. His goal had been to integrate his young charges into church life, but it wasn't working. They went with him once but that was all. "We'll come and listen to you," they said, "but don't ask us to go there again!" Phil Williamson was one of them (who much later became the much-loved headteacher of the Christian Fellowship School in Liverpool, associated with the Liverpool Christian Fellowship). Norman was dismayed. The increasing number of youths milling in and out of his home, I discovered, weren't only local boys whom Norman was helping, but an ever-growing number of students like me.

One night, desperate to get closer to God, I climbed one of the apple trees, armed with only my torch and Bible. No-one could see me. I called out to Him from among the branches. Up in the tree, peace flooded my soul as I had never known. Scrambling down, I slept soundly until the morning, when I rose to pray and found rivers of worship flowing from somewhere deep within. The Holy Spirit had come! Later, entering the 'hangar' to attend the evening meeting, I stepped through something that I can only describe as a curtain of joy into God's presence. How do you explain that sort of thing? It was as real as anything I had ever known. I was an artist, remember – I was into feelings. Liking what I felt, I went back out to try it again. It didn't happen a second time. Does God ever repeat Himself? What days! Catch me in heaven sometime – I'll tell you more!

As one of those precious 'leaves', the Lord wonderfully led Andy to Sweden many years ago now, where he lives with his wife Lorna, the sister of Pete Moffat, one of the senior elders of the Devonshire Road Fellowship. There has been much fruit and growth there, which we hope to share in much more detail in the second volume of this book, which will concentrate specifically on how God has been fulfilling His vision in so many countries abroad.

It is always interesting to hear how the Lord prepares the hearts of those surrendered to His will for all that He has planned for their lives. Every person's story will in many ways be very different. We are all unique, all from different backgrounds, all with different personalities.

Julie Grates (née Ray) was born into a Hungarian Jewish family, and first met her husband Len at the Auchenheath Fellowship in Lanarkshire, Scotland. Both her parents came to know the Lord, as did her brother Andrew, married to Peggy, originally from America, who was an elder at the Winchmore Hill Fellowship in London for many years and currently remains in leadership in another church, also in London.

Since their marriage, Len and Julie have been much used in a variety of ways and in a variety of places, beginning in Liverpool, then in

Bournemouth, and then for a time in Israel, where their children live. As Julie herself now shares, one of the key factors of the Fellowships that thrilled her heart so much was their missionary vision to serve, to include every nation on earth. She needed little encouragement.

Born to serve
Julie Grates

66 My story with the Fellowships began in 1969 whilst studying at Manchester University.

In my first year, one of the 'Kendal girls', Margaret Jones, who was then vice-president of the Christian Union, invited me to a conference at the so-called Devonshire Road Fellowship, which I had never heard of. Neither had I ever been to Liverpool, so it was an adventure from beginning to end.

I had already received the Holy Spirit, but had been dis-appointed with the only others I had met who claimed to be baptised in the Spirit. Somehow their lives did not seem to match the quality of 'Holy'. So I searched for more.

I distinctly remember the fact that God was there and that the people loved Him and each other. That was all I was looking for and I had found it: radical, wholehearted, total abandonment. Then I saw the noticeboard with "Leaves for the healing of the nations" written on it, and I was even more excited that the nations were in the heart of this movement.

For the next three years in Manchester, together with others, we saw the birth of another house church at 'The Nook', which was the home of Heather and Ocsi Angyal. We had close ties with Devonshire Road and other such house churches which were springing up like mushrooms...

The hallmark of these Fellowships for me was the fact that this gospel was all-encompassing, affecting every area of my life. It was radical and holy. The question was not *whether* we should go but *where* we should go.

We are *hugely* indebted to Norman and Jenny who have discipled us, not by written courses but by being living examples for us to read, touch and imbibe. We seek to impart the life of the Bible wherever we are sent and to also be living epistles for others.

The heart of God encompasses all. He is *"no respecter of persons"*[45], or, as the New King James Version puts it, *"God shows no partiality"*. It has been a privilege, although very demanding and not without its problems, to see another work emerge that has also originated in Liverpool, and that is of reaching out to many asylum seekers. This has grown and developed so much over the years; initially through one sister from the Fellowship responding to their desperate need as it gradually unfolded, but now being supported by many others, not only from Devy Road but also by other Christians in the area. Not a few have come to know the Lord for themselves – one of the greatest joys of all. It may also prove true that in time they too will become 'leaves' that the Lord will take up and use for His ultimate purposes all round the world.

In some ways this chapter has no end; there are so many who have been a part of the beginnings at Devy Road and the work in Liverpool, and who are now fulfilling the call of God upon their lives throughout the UK and across the seas. A special chapter near the end of the book has been reserved where further testimonies have been shared in more detail.

Although The Longcroft existed firstly as a private home, before the Fellowships at Queens Road and Devonshire Road came into being, the timing of the Lord in its preparations to become a church and an integral part of the Fellowships was, as always, something that could not be foreseen. It will be another chapter that will have no end, but the miracles that have been witnessed and the lives that have been changed through those who have faithfully laid their lives down over the years in this much beloved and treasured home need a mention.

[45] Acts 10:34 (KJV)

6

The Longcroft

A vision outworked

Gather My saints together to Me;
Those who have made a covenant with Me by sacrifice.[46]

When The Longcroft was first built for the Milner family in the early years of the twentieth century, they would not have been able to envisage the wonderful outworking of all that God had prepared in His heart for this much-loved home.

From a farm house on the Barnston Road, close to Storeton Lane, the Milners moved into their new home in the early 1920s. They were a God-fearing family and their heart was to see the Lord use their home for His glory. Before his death in 1947, Mr Milner, who had been considerably older than his wife, bequeathed the home to Mary, their second daughter. They had three children in all: Joan, Mary and John. The family had a 'living in' nursery maid to look after the three very young children at the time. The understanding was that their mother was to live and be cared for in the home until her death. With this in mind, during Mary Milner's time abroad in Sikkim as a missionary, and with the complete approval of her mother, it was decided to set up a trust that would be responsible for the upkeep and running of the house. There was much ongoing prayer, and the Lord began to speak very clearly to Mrs Milner from His word, gradually unfolding and clarifying His will and His heart for the way forward. Over a period of twelve years, between 1947 and 1959, five very specific scriptures were brought before her. The first was the scripture at the head of this chapter, Psalm 50:5. From this, He then spoke to her from Isaiah 56:

---

[46] Psalm 50:5

...My house shall be called a house of prayer for all nations.[47]

Then, in January 1948, from Ezekiel 48, in the Moffat's translation (MFT):

No part of this choice land is ever to be sold or exchanged or alienated; it is sacred to the Eternal.[48]

It was during this same year that the house was dedicated to the Lord, for the 'setting free of the captives'[49] and for all His unfolding purposes. Fourthly, in the October of the same year, He spoke from Jeremiah:

And I will give you pastors according to Mine heart, which shall feed you with knowledge and understanding.[50]

Finally, in 1959, to encourage and to confirm all that He had spoken:

"Be strong and of good courage, and do it; do not fear nor be dismayed, for the LORD God – my God – will be with you. He will not leave you nor forsake you, until you have finished all the work for the service of the house of the LORD."[51]

During these formative years, many people came to visit – some for just a brief stay, some for longer. Mrs Milner knew many people and not a few were well-known names such as Gladys Aylward and Arthur Wallis. The gift of hospitality was extended to all. Many missionaries on furlough found a welcome resting place and time of much-needed rest and recuperation within the walls and grounds of The Longcroft.

In 1951, Mary Milner came home on furlough. The family again enjoyed a much-valued time of renewed fellowship together and they joined their hearts afresh to seek the Lord and to pray, particularly with the thought of appointing some trustees who shared the vision of their home and would be willing to take responsibility for the upkeep of the property. Much prayer concerning the Deeds was made, to ensure that all that the Lord had spoken to them would be implemented. Wonderfully, trustees were found, and by 1964, The Longcroft was officially registered as a charitable trust and called 'The Longcroft Rest

---

47 Isaiah 56:7
48 Ezekiel 48:14
49 See Luke 4:18
50 Jeremiah 3:15 (KJV)
51 1 Chronicles 28:20

Home', envisaging the many and varied needs of those working abroad, as well as at home, to find a place of healing and restoration.

The beginnings of a church

It became increasingly apparent that the work that the Lord was establishing was more than what would be called a para-church. It was becoming a true and living house church. Christ's ministry, as first described in Luke 4, was continuing to be outworked, as others became involved in what the Lord was doing, and they began to meet together, especially on a Sunday morning. Mr and Mrs North, with whom Norman and Jenny had now become closely involved, were invited to live in the lodge of The Longcroft, and both he and Norman did much of the preaching, both at The Longcroft and at the Liverpool Fellowship in Devonshire Road. Prior to moving to The Longcroft, Mr North had pastored a church in Bradford for twelve years, having originally been the minister of a Baptist church in Kent.

The baptism in the Spirit and the gifts of the Spirit were issues that Mr North did not embrace as a young Baptist minister. He was familiar with the Scriptures and held traditional views that provided no room for anything Pentecostal (or so he thought) or Charismatic. Then one day, much to his surprise, when at a minister's meeting, someone spoke in tongues. The Lord immediately gave him the interpretation. His theological arguments against such things evaporated in an instant! No-one was more amazed than he was, but God had most clearly moved, and he now found himself being exercised in a way that was totally new to him. This ultimately led to him leaving the Baptist church and moving north to the Calvary Holiness Church in Bradford. It was a church that was governed by a board living in America, about which the congregation were not too keen, so it was decided that they should become an independent fellowship, renaming themselves the New Covenant Fellowship, Bradford.

Mr and Mrs North moved into the lodge in 1963 and were resident there for approximately three years. During this time, he not only ministered locally but used it as a base for a growing itinerary throughout the UK and abroad. An outcome of this was that they were invited to Exeter, to where they moved towards the end of 1966.

"I will build My church..."[52]

---

[52] Matthew 16:18

From early in 1966, a handful of people had been meeting to pray regularly with Norman, seeking the Lord with a real desire to know what was on His heart and a hunger that knew no bounds. As mentioned, they would gather together on a Sunday morning for a time of fellowship and the 'breaking of bread'. In the evening they would travel over to Devonshire Road in Liverpool and join with the saints there for an evening meeting.

The responsibilities of not only needing to minister and travel between the Fellowships, but also the added needs of caring for and overseeing the continual demands of The House, caused Norman to consider the possibility of moving out of the Fellowship in Liverpool and trying to find suitable accommodation within the vicinity. This would help to alleviate some of the pressure laid upon him. Within a short time, a three-storey flat with a garden, in Sefton, was brought to his notice, and which seemed an ideal solution.

Just prior to this, he had said to Jenny, "If the trustees of The Longcroft were ever unanimous and asked us to go and live and work there, I would seriously consider it." In one sense, it was quite a 'safe' comment because the trustees had never been unanimous about anything!

Jenny exploded, aghast, "You're not taking me *there?*" To her horror, at their very next meeting they unanimously asked him to do just that.

Mr North had by this time moved down to Exeter, and the lodge was free. Needing absolute clarity and confirmation, the Lord spoke clearly to Norman the very next morning: *"The gate of the house is towards the east."*[53] This was exactly where the gate of The Longcroft is!

'Meeten's Monastery'

Within a few days, Norman and Jenny hurtled through the Mersey tunnel yet again; this time with their limited possessions, on their way to the Wirral. No mean task! Due to work needing to be done, they were continually relocating between the lodge and the house. Furniture was stored, then moved, then back again to the house, and then finally, with the help of a wheelbarrow, brought to its final resting place. It was the beginning of a new era that was far from idyllic but ordained of God.

The challenges of living within a community are continuous, and The Longcroft was no exception. The phone remained red hot; the flow of

---

[53] Ezekiel 43:1

needy people rarely ceased; daily demands on their time were relentless; not to mention all the issues from a board of trustees who seemed unable to agree about anything. It was not easy.

Next to the lodge at that time was an orchard, and within this, hidden by hedging, was a potting shed. This was soon transformed into a much-needed 'bolt hole' and getaway, to where Norman would retreat into his much needed and valued 'haven' to pray and study. Jenny would be able to truthfully tell people that he was not in the house!

During one such time, when Norman was before the Lord and agonizing over the ongoing (and what appeared almost insurmountable) problems confronting him, a 'ray of light' broke through! Let Norman recall this in his own words:

   One morning I was praying. My reading that morning was the first chapter of John's Gospel, and this scripture seemed to leap out of the page. This is the difference between learning and gathering information from the Bible and the Spirit of God quickening that word. It was a revelation to my heart. The scripture said, *"Can any good thing come out of Nazareth?"*[54] However, I didn't read "Nazareth" that morning – I read "Longcroft", and then right deep down in my heart, I heard the Holy Spirit say, "Jesus!"

   From that moment on, the tide turned. Sometimes, just a single word can reverse a whole situation. Up to that time, it had almost been an intolerable burden to bear. I guess we all, at different stages in our life, in different situations, go through similar experiences where we feel something to be impossible – and then God speaks. ...

   No-one else was up; it was about six o'clock in the morning – and I danced round the orchard. I was ecstatic with joy.

One would think that the demands and commitments on Norman's life to this point were more than sufficient: ministering between The Longcroft and Liverpool each week; overseeing, as a trustee and young leader, the work that was being established at The Longcroft; being available for personal ministry to those in need; as well as giving time, when possible, to dear Jenny. However, it was about this time that Mr North, now in Exeter, embarked on his first visit abroad to India for six months, and asked Norman if he would look after his itinerary – a

[54] John 1:46

'leaving' present: his diary! Initially he had even asked Norman if he would accompany him, but on the three occasions that he was asked, the Lord clearly said no, he wasn't to go.

As the church at The Longcroft gradually began to grow, it was needful for more leaders to emerge and to be recognised as elders. These included Dr Benjamin Storey; Arthur Thomas, with his wife Jessie, who had moved from Liverpool; Dr David Vine, engaged to Ann; and then Eddie Horner, who had moved from his hotel business in the Cotswolds.

Dr Storey had a special place in Norman's life, as he had recently married Jenny's mother, who had been widowed some years earlier. She had fallen and broken her wrist, followed by a lung infection, and Dr Storey had been called as their local doctor for some help and advice. He too had been widowed. The sad part of the story, humanly speaking, was that he only had five years with his new wife before he unexpectedly died – but not before God had truly met with him as a result of Norman praying with him. As they shared together in the lounge one day, and at Dr Storey's request, they both knelt to pray and the Lord came. He had knelt down as Dr Storey; he rose as Norman's true brother in Christ.

He had been a highly respected conference speaker and he was a tremendous expositor of the Scriptures but, at his own confession, had never found what he was looking for. He had never known what it had meant to be loved, and therefore never had the ability to love. He had even been honest enough to admit that when he was walking up the aisle with his first wife-to-be, who was a Roman Catholic, he knew that he was marrying the wrong person but had never had the courage to say so. As Norman and others have so clearly expounded to us over the years, and to this dear man too, we all need to know and experience a true circumcision of the heart which liberates and delivers us from all the tragedies of our past, whatever they may have been. This is the genuine new birth, a true baptism in the Spirit. "If this is not preached," says Norman, "then what is preached is not worth preaching."

Another move

It is probably not possible to accurately count the number of times both Norman and Jenny, together as well as on their own, have travelled across from Liverpool to the Wirral and back again. Norman was a frequent commuter through the Mersey tunnel even before he was married, ministering in both the Wirral and Liverpool 8 as well as other places, often several times a week. They had now been living in the lodge for four years, until 1975, at which point they felt that as so much time was still being spent over in Liverpool as well as away, with requests from abroad emerging, they were not justified in occupying the lodge any more.

This decision proved to be very timely as it gave opportunity for Dr Storey and his new wife to be on hand in his role as an elder; and he relinquished his privacy and private home in Heswall. He was seventy-five at the time and his new wife seventy. Up to this point, she had lived in the family home in Crosby, and it was to this house that Norman and Jenny now moved and where they have remained. Much of the time, Norman was away in India and Nepal, as well as other countries, while Jenny faithfully continued to travel backwards and forwards, often several times each week.

Dr Storey and 'Mummy', as Jenny's mother was affectionately called, had five very happy years together on the Wirral before he unexpectedly died. A word that God had clearly spoken to him, just one year before this, was from Isaiah 22:23-25:

> *And I will fasten him as a nail in a sure place ... and they shall hang upon him all the glory of his father's house ... In that day, saith the LORD of hosts, shall the nail that is fastened in the sure place be removed, and be cut down, and fall ... for the Lord hath spoken it.*[55]

Long-term commitments

One of the noticeable things of The Longcroft is that many have been there for many years and have been serving the church so faithfully.

A dear couple who have remained very faithful and have laid down their lives to be a part of what God has been doing, and is still doing, are Lee and Lynda Cheung. Lee had originally been attending a Baptist church in Liverpool where he used to live with his family but, through a friend of his, was introduced to Devonshire Road. Here is part of his testimony:

66 Although I had made commitments to God and was often blessed during the Sunday meetings at the Baptist church, I became aware that during the rest of the week, I was basically unchanged.

[55] AMP

"...what I will to do, that I do not practice; but what I hate, that I do."[56] I knew that although I tried to be a good Christian, there was still sin in my life. ...

The Holy Spirit was moving in the meetings at Devonshire Road, and I decided to move to the Fellowship after having initially gone to both churches. I realised that I needed that which the young people there had – which I later realised was the Holy Spirit – in my life. I remember a particular meeting when Norman was preaching and it was as if God was speaking life and truth directly to me – which He was. When Mr North visited, the meetings would be greatly blessed and there was a powerful atmosphere of love, during which time the Holy Spirit was present in a very real way. Young men would be standing with their arms outstretched above them whilst worshipping. This spoke to me of the reality of their spiritual experience.

Some years later, Lee moved with his family to the Wirral, although staying on in Devonshire Road for some years. After a time, he sensed that the Lord wanted him to move on, but he had no idea where to. He had wondered about Hong Kong as he was half-Chinese by birth. However, the answer came in an unusual way. During a visit to The Longcroft the following year, to share some of his personal concerns with Dr Storey, they had prayed together, after which they both went into the meeting room. He immediately called out to Lee and asked him if he would join them at The Longcroft. Lee knew instantly that this was where God was calling him to, although he had never somehow considered it to be the church to which he would be going. That was forty years ago. He, with his wife Lynda, are now both deacons, and much valued. They had met originally in Devonshire Road in the early '70s, and married in 1982. Shortly after that, they were asked if they would be willing to be resident at The Longcroft, to help with the work, and in fact remained there until February 2000. Although now living a short distance away, they both remain fully involved. Their eldest daughter, having worked in China for some years, has now returned and is living with them again; and their middle daughter, who also moved to China with her husband and two young children, returned some months ago and is living once again on the Wirral. Their son has 'flown the nest' and currently lives with his wife and young son in Austria.

[56] Romans 7:15

Another faithful couple have been Chris and Julia Powys, who, apart from some time away, first attended from 1973. Chris was a professional horticulturist, and what he did not know about this very specialised field (if anything) is certainly not worth knowing! The Longcroft stands in nearly five acres of ground and takes a great deal of time, love and effort to maintain it to the standard that Chris would like. He was resident there from 1973 to 1979, during which time he was responsible for all the grounds and produce – a very full-time job. In addition, however, he laboriously maintained all the log fires in the house, of which there were at least three; cleaned, laid, chopped and lighted the wood; pruned all the trees in the orchard; looked after the hens; and also, once back inside, set out all the chairs for the next meeting. His energy and commitment knew no bounds, and he revolutionised and artistically created areas that had been patiently waiting for his expertise! Others now have joined the task force, and although not primarily responsible for overseeing the work, he nevertheless continued to give himself wholeheartedly to its maintenance, as well as helping others with their gardens on those rare occasions when not at The Longcroft.

Chris, with his wife Julia, have now more recently moved to the Cotswolds to be nearer to some of their children, and needless to say, he has continued to totally immerse himself into many landscaping ventures both near and farther afield!

Set free – to serve

Another dear lady who has been serving faithfully for over thirty-four years testifies so clearly of how the Lord drew her and the joy that has ensued ever since.

She had been invited to a conference in Liverpool in the May of 1968, which was used to change the whole course of her life.

66 It was not so much what was being preached that weekend but what I observed in the believers. They had a deep joy, a purity and clearness of spirit, plus a real love for the Lord and others – like me, who was a complete stranger. This is what spoke to me, as it was reality and what I had been seeking.

For the next few years, she travelled ninety miles as often as she could, and although she confesses that the preaching was beyond her, she knew that she wanted what they had. In 1969, a friend took her to another conference. Mr North was preaching, and when talking to him afterwards, somewhat "incoherently" as she puts it, he simply said to her, "Let go!" and prayed for her.

66 Instantaneously, I knew a release in my spirit and a joy welling up within me. I was free of self and dead to the world. I have never looked back, but have known a faithfulness and consistency of this life in Him ever since. The Fellowships, therefore, mean a lot to me. They gave me not only a whole new purpose, but have also opened up opportunities to serve Him, both at home and abroad.

In 1983, she was asked by the eldership if she would be willing to come and help them on a full-time basis and to be resident for two years. After a brief struggle and needing real clarity and confirmation that this was of God, she agreed. There were certainly challenges – much 'pruning' and steep learning curves – but she has in fact remained with The Longcroft ever since, being an integral part of the life of the church and full of praise for the Lord's faithfulness.

66 Being a part of the Fellowships has shown me the importance of *serving* one another wholeheartedly; holding the things of this life and of the world lightly; being in the background, quietly getting on with things unnoticed and unrecognised; living the life in Jesus as His Holy Spirit directs; not neglecting one's natural family and friends, but seeking their salvation too; honouring those men and women of God who both currently and in former years have faithfully shown and taught the way, the truth and the life; and finally learning to sing the *song*, not just the *words*.

Children have always been an integral part of any Christian group, however small or large. From the moment a baby is born, and throughout his or her developing years, right through to adulthood, the heart of God is that with the right help, teaching and support from their parents and others, including His body, they will find Him for themselves and be brought into and be part of His kingdom, on earth as well as for eternity.

To this end, God has been utterly faithful in His provision of willing and committed people who have shared in this work and faithfully made themselves available for all age groups; from crèche work right through to the older teens.

All those who have been involved with the children's work at The Longcroft will admit that this can be both demanding and challenging, but also bring with it much joy and reward. The tender heart of a young child is soft, open and teachable. Adults possibly have much to learn from them. Jesus Himself said, *"...whoever does not receive the kingdom of God as a little child will by no means enter it."[57]*

As the church began to grow, so did the work with the children. Many have been involved over the years at every level, and much seed gently planted in 'good soil'. A couple who are still with The Longcroft, from those early years, were part of this and saw it grow rapidly.

Children's work
Morris and Joy Rowlands

❝ In 1986, nine parents of seven- to ten-year olds had it in their hearts to start a children's group on a Wednesday evening, which they called the 'J-Team' ('J' standing for 'Jesus'). In the very first week, they had the joy of welcoming fifteen children, all from The Longcroft. By the second week, some of their friends also came along, increasing the number to twenty-two. The numbers continued to grow until sometimes there were over sixty attending.

The evening was comprised of games (as noisy as possible!) along with crafts, and finally, partly to calm them down sufficiently before returning home, an epilogue was given about the Lord Jesus. An annual overnight camp on the lawn was always a highlight and a great success, along with the occasional outing.

One of the most popular evenings was spent on the front lawn, jumping in and out of paddling pools, and water games that almost knew no limits. It was in fact obligatory for all the leaders to get a thorough soaking. There would also be an evening when all the families of the children were invited for food and games on the lawn, at the end of the school year.

After a couple of years, it was realised that there was a need to cater for the eleven-plus age group, as many of the J-Team children were beginning to outgrow the particular age-related activities; so a second group was started on a Friday evening called J-Force. Again, this proved highly popular, and numbers grew rapidly, so requiring a further group to be formed. 'J-Force Juniors' emerged for the eleven- to thirteen-year-olds, and 'J-Force Seniors' who were fourteen to fifteen years old, who met together

---

[57] Mark 10:15

once the Juniors had finished and gone home. Both these groups followed a similar programme to the J-Team, but age-related.

Periodically all teams and ages combined for trips out – another popular and enjoyable enterprise. Eventually these evenings out evolved to an annual weekend away to Beechwood Court in Conwy, North Wales, where fifty to sixty youngsters accompanied by twelve or more adults spent time on the beach, playing games, bob-sledding, go-carting, swimming, tennis, as well as perusing the shops. Weather permitting, a barbeque would also be enjoyed by all, with Keith and Christine Kelly taking the evening epilogues. There was always a good response to these.

Amongst the many positives that came out of these groups was that many of the local families belonging to these children were invited to come along to watch what their children were doing. This had the effect of demystifying The Longcroft in the local community, and put it on a par with the Scouts, Guides and Brownies, and therefore acceptable! That the children heard the Good News of the Lord Jesus week by week did not seem to deter the parents from allowing their children to attend. When the youngsters were too old for J-Force, many would go up to the long-established Friday club for the sixteen-plus age group.

The J-Team ceased around 2010, but the Friday Club still continue. Many hundreds of children, some now in their forties, have come through these clubs, all being given the opportunity of hearing the gospel week by week. They are now scattered far and wide, many having made a response to the Lord. What started as a need to provide a club for the Fellowship's children, God had used for the furtherance of the gospel on the Wirral and beyond.

Chris Knight, married to Carolyn, has also faithfully given himself to working with the young people, in particular, and has been responsible over more recent years for overseeing the young people's work. He too has testified to God's faithfulness at all times.

From his perspective, he would see the role of any youth worker to be one of encouragement, coming alongside them as well as being an additional support to the parents. Teamwork for him is of real importance – everybody working together to help each young person to not only come to faith in Christ but to increasingly help them to learn how to walk and appropriate their faith in a practical way. The pressures upon our young people today are considerable, and they all need our help in an unthreatening atmosphere.

The way that this can be realised most effectively is to have a praying church supporting all the work undertaken. The Fellowship at The Longcroft has certainly been a praying church from its very beginnings, and frequently people have testified to this, knowing so often that they have felt upheld at particular times as prayer has been made.

During the earlier days, more formal links were also made with the Jucos and Covenanters for the youngsters and teenagers, which proved both helpful and valuable. For the older teenagers, inter-church meetings were also introduced and run by Dave Vine, which covered the Merseyside area and beyond. Young people enjoy mixing together with their peers from other churches, finding this both stimulating and refreshing.

As mentioned earlier, the J-Team and J-Force groups joined together each year for a weekend away in Conwy, North Wales. It was during one of these weekends, on June 27th, 1999, that the Lord gave the following prophecy, given by Dave Vine:

"I have sown My seed and I have sown My seed far and wide, and there will be a gathering. There will be a gathering from that seed. For the seed will have grown and will have brought forth fruit unto Me. The seed will have overcome the obstacles of the world – the temptations which are many – and will have endured, from that good ground. And there will be fruit from that seed, and I will draw in and gather in the fruit which I have perfected over many years, and I will present the fruit and the riches thereof which are of Me unto the Father when it is perfect. It will be of Me; I *will* have tended it and kept it from the world and presented it perfect unto My Father and there will be much rejoicing in the heavens."

Steps of Hope
One of the helpers

66 Steps of Hope began with a young lady who had been in the Sunday school at The Longcroft. She was walking home from university one evening and saw a homeless man sitting outside a shop. She bought him a coffee and sat and talked to him. He was

so grateful – more that she talked with him than for the coffee – and this moved her to get involved with homeless people. She began by preparing Christmas bags for the homeless, and several people from The Longcroft joined her in distributing them.

From this small act of caring, a work has developed and a team now go out onto the streets of Liverpool twice a month in the evening to give out drinks, food and clothing to their homeless friends. They talk to them about 'making steps' to get off the streets and into accommodation. As the work has grown, groups now from several denominations work together, sharing God's love.

> *"Then the righteous will answer Him saying, 'Lord, when did we see You hungry and feed You, or thirsty and give You drink? When did we see You a stranger and take You in, or naked and clothe You? Or when did we see You sick or in prison, and come to You? And the King will answer and say to them, 'Assuredly, I say to you, inasmuch as you did it to one of the least of these My brethren, you did it to Me.'"*[58]

An extended family

An integral part of the life of the church in more recent years at The Longcroft has been a special secluded and allocated area at the top of the front lawn (originally a vegetable garden) for Jo's 'extended family'! Initially, a very kind family living next to The Longcroft were willing to provide a 'home' for these very special 'residents', but they were relocated to The Longcroft when their home was sold.

Jo is a precious and multi-talented lady who has been there for many years, living in the main house and available for almost anything. In the early days, when it was specifically a rest home, Jo would be at the hub of all the activity – the kitchen. There she would care for latecomers, making them hot drinks, huddled against the source of all heat – the Aga! Everyone else had usually retired for the night, asleep in bed, but dear Jo would ensure that visitors were always made welcome and provided for before they too were given a bed for the night.

However, it was not only visitors who benefited from her kindness and hospitality; it was the many and varied long-term residents from a variety of species, who squawked, quacked, squeaked and bleated,

---

[58] Matthew 25:37-39

making themselves known in their undeniable ways, and all housed appropriately behind a hedge at the top of the garden.

Sian the sheep was possibly one of the favourites, together with a few goats, geese, chickens, ducks and rabbits. Sadly, Sian has now been laid to rest there, and the geese and goats have bid farewell, as have the ducks, but a few chickens and rabbits remain, slightly nearer to the house. The chickens have been well trained, providing many with their free-range eggs – six for £1. Today, this whole area behind the top hedge has been transformed again into a quiet and peaceful haven to which one can escape for some treasured moments of tranquillity.

Jo's IT and computer skills are also greatly valued, as well as her being able to help out with the endless domestic duties and demands needed when running and maintaining a large home.

Transformations

All those who knew life at the 'Longi' in the early days will know that many adjustments, renovations, building and decorating have been ongoing as the work has expanded. Walls have been knocked down, flooring renewed, the roof repaired on several occasions, as well as a new build adjacent to the main house to provide a well-equipped crèche area and a first-floor meeting room for the young people.

It has been invaluable to have, as one of the elders, someone who was a qualified surveyor, and whose expertise has been drawn upon and appreciated on many occasions. Transforming the three small rooms that had made up the kitchen area into one large room was a major challenge and gave the strong lads of the day much opportunity to learn and practise their DIY skills under the guidance of their in-house professional. For some, it was so much easier to smash through the many layers of old tiling rather than to carefully hammer away in a more orderly fashion. Much discussion was needed regarding the Aga – should it be fired by gas or electricity? What about the plumbing? But in all of these issues and labours of love, they knew a unity of heart and spirit, and the Lord truly blessed and worked in them all.

Comparing current photos with the originals, so many areas have changed almost out of recognition, but the testimony of God's love and the vision that He originally gave to the Milner family continues on undeniably. Wonderfully, all needs have continually been met as the need has arisen, the Lord being so faithful to all of His promises.

The Longcroft today

Missionary support and outreach

The vision that the Lord first gave to Norman in the early '60s of a tree "whose leaves were seen burning together in a heap for a time, and then being caught up in the wind, spreading out and becoming a canopy over the whole globe, with the leaves falling down into every nation" has certainly been increasingly fulfilled over subsequent years. Countless people of all ages, whose lives have been so radically transformed through the life, teaching and ministry known within the Fellowships, have responded to God's call upon their lives and ventured forth to well over seventy countries worldwide, laying down their lives for the gospel.

As one walks into the meeting room at The Longcroft, a large world map is clearly seen on one of its walls, with photos of missionaries specifically linked with the Fellowships and for whom much prayer is made week by week, both in the weekly prayer meeting and also in additional and varying monthly groups, as well as for the countries and needs that they represent. There are also those with a strong intercessory ministry who are known to spend much time in prayer for those countries and people who have particularly been laid on their hearts. Norman, even until his late 80s, continued to travel out to India and Nepal twice a year for weeks at a time, as well as supporting and visiting churches in Sicily, France, Cyprus and, more recently, Armenia and other places, as opportunity (and strength) were given.

As mentioned previously, a much more detailed account of the history of The Longcroft is currently being prepared, but this will have hopefully given some insight into how the Lord has miraculously and wonderfully moved and established His purposes through initially a very God-fearing family – the Milners. Only eternity will reveal the full story.

7

Expansion and Growth

A spreading flame

Birmingham; Victoria Park Christian Fellowship, Manchester; further outreach, Manchester

It wasn't too long before things began to happen in other parts of the country. Those who had travelled into Liverpool almost every weekend, hungering and thirsty for more of God and all that He was doing there, returned to their homes late on a Sunday night or within the early hours of the following morning, often miles away – north, south, east and west. Those weekend 'conferences', with often no beds to sleep on, little food, primitive cooking arrangements, and where the only seat available may have been the landing floor or staircase, had in no way deterred them. They had simply picked up the phone and said, "Can we come?" They had been wonderful times, and God moved freely and powerfully.

Birmingham

One of the first Fellowships to emerge outside of Liverpool was in Birmingham. Initially it had simply been a group of young teenagers whose lives had been changed through listening primarily to the ministry of Mr North and Norman in Liverpool. They worshipped, prayed, shared and evangelised, the Holy Spirit enabling them to live out all that they had received, week by week.

In another part of Birmingham, at the Birmingham Bible Institute, students were also seeking the Lord, some of whom had also heard of the move in Liverpool and had travelled up to experience this for themselves. Two of these students were Derrick and Barbara Harrison, along with others from the local university. The thing that drew Derrick more than anything and that had resonated so deeply within his heart, was the scriptural teaching on holiness and freedom from sin, which was central to all the teaching and ministry so clearly being expounded. This was surely God's heart for all of His people.

Returning from further missionary training in the States, Derrick and Barbara began to meet with these other small groups, opening up their semi-detached home for times of informal meetings and Bible study on a Sunday afternoon and during the week. John Simkins and Sandy Frame were two of the brothers who were with him at that time.

It soon became apparent that their semi-detached home was causing not a few of their neighbours to complain; not only because of the noise, but also because of the number of cars blocking the road. Sharing the problem with Norman, they began to pray and seek the Lord for an answer. A house in Wentworth Road became available but, as is so often the case, financially out of reach. They continued to pray, and the answer unfolded into a situation that has remained unique to the Fellowship there ever since. They had what they called 'a squeeze'. Each member of the Fellowship would live on the basic minimum, both food and clothing, over a period of six to twelve months. They would buy no new clothes, no luxuries, no 'extras' of any description. Norman recalls:

66 I knew one family who for six months of the year virtually lived on bread and milk so that they could give ninety-five per cent of their income towards what the Lord was doing. They have, as a Fellowship, done this again and again, both for the work in Birmingham and for work overseas.

He remembers a time when someone from eastern Europe came to speak, and before he left, he took with him three carloads of clothes. The whole Fellowship gave literally everything that they possessed apart from the clothes that they were wearing.

As a result of such sacrificial giving, together with the selling of their home, they eventually found a house in the Harborne area that was not only a real provision for this growing church (now over sixty adults and thirty children), but it was also discovered that it had received planning permission for religious meetings – an added bonus and confirmation.

They continued to meet in Harborne for twelve years, after which it was felt that they should move to a more needy area of the City. As a result of another 'squeeze', with families selling their own homes and giving so sacrificially of all that they possessed, they were able to build a new church and a home for Derrick and Barbara in Smethwick. Every evening and Saturday morning saw many, not only from the Birmingham

Fellowship but from other Fellowships too, join forces and roll up their sleeves to take on this major work. Bricklayers and plasterers were the only outside help that they employed. Derrick recalls how "Mr North proudly opened the new church in January 1987".

A few years later, resulting from encouragement again from Mr North, it was felt that it would be of real value to provide specific teaching and training for future leadership, and the Christian Workers Programme (CWP) was launched in 1993, extending over an eight-month period from January to August, culminating with the students travelling down to Devon to help set up and be involved with the annual summer conference within the grounds of the Rora Fellowship in Liverton. Mr North was always in his element when surrounded by students eager to learn and study the wonderful biblical truths that had so revolutionised his own life, as well as being able to impart the immense depths and riches experienced by him over so many fruitful years of ministry. Other elders, leaders and experienced mature Christians were also invited to help and have a specific input into the curriculum, which was not dissimilar to that found in the more traditional Bible colleges. The average annual intake of students was usually between nine and twelve, all of whom were accommodated within families belonging to the Fellowship. It continued on successfully for seven years until 2000, after which it was felt, for a variety of reasons, to discontinue it; but during that time, much was accomplished and many gained a very valuable insight not only into the Scriptures but also an outworking of these truths in their individual lives.

Two other groups also began to meet in Birmingham, one in south Birmingham under the leadership of Ron Bailey, but both now have discontinued. Some joined the Fellowship in Smethwick, and others alternative Fellowships or churches. Many others were also coming into being such as in Ledbury, Bristol, Leamington Spa, Leigh, Otley, Tiverton, Whitley Bay, Leominster, Nottingham, Grimsby, Warrington, Bramhall, Manchester and Leeds. Some have continued and grown; others have remained but smaller, or have discontinued, but each were vibrant groups of believers who had come into the life of God in a way that they had never previously known and that had transformed their lives.

One such testimony is from a dear brother – John Shaw, married to Martha, whom the Lord has quietly and unobtrusively used both in the UK and abroad in Africa. John is a quiet and unassuming man but with a strong gifting in teaching and leadership. He has faithfully served as an elder in the Epsom Christian Fellowship in Surrey as well as the Lanark Fellowship in Scotland, and was very involved with the Auchenheath Fellowship.

The faithfulness of God
John Shaw

❝ Our first encounter with the Fellowships was hearing Derrick Harrison when he came to speak at a small meeting in Leamington Spa. The Christianity that we had was not giving us the answer to the needs of our lives. Soon we were travelling four times a week to the Fellowship in Birmingham. When Martha came back from a conference in Auchenheath, Scotland, where Mr North had been speaking, she was a changed woman, and I knew that I needed the Lord to change me. We subsequently moved to Walsall to be near to the Fellowship there. I gave up my teaching job and we gave ourselves to seeking the Lord. In 1977, at a conference at Rora House in Devon, the Lord came into my life and I received the Holy Spirit.

In 1984, after being fully involved with the Fellowship at Walsall for a few years, the Lord opened the way for us to join John and Celia Valentine at Ameva Farm in Zimbabwe. We spent two and a half years setting up the primary school, before returning to the UK.

We helped at the Auchenheath Fellowship in Scotland for four years before the Lord graciously opened up the way for us to return to Ameva to set up the secondary school. So often, the Lord gives us a second chance when we have not handled things as well as we should have done.

We thank the Lord for the wonderful staff and helpers He provided for us, for all their hard work and managing to overcome so many difficulties.

At the beginning of 1999, Shepherd Ziramba took over as headmaster of Ameva Secondary School. He has competently steered the school through turbulent political times and is now introducing 'A' level studies at the school. Later in 1999, we were refused our application for our permanent residency in Zimbabwe, and we returned to the UK. Hem and Kathy Bunten kindly adapted their home to enable us to stay with them in West Ewell, and we spent three happy years in the Epsom Fellowship.

In 2002, the Lord spoke clearly to me that we should move, and a few days later we received a letter from Mickey Wright, inviting us to help him at the Lanark Fellowship. The Lord wonderfully provided enough money for us to be able to buy a small flat in Lanark.

Our testimony is that the Lord has been with us in so many varying situations and has always proved to be a faithful and loving Father.

John and Martha have recently moved back to Scotland from Northern Ireland, where they have been caring for family members of Martha's, who sadly have now passed away.

Rise, take up thy bed and walk!
Peter Coates

66 I was regularly attending another Fellowship in Walsall. In one unforgettable meeting there, everyone was taken up in ecstatic worship of the Lord and His presence was unusually evident. As many sang and prayed aloud, I heard the voice of the Lord again clearly say to me, "Will you risk your life for Me?" I was a little taken aback at first, but then, because I knew that God would see me through whatever might happen, I gladly said yes.

A week later, a lady in the church asked me if I would take her young son and his friend to Sandwell Valley County Park to swim in the lake there. These boys were both deaf and dumb. When we got there, the boys went straight in for a swim, then came out and started to kick a football on the grass nearby. I then went in for a swim and noticed that the lake was shallow at first but then suddenly became very deep.

When I came out again, one of the boys kicked the ball about twenty yards out into the lake. I turned around and ran back through the clear water and did a racing dive as flat as possible, aiming to arrive at the very deep part. I did feel a very slight bump on my forehead but drifted out, face down, towards the ball. However, when I came to take a stroke and turn to take a breath, I was unable to do either. I could open my eyes and still hold my breath and thought that maybe I had hit the rim of the lake and was experiencing concussion. Seconds ticked away, with me still drifting out, and I was running out of breath. Just as I was about to really struggle, I felt the presence of the Lord just as if I were back in that meeting the week before. I realised that this was what the Lord had indicated and wondered if any second I would be in Glory. A second or two later, I was lifted out of the water. I saw the sky and shore and then passed out.

I came to, lying on my back, still completely paralysed from the neck down. A group of people came along and two men approached me to pull me up, but a lady behind them screamed out, "Leave him alone! I'm a nurse. He may have broken his neck!"

They called an ambulance and I was whisked off to hospital where an X-ray confirmed that indeed I had broken my neck. Martin Williams, our elder, and my brother Stephen came to visit me and prayed for me. I knew that the Lord would heal me and that I would walk again. I was put on head traction and in a couple of days was taken slowly by ambulance up to a hospital in Wales to a specialist spinal injuries unit in Oswestry.

Many visited me from the Fellowship, and someone told me how the boys had indicated to their sister that they could not understand why I had not continued to swim out to get their ball. Then they had seen two lifeguards run around the lake, who had rushed into the water, lifted me out, laid me out on the bank and then run off again!

After a few days a young lady from the Liverpool Fellowship, Wendy Dooley, had an accident and fell part of the way down the Llanrhaeadr waterfall in Wales. She fell onto her coccyx, damaging the nerves in the base of her spine. She fell into a 'dish' of rock where the very cold water helped to numb the pain a little until the fire service arrived to fish her out. She was also admitted to the same ward as I was in; ladies one end and the men at the other. All patients on this ward were considered either paraplegic or tetraplegic. Wendy had many visitors as well from her Fellowship. So many visitors! We both felt tremendously uplifted, encouraged and supported as well as by people praying. Suffice it to say that we were both healed of paralysis and learnt to walk again.

Victoria Park Fellowship, Manchester

The Fellowship in Manchester first originated through a group of Christians who had come over from Hungary. One family had been involved in missionary work, particularly in India and Nepal, before they came to England. One of the daughters was Julie Grates (née Ray) who married Len, who subsequently became an elder at the Devonshire Road Fellowship in Liverpool for a time. The group met in a home called 'The Nook' which belonged to Ocsi[59] and Heather Angyal. Julie has shared part of her testimony in Chapter 5.

From The Nook, a larger premise was found, which is still used by the church, together with another building that first needed to be exorcised and renovated as it had belonged to some spiritualists. An in-house architect helped to transform it into a very welcoming venue. Many have been involved in the leadership of the Fellowship at different times, including John Carter, Roger Shuttleworth, Bob Peck, Les Wheeldon, Dr Malcolm Brooks and Brian Rainford. Dr Malcolm Brooks, along with Peter March, are still there.

One lady who was a part of The Nook and is now in full-time missionary work shares her testimony.

Drawn by God

66 In the late 1960s, God began to draw me with cords of love to Himself.

I was walking in Switzerland and in a small village church had found the Bible open at Ezekiel 47, which tells about the river flowing from the throne of God. I did not understand it but felt drawn by God to its meaning.

Later, returning to England, I met someone who invited me to a small House Fellowship known as The Nook. At the first meeting I went to, Norman Meeten stood up and said that he wanted to talk to us that night about the river that flows from God, from Ezekiel 47. As he spoke, I knew he was in that river and the river was flowing out of him. He explained from John's Gospel the words that Jesus spoke: *"If anyone thirsts, let him come to Me and drink. He who believes in Me, as the Scripture has said, out of his heart will flow rivers of living water."*[60] God

---

[59] pronounced 'Urchi'
[60] John 7:37-38

was revealing His great truth to me. I never stopped going to the meetings after that.

I continued going to this small House Fellowship, and after a few weeks the leader's wife asked me if I would like to receive a pure, clean heart and a new spirit.[61] I was amazed that God would give that to me. She explained that I could receive it just as Mary had received the word of the angel when she said, *"...be it unto me according to thy word."[62]*

I received it as a gift and I felt clean from head to toe; I felt like I was wearing bright, clean wedding garments.

I believe it was after the first meeting that I had ever been to, where Mr North had been preaching, that he stopped me as I was leaving to go out. He told me that the Lord had given him a word of knowledge for me. I was amazed, as he had never met me before. He said, "You have never known a father and it is as if you have been walking around with only one arm, and God wants to fill you with His love, the love of a Father." He prayed for me and I was filled with God's fatherly love to overflowing. My earthly father had died thirteen days before I was born; wonderfully, he had known the Lord and had been involved in missionary work.

Another couple remember with gratitude the ministry they experienced and received when they were with the Victoria Park Fellowship in Manchester.

Introduced to the Lord Jesus
Tony and Linda Stronge

66 We do recall the amazing depth of fellowship and teaching we received from Norman, Mr North, Bernard Hull and others when they visited Victoria Park Fellowship over the years. However, the biggest impact on our lives was the daily contact with, and love from, our more mature brothers and sisters in the Fellowship who bore with us when we were ignorant and arrogant. They pointed us to Christ. We had both been fervent, sincere church attendees for many years, but had never come across people who had 'died to self'. We witnessed them living everyday lives by faith with

---

[61] See Ezekiel 36:26
[62] Luke 1:30,38 (KJV)

Christ at the centre, and eventually we yielded to Him too. They were very precious years and the bonds are still there. When we meet up with them, we just carry on where we left off.

Tony does recall (with some embarrassment) meeting Norman for lunch in the early 1980s. Tony says he felt that it was like having lunch with Jesus, who was very gracious while Tony talked about himself. That made a lasting impression on him.

Bramhall Christian Fellowship
Mark Langley

❝ The very beginnings of Bramhall Christian Fellowship can be traced back to 1974, when Alan England (who had at that time been a part of the leadership team at Victoria Park Fellowship, Manchester) developed contacts through a church in New Mills where he had been invited to preach. As a result, a number of people started travelling to Victoria Park on a Sunday, and eventually mid-week meetings were started south of Manchester in a village called Mellor. From here, they moved to nearby New Mills. Sylvia Davies, who was also a member of Victoria Park, came along to help with the children during the meetings.

As the group grew in size, the meetings moved to a suburb of South Manchester called Bramhall, initially in the home of Eric and Jane Vickers, and then in the home of Bob and Joan Barrel.

These meetings in Bramhall were only intended to be a mid-week house group, an extension of the church in Victoria Park, but during a time of prayer and fasting at the end of 1982, the Lord spoke clearly to a couple in the group called Alan and Janet, that His heart was for them to move to Bramhall where He would establish another Fellowship. This seemed an impossibility, as they were living in inner-city Manchester and the prices in Bramhall were way beyond their reach. However, the others in the group embraced this vision. Alan and I met early one morning in a car park to sign the papers for a bank account to be opened in the name of Bramhall Christian Fellowship.

Alan and Janet put their house on the market in Longsight, and over the next three years the house sold five times, only for the sale to fall through yet again before the final completion. Finally, at the sixth attempt, it sold for £19,000 to a man who was only interested in the garden as it was apparently ideal for growing dahlias! He never did bother to view the inside of the house before buying.

Miracles!

During this same three-year period, much was done by the group to try to raise sufficient funds to purchase a suitable property, such as selling jewellery and other personal assets, but even with these sacrificial endeavours there was still a considerable shortfall. However, the God of all miracles was still at work. Other Christians, whilst praying, were also prompted to sell their possessions in order to give financial gifts. There were also large anonymous gifts of cash posted through letterboxes and monies passed from sources that are unknown even to this day.

A Christian widow who had heard about our situation turned up at Alan and Janet's door one day and passed over her engagement ring to them to sell. Humbling beyond description, no amount of persuasion could make this dear lady change her mind. On another day, a friend from the Victoria Park Fellowship delivered a truck-load of antique furniture and explained that he had been doing a plumbing job for a retired and very highly ranking officer in the Greater Manchester Police. He had never married, had no relatives, was very wealthy and was moving to a retirement home. He had told our friend that he had too much money, that he didn't need it, and wanted to sell some of his furniture and give the proceeds to "a Christian work". Could his friend suggest anything? Bramhall Christian Fellowship came to mind. The furniture, which included a floor-to-ceiling oil painting similar to those on display in stately homes, was auctioned and yielded so much money that we offered to return the proceeds, thinking that he had not really realised its worth. However, the message came back, "Keep it for whatever you are doing!" We actually never met this man or knew his name.

Looking for property

The group began to look around for properties. In 1983, one of our members, Janet Ince, noticed that 67 Bramhall Lane South was for sale, but initially we dismissed the idea because although we had raised a substantial amount, the asking price of £104,000 seemed far out of our reach.

During one of the group's regular times of prayer and fasting, God gave a prophecy saying, "I will show you the house. Two or three will also be going for it, but I will give it to you. And I will tell you how much you should offer for it." After some of the group viewed the house, we were sure that No. 67 was the right property. We had not made an offer at that point, and it was decided that each member should seek the Lord independently (no conferring!) about what to offer. The group was just over twenty-strong at that time and everybody was within £500 of the figure the Lord had given to Alan and Janet, which was £87,000. Two other interested parties came and went, and our offer stayed on the table. We waited for the third person to arise, and sure enough they did, with a cash offer £500 above ours. Nonetheless, we felt that we should stay with the amount God had said, even though it looked as though we would lose it. The owner decided that as we'd been honest with him, he would accept our offer. Unbelievably, the house was ours and the Bramhall Christian Fellowship had a home.

Then the hard work started. The building had been empty for nine months and needed a lot of renovation. Again, we had no money but God always provided just what was needed. A major expense was for a new boiler for which we needed around £1,000. One day a letter came from a lady in Manchester whom we didn't know. She had received money from an insurance policy and had asked God what to do with it. He told her to give it to us.

People we knew with building and plumbing skills gave their time for free, and we had work parties all day every Saturday and on Wednesday evenings. If we didn't have a skill then someone would go off and learn it.

Walls were knocked down, chimneys removed, doors stripped and varnished, the house painted, replumbed and rewired, the driveway restored, and the whole inside stripped, repaired and redecorated. The kitchen was completely stripped back to bare brick before being replastered and painted. Finally, in January 1986, we were ready to have our first public meeting as Bramhall Christian Fellowship.

Once we were up and running, many other people joined us, and at times we didn't have enough chairs or room to seat everybody. We have seen many lives changed over the years and many people arrive and move on; some to go on with the Lord, and others sadly not. Several people have gone on to work for the Lord overseas or have become involved in active ministry in other churches. There have, of course, been difficult times, some quite traumatic to the church and that could have destroyed us, but our testimony is that God has always been faithful and has kept us.

At the time of writing (2018) we have been going for over thirty years. We are still in the same building that God gave us so miraculously at the start and we still have a few members who have been here from the beginning. Our numbers are fewer than they have been in the past, but our confidence is that He who has begun a good thing will bring it to completion.

Further outreach in the Manchester area

Keith and Christine Kelly have had a significant input into many of the Fellowships over the years, as well as abroad in numerous countries. Keith has shared part of his testimony, recorded in Appendix 1. Similar to Dave Wetherly, there is no hint of the heartaches he experienced in his earlier years related to financial restraints on his parents and the ill-health of his father. He is an exceptionally gifted evangelist, and has seen the Lord move miraculously again and again as he has simply moved in obedience to God's leadings.

8

Further Growth and Expansion in the South East

The fire burns on

Crystal Palace; Hotton Kirby; Topsham, Eltham Green, London; Winchmore Hill Christian Fellowship, London; Earley Christian Fellowship, Reading; Worthing Christian Fellowship, Sussex; Beaconsfield Christian Fellowship, Broadstairs

In a large house in Hotton Kirby near Dartford in Kent, back in the 1940s, lived a dear couple called 'P and J' – Peter and Joy Palmer. One of Joy's precious legacies is that wonderful hymn, one of many which she wrote, 'Thou dost seek a Bride all pure and holy', that so many have come to love.

They spent much of their time there ministering and caring for Finnish girls. In 1946, a small house church was formed, led by Donald Reeve, who had been an Oxford Don and previously a member of the Quaker movement, until the Lord met him and filled him with His Spirit. After a time, they began to meet in a Congregational church in Crystal Palace, and then later in Penge.

Peter and Joy knew Mr North, who at that time was living in Maidstone, pastoring a Baptist church. From time to time they used to travel to a nearby town to where he had occasionally been invited to speak. They were also in touch with Dave Wetherly and Dick Hussey, both of whom became elders at the Devonshire Road Christian Fellowship in the 1960s. One of Peter and Joy's children, Di – who later married Paul Moss – remembers being baptised with her brother when she was just twelve years old, by Dave Wetherly, in a local river!

In 1947, they moved to Devon, to where there was a similar house group in Topsham, although close links with Hotton Kirby continued throughout the 1950s. Two well-known preachers at that time – Edgar

Parkyns and Cecil Cousins (from Bradford) – were often invited to minister there, with Ken Jackman and David Lily being the two leaders.

Peter and Joy travelled a lot in their Christian ministry, establishing close links with the Exeter and Liverpool house churches in particular. Their children were involved in full-time Christian work, both in Southampton and the North East, as well as Paul and Di living and working in Hong Kong for over forty years. Paul is now with the Lord and Di is part of the Fellowship in Reading.

Further house groups also came into being in the London area, namely in Bromley, Eltham and Winchmore Hill. Penge and Bromley have discontinued, but Eltham and Winchmore Hill (now known as the Chase Family Church) are still growing; the Chase Family Church are now not so closely connected to the Fellowships, as such, but are still of the same heart.

Eltham Green Fellowship

Terry Watson has shared the first part of his testimony in the first chapter. His full and amazing story can be found in the introduction to his book *The Pastoral Ministry*, which is available free of charge.[63] He has kindly given us permission to share with you anything that we feel may be helpful and relevant. Here is another excerpt shedding some light on how the Lord was graciously preparing him for full-time Christian ministry and leadership.

66 Having been blessed of God, secular work began to be an obstacle. In my heart arose a real desire to serve God and I was in conflict. ... It wasn't long before God's word came to me from reading the Scriptures, from a passage in Chronicles: *"...who lodged in the chambers, and were free from other duties, for they were employed in that work day and night"[64].*

I wanted to serve the Lord without restraint, and without having to go up and down to town every day. I understood later that this was the call of God to me to be involved in His work and be available full-time. It seemed right for me to give up my work and make myself available. ... I was desperate for something more, so we began to meet with a few folk in the home of Lionel and Nora Hemmings, who were involved with Mr North. My

---

[63] Terry Watson can be contacted at *terry@terryandfran.info*
[64] 1 Chronicles 9:33

decision to give up work was totally alien to most of our friends and family. My father-in-law expressed the opinion that I was irresponsible to abandon my family to the insecurity of serving God and that I would be giving up a good salary and putting at risk the beautiful three-bedroom house we had bought over-looking Ladywell Park. However, in spite of such opposition, one morning in July I gave my manager a month's notice to terminate my employment. To his question, "How will you live?" I replied, "By faith," although at the time I didn't really know what living by faith meant.

For a time, Terry worked as a double-glazing salesman, recalling the dread that he felt in considering such a task as knocking on strangers' doors seeking to sell them something that he was sure they did not want. However, he realised that he was in God's school, learning to communicate with men and women.

66 For three years I remained in this learning place, at times even being top salesman in London for three consecutive months during my time there. In 1973, I gave up this work to be available full-time to the Lord. During this time, we had begun to meet in our home in Crofton Park. How strange it is thinking of those early days, because at no time did we plan to hold meetings. No-one would have considered that this shy, introverted man would have qualified for a leadership place in the Lord's church, but people were being sent by God from quite a wide area, for encouragement and counsel, and it seemed that God graciously gave us answers to their needs.

Eventually, after a few difficult situations, house moves and a variety of meeting venues, with steep learning curves, the Lord clearly led them to a home in Eltham, and in June 1975 they began the Eltham Green Fellowship, knowing afresh that they were in the blessing of God.

66 Within eighteen months of gathering, a hundred of us squashed into our living room using chairs and stools, babies on our laps and with some floor space for the children, all eager to learn of God. Eventually we had to move up three doors into the house of Alan and Betty Stewart at No. 1 Eltham Green as they had a larger living room, moving the Sunday school to our own home. We had now grown to a hundred and thirty and began to upset the

neighbours who lived in houses 2 and 3, who were becoming distressed by the activity on Sundays as children and adults moved from house to house.

Once again, it was needful for them to find more suitable accommodation, and by the end of 1979, with the Lord overruling miraculously, they were allowed to use an extension of one of Eltham's Anglican churches on the other side of the town. Then in 1982, after much prayer and fasting and heart-searching, the Lord wonderfully enabled them to purchase their own property, which had been a Methodist church.

66 The vision God gave to us was a place where we could live, meet and fellowship. Over these past fourteen years (and still to this current day) we have been able to enlarge the property, providing extra facilities including a baptismal pool, new toilets, kitchen, lounge and Sunday school rooms, together with a three-bedroom and two-bedroom flat. Surely true evidence of God's goodness in His leading us as His church.

Winchmore Hill Christian Fellowship, North London
Ken Swan

66 During 1964, although I confess dates are not my strong point, I experienced a very real thirst and desire to know the power of God in my life. I read in the New Testament about a vibrant Christianity that did not appear to be the case in the church circles I was in. I had experienced the 'deeper life' teaching and welcomed the association with those whose lives challenged me to service and sacrifice, but I was faced with a Bible that seemed, to me, to teach a filling by the Spirit which did not rely on my achieving a holy life first. In fact, it was only by the filling of the Holy Spirit that we were able to live the life that Jesus promised, and not by my efforts. It was by His impartation. I looked for a marrying of the word and the Spirit, holiness with power.

I started seeking for a baptism in the Holy Spirit, which was an unpopular decision amongst my fellow believers.

I heard of meetings being held by a man called Richard Bolt, who had trained for the Anglican ministry, but was working as an evangelist with the Assemblies of God. I asked and received prayer, and although I had no great experience, I had an assurance that God was at work. Then things started to happen. I had been accompanied to this meeting by the wife of one of the youth leaders in my church. She did not receive prayer but wanted to watch what happened. Bolt sent her to the back of the meeting saying he wanted no spectators!

Her son, who was my age, was at Bible college and we did not get on. He was a very nice person, brought up in a Christian home. I, on the other hand, was a rough ex Rock and Roll drummer, still learning the ways of a polite Christian society! (I am reminded of a story of John Wimber who, when asked, "When were you washed in the blood, brother?" replied, "When do they do that, then?")

This son approached me, obviously upset, and informed me how wrong I was to have taken his mother to the meeting (she being twice my age!) He had been so upset with her that he went away to ask forgiveness for his anger, and whilst on his knees, God filled him with His Spirit. He was bewildered!

The outcome was that the two of us started to meet together for prayer. Soon we were asked to pray for others, and slowly a group of us were meeting midweek from different churches. We called ourselves the BITS group (Baptised in the Spirit). One of those who came is now Yvonne Medlock.

We were completely unaware of any other group like ours, little realising that God was doing a similar work all over the country.

It came as a bombshell to find that one of our number had a brother who attended a similar group in Beckenham, in South London. We visited them, and met Derek and Hilary Wilkes. They were associated with a meeting in Buckingham Street, central London, held in the offices of a businessman called Foote. They introduced us to the principle of body ministry, something about which the Lord had been teaching us, based upon 1 Corinthians 14:26.

During this time, I met Bernard Hull. Bernard was in the local Brethren Assembly. He approached me to ask if I would consider joining a gospel band for working with young people, many of whom were addicts. After a short time, Bernard asked me to pray for him for the baptism in the Spirit. He also joined the BITS group. I was still in the Baptist church, but the midweek BITS group continued to grow.

One Sunday, Dave Medlock turned up at the Baptist church. An uncle had just died and this had had a profound effect on Dave, challenging his backslidden condition. To cut a long story short, he ended up being filled with the Spirit and joining us midweek.

Bernard and I, with the gospel band, often worked with an evangelist from the National Young Life Campaign. During the summer of 1966, they took over a school in the Lake District called Witherslack Hall, for week-long holidays and house-parties. I took a party of young people. It was here that I met Barbara and got to know her better. We married in April 1968.

During the summer of 1967, we were both on the staff at Witherslack, as was a young man called Andy Hunter. Andy was at teacher training college in North London, and another Brethren man. Andy asked Bernard and me to pray with him, and he too was filled with the Holy Spirit. We met Margy, who was to become Andy's wife, after Witherslack.

Dave married Yvonne in early 1968 and moved to Reading. Some of us would go at certain weekends to Reading, and eventually a church started there. Bernard went to Bible college in Glasgow, where he met Hazel. Andy and Margy married in late 1967, and Andy enjoyed a fruitful ministry in the college until they moved to Kent.

After our marriage, Barbara and I sensed the call of God to start meeting on Sundays. We left the Baptist church very amicably and started to meet in our three-roomed flat. In fact, the only place left in the room where Andrew Ray, who was to play a major part in running the Fellowship, could sit was under the table!

Through a series of miracles we managed to obtain two houses next to each other in Green Dragon Lane, Winchmore Hill, in North London, where God did many wonderful and marvellous things.

We met Mr North in 1968, although Barbara had met him and Norman at one of the very early conferences on the Holy Spirit in Haldon Court, Devon in 1964/65. He invited us to a men's conference at Rora, where we met for the first time men from other groups like ours, known as the Fellowships. There was much reconciliation going on between brothers from Liverpool. This was our first contact with people like Ken Moffat and Dave Wetherly, Terry Watson, Derek Gitsham and Jack Kelly.

Over the years, we have had the privilege of having many prominent leaders come out of the Winchmore Hill Christian Fellowship (now known as the Chase Family Church) like Andrew Ray, Dave Latham, Les and Vicky Wheeldon, Dave and Heather Snow, as well as those already mentioned.

I have kept to the bare bones and left out details of houses and mission work, and the many people whose lives have been touched by God. All the glory goes to God who raises up works to make the name of Jesus known. We have experienced so many miracles of God's grace, meeting lovely people; and the fact that God used us *despite* my best efforts, not *because* of them, shows us that He alone deserves the praise.

Earley Christian Fellowship beginnings, Reading
Dave Medlock

66 In autumn 1969, a group of young people and students from Reading University began to seek the Lord for a deeper experience of His love and life-changing power. Initially there were about twelve people who began to meet regularly, but as the months passed, God added new souls who were hungry for more of God. Some of the Reading University Christian Union executive came to find out what was going on in this 'house' near to the university grounds, as wild stories began to circulate and there was growing opposition through misinformation and sometimes prejudice from some established churches. In hindsight, the leadership of the group were not as generous as they might have been to this reaction.

The real growth which followed was triggered when a young student came for prayer and God delivered him from evil spirits. He was so transformed that when he returned to the university, about forty new people turned up at the next meeting to see where and how this transformation had taken place. Many joined the group and the growth continued. We were all in our twenties and not very mature in Christ, but were greatly helped by occasional visits from mature itinerant preachers who taught the Scriptures and ministered Christ to us. The growth continued and we alternated the meetings between the different houses to give our neighbours some respite from the numbers and the singing. As we grew, we hired school premises on Sundays until, after some years, we purchased two large houses to live and meet in and eventually built a multi-purpose meeting room in the grounds.

One of the university lads who went along to the Fellowship describes the very positive input that it had on his early Christian life, and that has remained with him ever since.

Solid foundations
Rob Betts

❝ I first began to attend the Reading Fellowship during my final year at university in 1976. I can remember how quickly I felt at home in that church. It was quite unlike the rather traditional church I had previously attended in Reading and my home church in Salisbury. The things that particularly struck me about the Reading Fellowship were: (1) the spiritual and pastoral wisdom of the leadership; (2) the freedom given in the gatherings for others beside the leadership to share, for example, from the Scriptures or through prophecy and other spiritual gifts; and (3) the depth and spiritual understanding of the Bible teaching. It was a time of real building up as a Christian. Another thing that I remember and benefited from hugely was the pastoral care that I received there.

Worthing
Jenny Baldwin

❝ *"See, I have set before you an open door, and no one can shut it."*[65] This verse has been foundational in the life of the Fellowship in Worthing, now known as Clifton Community Church. The Fellowship began in the late 1960s when a group of about eight boys in high school were moved on by God and began meeting in the home of a local Christian couple. After about two years, a few other adults who had joined them together bought a detached property. This gave greater freedom in worship as they were able to sing without disturbing neighbours.

[65] Revelation 3:8

After some years, the original leaders and some other members moved away, and a small group continued meeting in the home of a young family. Later, another couple joined to take up the leadership. Numbers grew, and after some months of meeting in a rented hall, the church rented premises from the Council, which offered good facilities for the flourishing Sunday school.

With a long lease, future accommodation seemed secure, until the Council sold the site to a property developer. With many months of the lease left to run, the church received a sum of money which enabled it to buy Clifton Hall, its current home. An extensive building project was launched to convert the church into a two-storeyed building, with the main meetings taking place upstairs; with Sunday school rooms downstairs and two extensions housing toilets and kitchen. Having joined the church some months earlier, I was able to witness the sacrificial way that many gave themselves to this project, including some giving up paid employment to do so. It proved to be a time of deep fellowship as different ones learnt to work together as well as learning some new and varied skills.

The new building gave opportunity to continue the work among children, many of whom were from non-Christian homes and had been reached through tent missions held in a local park. Now it was possible to hold holiday clubs. For some years it was also used for annual Christmas parties for children from Christian clubs in four schools and run by members of the church.

Another initiative at this time was the provision of English language classes for Christians from overseas who needed English to serve the Lord. The students, who came from a broad range of countries, were hosted by members of the church whilst other members were able to help with the teaching. This in turn led to reaching out to overseas people in the town and running monthly international Friendship Evenings. Some of those with whom we made contact at that time joined the church, and to this day we have a lovely mix of nationalities. The students then left to fulfill their calling in different countries and some members of the church also left to serve overseas at about the same time.

Today, outreach work continues in the form of serving coffee and doughnuts in the town centre each month on a Friday evening and a weekly English language club for members of Worthing's growing overseas community.

Through the years, the Fellowship has increasingly joined with other Christians in the town in initiatives to reach out to the community. These have included ministries such as street pastors, Worthing Churches Homeless Project and joining with a local Anglican church for an annual Christmas carol service, continuing our schools work, and some Bible reading groups for members of other churches as well as our own.

Over the decades, the church has been served by many leaders, too many to mention here. All, in their faithful service to God, have blessed the church through bringing some to spiritual birth and helping others to mature in their faith. We owe them a great debt of gratitude. We have also been enriched by men such as Mr North, Norman Meeten (whose childhood was spent in nearby Washington and who has frequently been with us when visiting family) and Les Wheeldon. Others too have brought God's word, but space doesn't allow mention of them all. However, we are grateful to all who have challenged, exhorted and encouraged us.

Above all, we are so thankful to the Lord Himself, who has been our true shepherd and has proved so many times, through both the encouraging as well as the challenging seasons in the life of the church, that He really has opened a door which no man can shut.[66]

Beaconsfield House Christian Fellowship, Broadstairs
Andy Hunter

66 Beginnings

In the summer of 1967, Margie and I were both baptised in the Spirit, and then in the October we were married. Our background had been with the Christian Brethren, but quite quickly it became apparent that at that point many of the denominations were uncomfortable with the gifts and ministries of the Spirit.

We were meeting with Ken and Barb Swan, Dave and Yvonne Medlock and Bernard Hull and some others in Ken's flat on one night a week and in our flat in New Barnet on another. Also, there had been a significant move of God in the local teacher training

66 See Revelation 3:8

college at Trent Park where I was training. Students from there met with us as well.

On Friday nights it was common for us all to go to Dave and Yvonne's house in Earley in Reading for the weekend. We would read the Scriptures together and pray for others who were in need. They were weekends of wonderful fellowship together. From Dave and Yvonne's home there, the Earley Christian Fellowship developed.

Meeting together

We met together on the biblical principle of 1 Corinthians 14:26: *"Whenever you come together, each of you has a psalm, has a teaching, has a tongue, has a revelation..."* We met together and prayed for the sick and for those who needed deliverance. We worshipped the Lord and looked at the Scriptures together.

At that point we knew no other groups like ourselves, but when Heather Jones went to Liverpool, she met Norman Meeten and reported back that the same thing was happening there, and slowly we became aware that the Lord was at work in a similar way all over the country. After a while we became unofficially associated with similar groups from every part of the country and often abroad.

Meeting on Sundays

We had been careful not to organize meetings on a Sunday which would have encouraged people to leave their local church.

I had been encouraged by our own local churches, to continue our work among the students, together with Ken and Barb, so we began to meet on a Sunday morning in their flat. News of our meeting soon became public and many others began to join us. We met in the only available space, which was our homes.

It was not a deliberate policy but there were many advantages of meeting in such a way, not the least being the opportunity to exercise hospitality.

Moving to Kent

As the Fellowship grew at Ken's flat, I started a job teaching, and then in early 1970, Margie and I moved down to the Kent coast. I worked for some years in special education and at the same time people came to know Jesus as their Saviour in our home. As numbers grew, we moved several times in Broadstairs and eventually bought 'Beaconsfield House' in Broadstairs, which became a home for Margie and me and the children and also for the growing church. As well as a growing adult Fellowship, we had a large children's work and a growing young people's work. We had three appointed elders in addition to myself.

Beaconsfield House

'Beaconsfield House' was a large detached house in approximately half an acre of ground, and with lots of work from everyone in the church and also from around the country, it was gradually transformed into a house where we were not only able to meet as a church but also to care for individuals who needed some time to heal and recuperate.

Because we lived so close to the sea, we were regularly able to baptise new believers in the sea at Stone Bay and Broadstairs, often during both the summer and winter.

Mission Abroad

We felt from the outset that the Fellowship was to be a source of blessing to others, and we encouraged people to go out to other places and countries to share the word of God. We sent brothers and sisters to Egypt and the Cameroon, India, Pakistan and Nepal. Because we were quite near to the port of Dover, many visitors came to stay with us via Beaconsfield, either coming or going overseas, to share the gospel and supply Bibles and Bible literature to other countries.

Over time, as the church began to grow, further extensions and living accommodation were added. Due to continuing growth, as well as regulations that needed to be adhered to regarding numbers, it was needful after some years to hire a local school hall for the Sunday morning meetings.

Prayer

Prayer was a significant factor in the growth of the church, with regular times of prayer together and a number of groups also meeting to focus on specific areas like finance and mission, children's work and the young people. We regularly met for days and weeks of prayer with fasting, and these were really important in the growth and strength of the church.

The word of God

As well as meeting together with the use of the gifts of the Spirit, we always focused on reading and teaching from the Scriptures. On the principle found in 2 Timothy 2:2, *"...and what you have heard from me in the presence of many witnesses entrust to faithful men who will be able to teach others also,"* we sought to teach the basic Bible truths to others so that they could be teachers themselves.

A foundational principle of our existence was in seeking to fulfill the command of Jesus, found in Matthew 28:19-20: *"Go therefore and make disciples of all nations, baptising them in the name of the Father and of the Son and of the Holy Spirit, teaching them to observe all that I have commanded you. And behold, I am with you always, to the end of the age."*

Changes

Over the years, there have been different emphases in the work, and during the late 1990s there was a growing work among the older members of the community, with Margie and a team of us organising meals for up to forty at a time, whilst doing a short Bible study after the meal. A good number of older people came to know the Lord in their latter years.

More elders have been appointed and encouraged to gather in their own homes. At this time there are four elders, and meetings are regularly held in their homes, while everyone meets together in the local school on Sundays.

It became clear that in order for the church to grow and develop, it was necessary for Margie and me to move on, allowing room for growth and change. I was still preaching and teaching in churches in the UK and also abroad, particularly Africa and Scandinavia. In 2006, we decided to open a bed and breakfast business as 'tent-making', so enabling us to support ourselves financially.

By a series of miracles, we were able to buy, in 2007, a large house called 'Brook Cottage'. It was in a picturesque village on the edge of Dartmoor, where we ran the bed and breakfast business for several years. We built a good relationship with the village, hosting the annual Methodist church fete for many years.

I continued to preach and teach locally, across the UK and abroad. Then, after a few years, Margie became seriously ill and died.

After a while, Andy sold his home in Devon and moved to the south of England to support the church there as well as continuing to minister and preach in the UK and also abroad.

"For those who honour Me, I will honour."⁶⁷

When the Lord gave Norman the vision of leaves of a tree first burning together and then spreading out across the globe and falling in different places, he would not have envisaged the full extent or detail of how this would unfold.

Ever since this vision was first given, there has been a miraculous outworking: 'leaves' being blown across the UK as well as abroad, bringing much honour to the one whose gospel they carry and are faithfully preaching and living.

Each Fellowship may have its distinctive and unique features, but the golden thread that runs through each is the same: the supernatural life of God. Somebody once described it as "the same ice-cream but different flavours"!

In the next two chapters we will see again how the Lord clearly prepared and led many more of His precious 'leaves' to the South West, and raised up His church there that blossomed into a work that had far-reaching consequences throughout the world.

⁶⁷ 1 Samuel 2:30

9

Exeter

I will build My church

The workings of God in each individual life are unique. The way He prepares us for His purposes are truly tailor-made.

Before I formed you in the womb, I knew you.[68]

When Bob Love first met his future wife-to-be in Bombay, India, shortly before the second world war broke out, he was working in the Mercantile Bank of India, and Norah, together with her sister Ida, had embarked on their general nurses' training in St George's Hospital, Bombay. Neither of them knew the Lord and were enjoying a somewhat worldly and social life at the time. A further account and tribute to them both has kindly been provided for us by Sue Heathcote, one of their daughters, at the end of this book. Suffice it to say that after much travelling and living in Pakistan, Ceylon, Singapore, Australia and Hong Kong, they finally settled in England in 1956, living initially with Bob's mother in Fleet, Hampshire and then moving to their own bungalow in the neighbouring town of Farnborough.

Heart preparation

As has already been seen, there was a significant move of God throughout England during the early '60s, and people were hungry to know God in a way not yet experienced. Bob and Norah, with their family, had been attending an Anglican church since arriving in England, but as time went on they often visited Pentecostal churches, as well as holding prayer meetings in their home for those who were seeking to be filled with the Holy Spirit. Not a few were from the Anglican community. God began

[68] Jeremiah 1:5

to meet with them, and in turn this led to them realising their need to be baptised by immersion. The local Frensham Ponds became a baptistery, and along with many of their friends, Bob and Norah were also baptised. Quite understandably, this caused quite an uproar in the village!

It was also during this time that Norah heard about Mr North, who periodically was invited to preach in a gathering in Farnham, a neighbouring town. On one occasion, they were able to open their home to him. Before leaving for work on the morning Mr North was due to leave, Bob went into his room to say goodbye. As they prayed together, the Lord gave a prophecy that He would take the pen out of Bob's hand and put a shepherd's crook in it. How wonderfully that prophecy was to be fulfilled in the years that followed.

Moving on

Having been ostracised from the Anglican church, they needed much wisdom and guidance as to what they should do. Initially they joined a Baptist church. They had heard about the work that had developed in Liverpool, and they decided to travel up to Queens Road to speak to Norman. As Norman explains, "They just appeared! We didn't know them." However, this was almost the norm anyway. People used to often just appear! Bob and Norah had friends and contacts in Exeter, and they were wondering whether they should consider fulfilling a similar function there to what they had seen in Liverpool, working particularly with youngsters with addiction problems. Norman's reply was simple: "Well, what the Lord tells you to do, do it; but if He doesn't, whatever you do, don't do it. It's hard work if the Lord has spoken, but if you haven't got the word of the Lord, it will be a millstone around your necks."

Resulting from their visit to Liverpool, they did find themselves packing up and moving down to the West Country. To begin with, they lived on a farm with friends in South Devon. From there, after a year or two, they moved to 23 Belmont Road, Exeter – a large Georgian house occupying five floors! They had in fact viewed this property before speaking to Norman and were thrilled to discover that on a subsequent visit the price had been dropped with no explanation given. They took this as confirmation that it was the Lord's choice. It was late 1965.

It wasn't long before a group of about a dozen friends began to join them for prayer and Bible study, whilst continuing to go to a local church on a Sunday. Their two daughters had now married; one living in

Cornwall and involved in Christian ministry and the other helping with the work in Exeter.

Whosoever will...

As in most cities, Exeter was alive with young people of every description, colour and background, bringing with them a multiplicity of deep-seated needs and problems. Having lived and travelled through many countries in his former years, as well as having a God-given love for all peoples, Bob and his friends were not slow in walking the streets and reaching out to them. Gradually they were rewarded and hearts responded. One evening, a group of youngsters made their way to 23 Belmont Road and knocked on the door. They were given a warm welcome, and this resulted in holding meetings for them. They were a wild bunch, but with open hearts. It soon became clear that more help was needed, and they prayed for someone to come and give them support.

Almost immediately, a young man named Peter Davey arrived on their doorstep. "I hear you need help," he said. Peter was not only training to be a teacher at the local college, but also a pianist. Wonderful! A man called Edgar Trout was also an encouragement, who regularly visited and shared in the ministry, particularly during the first eighteen months.

In 1966, Mr North was invited to Exeter to take a conference held in a local Methodist church, and stayed with Bob and Norah. At the time, he was still living at The Longcroft, on the Wirral. At one point he shared with them that he had been considering moving and was seeking the Lord for clarity. The invitation to join them in Exeter was a seed that was watered with much prayer.

Returning from church on a Sunday would see many join Bob and Norah over their ever-expanding dining room table. Their generous hospitality was a real testimony to their big hearts. One Sunday, it was tentatively suggested that rather than go to one of the local churches for their evening service, could they not remain where they were and have a meeting? This soon evolved into both a morning and an evening meeting, and again on a Thursday, which had always been their time of prayer over many years.

Where there is life, there is always growth, and the group began to grow. They would not have called themselves a church at this point – simply a group of hungry believers who wanted more of God. The love

He gave them for each other was bringing them together, and they simply made themselves available to Him to work His works in any way that He would choose. It was a very special time. As someone has testified, "His language was on the lips of all."

One of the early visitors to Belmont Road was a young man called Martin Williams, who later married one of Mr North's daughters, Marian. He, with his sister Jennie and her husband Phil, decided to call in. Here is part of his testimony:

66 In 1966, my sister (Jennie Glover), together with her husband Phil and me, went on our own to a meeting at 23 Belmont Road in Exeter, which was the home of Bob and Nora Love. We were welcomed at the door by Bob himself. My first impressions of the Fellowship were of a room full of young people praising the Lord Jesus. I had never heard anything like it. The hymns from the *Redemption Hymnal* were all directed to Jesus and His work on the cross at Calvary. Love and worship were being addressed to Him in a way that I had never seen before. Also, I had a sense of 'arriving' at something that in some way seemed to be connected to something Jesus had said: that those who followed Him would have companions in their walk, i.e. brothers and sisters, mothers and fathers and so on.

Exeter Christian Fellowship, Belmont Road

Conferences were held each month, bringing people from near and far. Mr North was invited to preach. The house was full. Lives were being changed. God was sovereignly moving in so many hearts, and the reality and miracle of true new birth and the baptism with the Spirit was being experienced and answering the heart-cry of many of those who came.

Many years later, Norah recalls a little of those early days.

66 There were all sorts of strange and wonderful events taking place in our lives, but I would like to say that we had no idea or intention of forming a church. We were both very young in the Lord. ... It was God Himself who started and built the church at No. 23. He sent people to us. We did not invite anyone to join us. We found ourselves surrounded by Mods and Rockers, young people from other churches who came to see what was going on, and many others. However, after about two years all this came to an end and we were more or less on our own. We had heard that Mr and Mrs North were leaving The Longcroft, so we invited them to make their home with us – not thinking that they would come.

We started Sunday afternoon meetings. When Mr North was there people would come, but when he went out on a preaching tour no-one came.

One Sunday afternoon, about three or four of us sat waiting and hoping someone would come to the meeting, but not a soul turned up. We started to pray and to ask the Lord to show us the reason for this. A little later Jenny Glover came in, and within a few minutes the Lord gave her a prophecy. She had not heard our prayer. In essence she said, "Be faithful in all you do. I will build My church. This is My work. Trust Me – you remain faithful." And so we were comforted and filled with joy and anticipation, and we believed that this was God's word for us.

Further growth

No. 23 was a large house, but as numbers increased, more facilities and rooms were required to include temporary accommodation mainly for those needing help and ministry. Further adjustments were made, enlarging the meeting room and dining facilities, but also, No. 25, in perfect timing, came onto the market, much to Norah's horror! The challenges of maintaining a five-storey house had been more than demanding; the thought of yet another property, equal in size, derelict, with no electricity, and with major work screaming at them from every corner, was almost a nightmare! However, God, as always, remained utterly faithful to all that He had promised. After much prayer, John Williams, father of Martin, bought the house, his heart being that it should be used "for the furtherance of a New Testament church" as seen in the Scriptures.

Coinciding with the purchase, God had clearly been speaking to Mr North concerning moving south, and so when Bob and Norah's invitation to join them came, he knew that this was the Lord's leading and agreed to join them in the work, although he would still need to be able to continue his itinerant ministry as situations arose. Exeter would be his base. No. 21 had also been bought by Peter and Joy Palmer, and initially Mr and Mrs North lived there, prior to moving next door to the top floor of '23'. It was 1967.

John Williams, with his son Martin, continued to lay down their lives for the brethren, as did many others. There was much skilled manual work required to refurbish and then decorate No. 25, as well as the ongoing spiritual input that was needed for the many people who came to them with every conceivable problem. Sadly, in the July of 1970, John suddenly had a major heart attack and died. God had called him home.

There had been much preaching on the whole concept of the church; its function, eldership and leadership, and all that pertained to living a holy and righteous life within the body of Christ. These Bible studies and expositions were foundational in establishing and officially recognising the church. Elders were appointed and prayed in; those who had already been recognised quite clearly as God's leaders amongst them by the lives that they had lived, together with an ability to minister the word of God. They themselves felt far from worthy, but then, if they had, it would have been confirmation that they were far from suitable.

It wasn't just in the meetings that the presence of God was so tangible and powerful. The whole atmosphere of the house was a testimony to the reality of God in their midst. There was a love and unity amongst those who knew Him. They were of one heart, one purpose and one vision: to make Him known and share His life, His love and His gospel to all.

A wonderful home of love

Peter Richards

❝ I came to the Exeter Fellowship in September 1972, and my wife Jane joined me in December. Mr North was an elder there at that time, with Bob Love, Martin Williams and Bernard Hull. Martin's father John had died, as had Wendy Gitsham (née Love).

Belmont Road was an amazing pastoral house, with all conditions of need accommodated. We were staying in one of the house flats the following August, when our first son died, aged just six months. The reality of our new birth, experienced whilst visiting the Manchester Fellowship two years earlier, plus the consciousness of God's love and the care of the Fellowship, sustained us.

Pat Coombs and Dot Twivey were crucial helps to Mr North in disseminating the message he had to share. Dot taped the preaching and made it available on cassettes. Pat laboured daily on his prolific writings. These were initially duplicated and later, as a team gathered to support her, printed and bound. They were sent free worldwide. It was a work of faith. She typed every word of his many booklets covering all aspects of church doctrine and the Christian life, including his longest book, *One Baptism*, which was put for printing in Crediton. She carried forward the work, which commenced with Jim Williams in Bradford, who had previously published three of Mr North's booklets and also the famous and much loved 'blue hymnbook', *Hymns of Eternal Truth*, a collection of Wesley hymns, including all the original verses and set to tunes that were often far better suited to the words.

Our recollection of the seven years we spent in Exeter was that the Fellowship was a place where we saw God at work. There were regular deliverances and evidences of new birth. It was a training ground for those who wanted to serve the Lord, a launchpad for people called to minister in other towns in the UK as well as abroad. It was a manifestation of the true family of God where love abounded – exemplified initially and memorably through the ministry of Bob and Norah Love. Of course, there were also problems, and not every aspect of the culture that developed was helpful. No church is yet perfect, but for the period that we knew it, Exeter Fellowship was in so many ways an exemplar of what a New Testament church should be.

Sounds from heaven

66 I came to hear about the Fellowship in Exeter through a friend in Ashburton. I was going through the trauma of a broken marriage at the time, with three little boys. My husband had walked away into another relationship and, through deception, had kidnapped my children. The police were involved, resulting in many court hearings.

Things were very black indeed. I was made to think that it was all my fault. I was close to suicide, but the thought of what this would do to my children prevented me. I wanted much better things for them. There was, as it were, a 'golden rope' suspended from heaven over the blackest and deepest pit, and I knew that I had to catch hold of this and swing upwards, holding up my legs, to keep me from being held in that darkness.

The situation continued for some months, during which time I was considering many things that I thought would help me, although with hindsight they would have caused even more problems. Each time I thought of meditation, the person of Jesus came to my mind, and with that, I decided to pray the Lord's Prayer, which amazingly brought me joy. I then met a friend in the street who shared the gospel with me. My heart was open; I was ready to listen. She invited me to a prayer meeting in someone's house, and although my initial reaction was to think that this sort of thing was just for old ladies, I did eventually go. It was also during this time that a well-known evangelist was conducting an outreach meeting in the town. I was becoming somewhat dazed by all these various encounters and the things that I was hearing. A Christian friend said that it was the Lord wanting to protect me with a blanket of love from all the terrible things I was having to go through.

It was also at this time that a dear Christian couple, Bob and Norah Love, were visiting Ashburton, as they had been invited to take some meetings in a friend's house. I went along. This proved another link in the chain.

I had begun to go to our local Anglican church. It had been the vicar here who had helped me through the very difficult court visits. One Sunday, he preached from Hebrews 4:12,13, explaining how God knew all that was happening in our lives.

God had been moving powerfully both in the Exeter Fellowship and in Liverton, at Rora House. Friends who were going down there met Mr North, who was their main speaker, as well as Bob and Norah Love, and they encouraged me to come down to the meetings, which I did whenever I managed to find babysitters for my children. The meetings were amazing. I found myself being irresistibly drawn.

It was at a small conference one Whitsun when, as people prayed, there was the most extraordinary and beautiful sound – like silver trumpets being played harmoniously. I had never heard anything like this, and it was so spontaneous. I tentatively glanced up, with some fear and trembling, and saw about six 'people' scattered at various places. It was the sound of heaven itself – never to be forgotten. I continued to go and be part of the church there. Sometimes, during conferences, when the weather proved too wet for people to camp, I had the privilege of having one or two of them stay with me. It was like having angels staying with me!

Passing through

Bob sometimes described the Fellowship as a 'filling station'. He saw people come, get born again and filled with God's Spirit, and then, after a time, be led on to 'pastures new'; often being called to full-time ministry, whether that be at home or abroad. This was a real encouragement for the leadership. It possibly should be the norm, wherever we are and whoever we are.

Two such folk were Tony and Mary Seaton. They met at the Fellowship and subsequently married. Here are their individual testimonies:

A prophetic vision fulfilled
Tony Seaton

66 Mary, who was working in an approved school near Exeter, came to the Fellowship in September 1969. I came in the January 1970, having come from Bangor University to Exeter to teach in the university there.

I was unchurched, in sin and into the pub, and deeply unhappy. A friend who had become a born-again Christian gave me the address of the Exeter Fellowship, saying that if ever I was in need of help, I could go to them. So as a New Year resolution, I said to myself, "I have tried everything else but I am still disappointed. I will try God." I was welcomed at the Fellowship door by Norman Mayes, who said to me, "Do you know that God loves you?" I said no, to which he replied, "You had better come in then!"

Here I saw and heard people worshipping in the Spirit with delight. I understood nothing of the preaching but was moved to tears. God was manifested and powerfully present. I was deeply moved, and after a few meetings (in particular when Mr North preached on 'The Shipwreck'), I talked with Bob, saying I just wanted to be like these people.

In one meeting, after Helen Thorman had shared that the Lord had shown her a picture of "a person going up a mountain", I immediately identified with this prophetic vision and cried out, "That's me! That's me!" and received the Spirit and was aware of His glory. I knew I had come 'in' instead of being 'out', and my desire was met.

The Fellowship was in the house of Bob and Nora Love, in 23 Belmont Road, and amongst those who came there were Martin and Marian Williams, the old John Williams, Derek Gitsham, Bernard and Hazel Hull, Peter and Jane Richards, Paul and Lesley Evans, Richard Curd and Lizzie Page, to name a few. Many shared and preached, and we had special weekends with Mr North. He spoke when he was at home, but he was often itinerating.

Mary and I were only in Exeter for three years, after which we moved to Epsom. At this time there seemed to be a move of God around the country, associated with the itinerant ministry of Mr North and Norman Meeten, resulting in the Fellowships moving in the Spirit.

A prophecy fulfilled
Mary Seaton

❝ I came to the Exeter Fellowship in August 1969 after completing a theological degree at Hull University, where I met Lynda

Hutchinson (now Cheung) whilst visiting a friend. She gave me the address of the Fellowship as I was then working in an Approved School for delinquent girls (but darlings) some of whom, plus staff from the school, came to the meetings and received the Lord.

Going to the meetings was an eye-opener. I thought I had gone to heaven! Initially I couldn't understand the ministry, although I knew all the words, but then God opened my understanding and set me free to love and worship Him. It was wonderful, as I didn't realise that that was what Christians ought to do. I heard that I could be free from myself, by the cross. I made lifelong friends.

Before going to Epsom, we were prayed for. Mr North prayed that I would be "a mother of boys away from their mothers", which the Lord fulfilled in Epsom, with a number becoming born again. June Claxton, who was also at Exeter, gave a word "that Jesus sent them out two by two into whatsoever place He Himself would come"[69].

That was also wonderfully fulfilled in Epsom.

Rooted and grounded in love
Gill Butler

❝ As a child I had sought to please God and regularly went to a high Anglican church, where I particularly loved the eucharist services. When my brother was drowned at the age of twenty, I was just seventeen. My life fell apart, and only later, when I knew Jesus, did I realise that I had not been properly rooted into Christ. I understood from the Parable of the Sower[70] that my 'soil' had been shallow and when tribulation came I had fallen away. I needed to be properly rooted and grounded in Jesus Christ.

This change was the beginning of my finding a direction for my life. I trained in English as a foreign language (TEFL) and this taught me to listen to others and to focus my attention on understanding them, in what they said and what they were. In Exeter I had a formative work and training opportunity that I knew clearly had been arranged by God and for His purposes later in my life. Working with children and young people and adults,

---

[69] See Luke 10:1
[70] See Matthew 13:5,20-21

sharing and doing Bible studies, I realise that what God had worked in me started at the point of new birth.

One young lad, Richard Curd, now a leading brother for many years, pays tribute to the much-appreciated ministry and teaching of Mr North and others as he briefly describes his first encounter:

66 Initial impressions are not always reliable, but they were when I met Mr North for the first time. We passed each other in the hallway as I was leaving Bob and Norah Love's house in Exeter, when I was just eighteen. We said little, but there was something about this man that stayed with me. In hindsight, it was as if the Lord were saying, "I just want you to meet someone who is going to be a great influence in your life."

Yet another young man, Dai Patterson, who also became an elder after many years, has a similar testimony.

66 I was a student at St Luke's College in Exeter from 1963 to 1966. I was introduced to Bob and Norah Love, who had opened their home at 23 Belmont Road for meetings. It was during my last year that I met Mr North and also the lassie who was to become my wife.

Over many years, I have come to value the truth I heard preached by Mr North and others, and am convinced that the declaring of the baptism in the Holy Spirit as the means to new birth is vital for true New Testament Christianity. I thank God for hearing such truth as a young man and for the reality of it outlived in brothers and sisters I got to know.

Signs following

During such sovereign moves of God (though not exclusively, by any means) many miracles are witnessed. Someone who was part of the Exeter Fellowship at the time describes one such miracle.

66 On one occasion, a young man who had come for help climbed up onto the scaffolding that was erected at the rear of Nos. 23 and 25 Belmont Road. John Williams and a young man, Brian Tombs, were working on the outside of the houses. They didn't see him climb onto the third level. A rope that was used to transport concrete up the scaffolding on a pulley was unattended.

This young man decided to let himself down on the rope, but there was nothing secured to the other end. He landed head-first onto concrete steps below. John and Brian ... dashed to him. An ambulance was called, but by this time the colour had gone from his face, his eyes were rolling and his breathing erratic. Despite the blood, John cradled him in his arms and cried out to God for him. By the time the ambulance arrived, he was conscious, sitting up, and the colour had returned to his face. He was only kept in overnight for observation and then returned to the house, complaining of just a headache the next day!

Opposition

Not everyone embraced what the Lord was doing, and there have continually been those who have struggled to accept or understand the biblical truths in the way that they were presented. A nearby Bible college adamantly forbade their students from going to any of the meetings. One such student at the time describes a particular incident.

66 We were in our first year at college. One girl in our set was daily in tears; desperately unhappy and finding life a real struggle. Friends rallied round but nothing seemed to help.

Then one morning, whilst faithfully carrying out our domestic duties, clearing up after breakfast, I wandered into the kitchen and saw our friend at the sink, washing up. She was not in tears. She was not upset. She was not looking down and dejected. She was singing like a lark with great gusto, a beaming smile across her face, and enjoying every moment that life was presenting to her.

"*Whatever* has happened to..." I asked, amazed.

"Shh!" came the reply, as they quietly whispered, "She went to *you know where* last night and she's been born again!"

I stared, utterly incredulous. What a transformation! I will never forget that morning.

Somebody else, who also struggled with deep depression which she feels she probably inherited from her father, also spent some of her formative years in the Exeter Fellowship, and shares the following:

66 Another very precious word from the Lord was that I would always have a song in my heart, and this has been true over the

years; from the moment of new birth. Every day I have sung hymns and choruses in my mind. God has worked to free me from depression, which was a strong tendency inherited from my father.

On more than one occasion, two witches came to stay. The powers that had worked in them, however, suddenly became totally inoperable as they were confronted with the power of the Holy Spirit that was so present. They walked into the kitchen and one of them immediately fell down on the floor. On their own admission they could not cope with the purity and righteousness of God that surrounded them. Sadly, neither of them was willing to relinquish their occult practices and they left the house unsaved and unrepentant.

Called home

Bob and Norah had two daughters, Sue and Wendy. Wendy was young and married and helped with the running of the house. It was a terrible shock to all that at the age of twenty-four, just ten days after she had given birth to a dear little baby girl, she suddenly collapsed and died. Although Wendy had been born with a heart condition, such situations are far from easy. She, with her husband Derek, had also adopted a little boy, so it was needful to make some very significant adjustments.

Bob's health had also given rise for concern over some years. He too was advised to have a time of rest for some months, after which he resumed his commitments to the Fellowship. However, just three years after Wendy's death, in July 1975, he too was tragically found by some brothers early one morning on the kitchen floor, having suffered a fatal heart attack. For a non-believing family, this would have been more than devastating, but although Bob was sadly missed, his memorial service celebrating his life saw several hundred people rejoicing and full of thanksgiving for all that they had come to love and appreciate in this dear and true saint of God. He was sixty-three. So joyous was the occasion, that a passer-by who saw everybody on the front and back lawn enjoying refreshments thought it was a wedding!

The following day, Mr and Mrs North had arrangements to fly over to Sweden for a conference. Realising that Norah would be needing care and support in the aftermath of all that she had gone through, they quietly bought a ticket for her as a surprise and she was able to join the conference with them and thereby benefit from some time away.

In her typical and stoical way, Norah continued to remain totally involved in the work, giving herself unreservedly to all the daily demands and challenges that never ceased. Her sister Margaret came to join her, and they managed to buy and share a house not far from Belmont Road. By this time, another elder and his wife had moved into Belmont Road and were responsible for overseeing and running the house.

Somehow the home-calling of Bob brought these formative years at Belmont Road to a natural conclusion; and coupled with the fact that there was now insufficient room to accommodate everybody in their already extended meeting room and dining room, much prayer was made as to what they should do. Gradually the Lord directed them to an old chapel building that had subsequently become a warehouse, not too far from the city centre, which was for sale. Much renovation and work was needed, but No. 21 along with 23 and 25 Belmont Road were gradually sold, and The Old Chapel in Westgate since the late '70s has now become their new home and wonderfully restored.

Westgate Chapel, Exeter

Spiritually released
Roger Jacobs

❝ As a nineteen-year-old I was off to Exeter University. I had been remarkably converted just seven weeks earlier and was going to a place where I knew no-one. This was in 1980. The student in the room above mine was a Christian and he invited me to The Old Chapel Christian Fellowship (as it was known then). I still vividly remember that Sunday morning. People prayed out spontaneously or began choruses of worship. It seemed chaotic. After an hour, some other students who had come with us walked out and beckoned me to come. I remember thinking I would wait for the preaching of the word, and if it was no good, then I would leave and not return.

There was a guest speaker that morning. It was someone called Eddie Horner. He spoke from the book of Hebrews. I recall little of the message, but I knew that what he was ministering was life and this is what I wanted. I drank it in. To my surprise, I felt released and began to pour out my heart in worship. A godly lady had been watching me (as she told me much later!) and saw the change in attitude as I had listened.

I committed myself to that church for the three years I was a student and a further twelve years whilst in employment in Exeter. Prior to my conversion, I knew practically nothing of the Bible. I devoured all the biblical teaching I could find – tapes, books, studies – as well as systematically reading the Bible through each year. I also read Christian biographies, the most influential of which was the old two-volume edition of the life and work of Hudson Taylor. My heart was inflamed and I wanted to be a missionary. I knew this was my calling. In 1982, through contacts in church, I visited Les and Vicky Wheeldon in Cameroon, which convinced me that Africa was the sphere where the Lord wanted me.

I would like to relate two further experiences (among many!) which happened while I was at the chapel. The first was speaking in tongues. The meeting was about to close, when a great surge rose up from within and quite spontaneously I began to speak in tongues. No-one laid hands on me. It just poured out. It could have gone on for at least half an hour. It was a great release and gave me a new confidence in prayer.

The second concerns a visit by Mr G.W. North for a long weekend of ministry. He had been speaking from Ephesians and the meeting had just closed, when the Spirit of God fell on me and

I just melted in tears, and was conscious of a very deep cleansing from sin and all the past.

Since those days, Roger, with his wife Helen, has spent many very fruitful years in Malawi. They have now returned to the UK and are part of the eldership team at The Longcroft, being highly respected and much loved. His teaching and preaching ministry are at a depth and of a vitality that is exceptional.

Pastures new

Peter and Jane Richards, who were close friends of Norah, had moved to Worthing from Belmont Road and were seeing the Lord establish a small Fellowship there. When Norah shared with them that God had clearly spoken to her that He wanted her to join them, they were thrilled. She was there in fact for over seventeen years, during which time she was also able to visit family and friends abroad as far as Australia, India and Canada. Finally, with advancing years, her daughter Sue, who was now living with her husband in Exeter, encouraged her to return and to live with them, an offer which she gratefully accepted. It was here that she ended her days, being lovingly cared for and provided for in every way.

The Fellowship in Exeter is still meeting today in The Old Chapel in Westgate. There have been some changes in the eldership as is usual in most churches over time, with new people coming and others moving on. In 1977, Mr North unexpectedly accepted an invitation from the Auchenheath Fellowship in Scotland to join them, from where he continued an extensive itinerary both in this country and abroad, as well as being part of the eldership there when at home.

Bob's 'filling station' was well-termed. So many came in empty and went out full. Many of the young men who came found themselves in positions of leadership and eldership in their subsequent years, and many others became involved in Christian ministry not only in the UK but globally.

God continues to sovereignly build His church. His promises remain as true today as ever, and wonderfully, *"He who has begun a good work … will complete it until the day of Jesus Christ"*[71].

---

[71] Philippians 1:6

10

"Give Me This Valley"

The story of the Rora Christian Fellowship, Devon

A young man of twenty-three stopped for three young ladies who were hitchhiking on their way to Salcombe, Devon. He graciously left them at their destination, but found himself returning the following morning with some eggs, cream and a bottle of wine, to take them to Plymouth. A young lady had arrived at this same cottage from London for her annual holiday, and as Malcolm was introduced to this eligible young Londoner, it was, as they both confessed, "love at first sight"!

Neither Malcolm nor Christine were Christians at the time. Both had had the privilege of going to good schools and were, in a limited way, familiar with the Anglican Church and, for Christine, a Bible class and Girl Guides.

Malcolm had been born into a farming family, which had been indelibly etched into his DNA. Apart from his two compulsory years in National Service, he gave himself wholeheartedly to working on the land.

Christine had left school at seventeen, working initially as a Mother's Help in various temporary posts, spent a brief time at the prestigious Norland College for Nannies, and finally was accepted to do her three-year State Registration training as a nurse at St Bartholomew's Hospital in London.

It was at a tent mission in Paignton, when he was just twenty-three, that Malcolm responded to the call of salvation and accepted the Lord Jesus Christ as his Saviour. He was the only one that particular evening. Christine became a Christian at the age of fifteen after a challenging conversation with one of her Girl Guide friends.

They were married in March 1958. Malcolm was twenty-four and Christine twenty-two.

Together for God

66 After our marriage, we lived in Bow Mill farm cottage, Broadhempston, and Malcolm worked for his father on the family farm. We occasionally attended a Baptist church in Torquay.

As the children came along, first Stephen in January 1959 and then Jeremy in June 1960, life became busier, and there was little attention to church, although we continued to pray and read *Daily Light* together each evening.

One significant event was when an elderly colporteur, Mr Santer, came regularly to visit us with his books. He had heard of us through some other Christians and came to encourage us in the faith.

Three years later they moved to Higher Whiddon Farm in Ashburton, but only occasionally attending the local Anglican church. A local salesman visited them, along with one or two others, to try to encourage them to attend church more regularly. This had some effect, and they became involved with the youth work and Christian Endeavour at the Ilsington Methodist Church.

66 During this period, a fortnightly Bible study was started at the farmhouse for all who were seeking scriptural holiness. The numbers grew rapidly and there was a regular speaker involved who was part of The League of Prayer movement. It was as a result of these meetings that we began to become hungry for the Holy Spirit, without realising what was happening in our hearts.

Rachel was born in May 1964, thus (as we thought at the time) completing our family with a little girl, but we only saw a small part of the picture!

It was at this time that two young missioners from Cliff College in Derbyshire were holding missions in the area. They made a real impact. For the first time, Malcolm heard the challenge of God to his heart, in a very personal way: *"Whom shall I send, and who will go for Us?"*[72]

[72] Isaiah 6:8

Significant events

❝ The teaching about holiness began to create a deep hunger in our hearts. We didn't know how; we just longed for it, but couldn't do it.

A timely gift of *The Cross and the Switchblade* by David Wilkinson urged them on. They were then given a tape by David DuPlessis on 'The Baptism in the Holy Spirit'.

❝ After many months, we finally knelt down one evening in the farm kitchen and asked God to baptise us with His Holy Spirit. In those days, we were very untaught and knew little of the Bible, so we waited for the *"rushing mighty wind"*[73] as spoken of in Acts 2. As nothing happened, we repeated the exercise the following night, and it was then that Malcolm said, "I think the Bible says *'Ask and you will receive.'* We have asked, and we will believe we have received." In our hearts we were very sincere, and we know that God was looking on our hearts.

The following month, some missionary friends on furlough from Thailand were visiting them. During a time of prayer, their friend prophesied that "God was doing a new thing and many would come to us from all over the world and be blessed" – somewhat impossible considering their geographical position and relative isolation, but wonderfully fulfilled in subsequent years.

The transformation in Malcolm and Christine did not go unnoticed in the Methodist church. The young people in particular were very challenged and drawn. Others were not so accepting and caused some heartache. After a time, it became needful to really seek the Lord very specifically to know what they were to do.

Miraculously, over a period of time, despite their lack of knowledge of scriptural truths, God spoke words into their hearts which they knew were from Him and which were not infrequently found in the Bible afterwards. They were gradually learning to recognise and to respond to that inward voice of the Spirit, which was very wonderful. He also gave them many visions and pictures. One such vision was of five of them in a boat with Jesus. He then spoke to them and said, "Draw up your nets. Cast them on the other side of the boat. Step out of the boat. Walk on the water towards Me, and I will not let you sink."

[73] Acts 2:2

Malcolm continues:

❝ We all knew what we should do, and although we had no idea what the consequences would be, we knew that God was telling us to come out of the Methodist church and to trust Him alone. The next day we wrote our letter of resignation, much to the horror of all those with whom we had previously been in fellowship. No-one understood and everyone thought that we had been deceived; *but God*, in His great power and wisdom, has fulfilled every word that He spoke during that time, however impossible it seemed then.

Their four-bedroomed farmhouse soon saw an increasing number of friends and family joining them for prayer and times of worship. How young people heard of us we do not know, except that it was by word of mouth and a sovereign move of the Holy Spirit. They came from near and far; some even hitchhiking, so keen were they to be a part of what the Lord was doing.

Norman recalls his first visit:

❝ When I arrived, it was like the old woman who lived in a shoe, she had so many children, she didn't know what to do! There were young people hanging out of every window! They were all over the place. Another dear brother from Exeter walked into the room carrying his invalid wife in his arms.

An invitation by a couple on a nearby farm to join them for one of their meetings was also a source of much blessing and where they experienced a completely new form of worship. It was here that they were also introduced to Bob and Norah Love, who in turn invited them to meetings in a Methodist church in Exeter where Mr North had been invited to preach. God has a wonderful way of bringing all the pieces of the jigsaw together – in His perfect timing.

Malcolm testifies:

❝ We were unprepared for the type of meeting we experienced there, but we were readily drawn to the dynamic and challenging preaching, and we knew that this was what we were looking for.

Mr North was then invited to their farm meeting and, at their request, they were introduced to others who would also be able to come and share these truths with them. Norman and Dave Wetherly became 'regulars'! Arthur Wallis was also one of their earlier guests.

66 Every meeting was packed with young people, hungry for God ... As the weeks went by, it was becoming more and more apparent that God was doing something new, just as He had promised us in the word of prophecy. Many new people arrived each week. The Holy Spirit was at work. ...

The move to Rora House

Learning to trust the Lord in all things and for all things, and not least in financial issues, can prove difficult, and often in their enthusiasm and inexperience, many mistakes were made. Malcolm and Christine were learning some hard lessons, but God in His faithfulness was gently teaching them and leading them on. They passed through some rocky waters for over a year until, after a time of prayer with Mr North, the Lord showed them clearly that they were to move.

As a result of a sequence of miracles, Rora House was purchased in May 1968; a large, attractive country home situated at the end of a rough lane and set in six and a half acres of garden and woodland. The final asking price had dropped to £10,000, with a promise of a fifty per cent mortgage! The house had formerly been the property of the Bournville family, who were Quakers. When the solicitor asked the purpose of the house, Malcolm simply explained that he was going to start a church. Three months later, one car, one van, two tractors and some accompanying trailers, after many trips, safely ground to a halt at the top of the lane, with nine very exhausted but happy people beginning their new venture with the Lord – the Ford family plus three young, strong men!

66 When we first moved to Rora, we were a motley crew of inexperienced Christians but with a burning desire to do God's will, whatever the cost. We had no idea what this would mean, but God saw our hearts.

He had spoken clearly to them on many occasions from His word, confirming that this move was of Him, and that was all that mattered.

A church is born

In 1969, two elders were officially appointed: Jim Rowley and Malcolm. Jim, with his wife, had faithfully supported the farm meetings along with another family, all of whom also had links with the Exeter Fellowship, to which they often travelled to join with them. They were exciting days.

66 Every step was a miracle of God and we were merely bystanders watching God at work!

Increasingly Rora became a hive of activity: boys' camps; girls' camps; brethren's meetings; annual Whitsun conferences; as well as other special holiday meetings – plus many visitors, not only coming to the many camps and conferences, but also those with real needs and needing help. Wonderfully too, as the work developed and expanded, the Lord added to them those who were able to help on a full-time basis, willingly laying down their lives. Conditions and circumstances were not easy, but they were only too willing to be a part of what the Lord was doing.

66 They just prayed and prayed and loved and loved. ... Together, all who worked and lived at Rora have given something special to the work and contributed to its ongoing and developing.

As the work continued to grow, they realised that more accommodation and facilities were needed. There were various options, but in the end the Lord spoke very clearly: *"Enlarge the place of your tent, and let them stretch out the curtains of your dwellings; do not spare; lengthen your cords, and strengthen your stakes. For you shall expand to the right and to the left..."*[74]

A planning application was submitted and they were given permission to build two much larger buildings, one on each side of the house. The work was slow and continued for many years. Not wanting to be in debt, they were able to proceed as finance was given, and if not, they stopped and waited. This was not always easy and there was a time when the church needed to repent because they realised that they had moved ahead of the Lord's timing. Important lessons were being learnt.

Further extensions and new buildings continued over the years, to include a new church building for meetings, youth work and small conferences, the original hut having long passed its sell-by date; catering barn; washing and toilet facilities; and so on.

[74] Isaiah 54:2,3a

136

During this time, Norman and Mr North approached the elders to see if they would be willing to consider hosting the main annual summer conference. Until that point it had been held in the grounds of Cliff College in Calver, Derbyshire, which now could no longer accommodate the growing numbers. The church agreed unanimously and preparations were instigated. The first summer conference took place in the July of 1986.

A new phase

Travelling had never been on Malcolm's or Christine's agenda. They had been quite happy in their role to oversee the establishing of a church, to care for their children as they were growing up and to work tirelessly on the house, building projects and the grounds; three full-time occupations all rolled into one! However, resulting from a trip to Romania in 1983 and 1984 with Open Doors, Christine had come home full of vision and enthusiasm. Malcolm too, in obedience to God speaking to him, travelled out to India, Thailand and Poland to visit some of their missionaries. This was followed by a visit to Czechoslovakia and East Germany in 1985, and a return visit to Romania in 1986, both of them this time travelling together.

Learning curves were steep, not only for Malcolm and Christine but also for the church. There were long-lasting lessons that needed to be learnt by all, some being far from easy if not deeply painful; but in retrospect it was accepted that God was in these times and was working out His purposes. It was often needful for them to come together as a church in humility and brokenness, to search their hearts before a God who loved them and seek forgiveness.

The account of how the work progressed in Romania, and which continues to this day, is another story in itself. Suffice it to say that a real work has been established there, supported not only by the Rora Fellowship but by many other churches and Fellowships, particularly amongst the neediest there – the dear Roma communities, who have so little and have responded in various ways to the gospel and to the love shown to them by so many.

In recent months, the regular visits have not always been possible, due to ill-health and major surgery for both Malcolm and Christine; but the work there continues, with full-time workers faithfully continuing on. Properties have been purchased, building and renovation work undertaken, and large containers regularly leaving our docks carrying much-needed equipment, clothing and other provisions to the churches now established there.

Back at Rora, with over sixteen more acres of ground now added to the original six and a half, the vision continues to be outworked. Many changes have taken place over the years – people leaving, others joining them, conferences, house-parties, children's camps, further improvements and extensions – all of which are demonstrations of God's continual faithfulness, love and grace. New lessons are still needing to be learnt, which surely will never come to an end this side of eternity.

In 2017, the last of the annual summer conferences was hosted by the Fellowship, as for several reasons it was decided to relocate it to Quinta, a Christian conference centre near Oswestry. It was a nostalgic time, as the grounds of Rora and Rora House had become that special place, spanning thirty-two years, with some very precious memories and where God had moved in many wonderful ways.

However, God remains the same, and what He accomplished at Rora, He will continue to do, perhaps in even greater ways and in new ways, at Quinta. The Lord continues to minister to the dear saints in Rora too and in all the many areas of ministry with which they are still involved.

66 Rora has become a training ground for many; in faith, prayer and hard physical work, as well as teaching us all how to work together in unity and love. ... He is building His church, and ultimately remains over all His work. All *we* are called to do is to be obedient and willing to serve Him.

Rora House today

11

Epsom Christian Fellowship

Love never fails

It was during 1969/70 that Tony and Mary, whilst at the Exeter Fellowship, came into the things of the Spirit.[75] They married, but soon Tony felt led to leave his lecturing post at Exeter University and accept a teaching post at Epsom College in Surrey, a boy's public school.

It wasn't long before they revived the college's Christian Union and started having meetings. As the Lord added to their numbers, the Epsom Fellowship was born.

Teaching Biology as a Christian brings with it a unique opportunity of sharing the miraculous through science, and the

Tony and Mary Seaton

boys soon began to open their hearts and pour out their questions. They not only began to realise the impossibility of evolutionary theories but, more importantly, were drawn to these two lives that so clearly were being lived out before them. The Holy Spirit was working.

One of Tony's mantras was "Just love people" – soundly scriptural and something that he had first seen lived out before him in Exeter. Mr North once described him as "a heart on legs", and how true that was. As Tony and Mary loved these boys, prayed for them, laid their lives down for them, many began to respond and they too were truly born of God, their lives changed.

[75] See Chapter 9

One of Tony and Mary's 'boys' was a lad called Phil Joannou. Here is his own testimony. Prior to coming to Epsom, he had been severely traumatised at his former prep school by the headmaster, supposedly an evangelical Christian, who was actually reported on in the *Guardian* in 2017 for thrashing and physically abusing many of the children several times a week over many years. The beatings were so horrendous that it was not unusual to see their clothes and pyjamas soaked with blood, not to mention the deep bruising. Another lad, Giles Fraser, also having attended the same prep school, joined Phil at Epsom a year later.

Early Fellowship days
Philip Joannou

66 In the autumn of 1974, I arrived at Epsom College a rather angry, mixed-up teenager who had been at boarding school since I was five and hated most of my time there. I was sent there by well-meaning grandparents who were trying to extricate me from the challenges of a broken home. Not to go into too much detail, I suffered with very bad eczema and asthma, and having been under constant fear of bullying in my early years, resorted to putting the shoe on the other foot in my latter time there. Somehow, I think because my grandmother knew the headmaster and placed a number of foreign students at the school, I became head boy before I left! Coming to Epsom, I was once again at the bottom of the pile – but was not going to start again if I could help it.

I, like Giles Fraser, who incidentally was a year below me, could have had a lifelong problem, but to shortcut out some of the gory details, I will take you to a teacher who had a life-changing influence on me.

Biology lessons… Well, what is there to like about any lesson, except that in these, the interesting part for a teenage boy was the human biology side. Anyway, we had what we thought was a rather eccentric teacher in a gentleman called Mr Tony Seaton; relatively new to the school, I believe, when I arrived. Mr Seaton, as I shall call him now, had the odd facet of actually being interested in his subject and interested in conveying it to his student; a bit of an enigma! His passion caused us rebellious teenagers to want to take advantage and cause as much mischief as possible.

A low humming buzz would emanate from twenty or so young adolescence mouths, at which point Mr Seaton would shout, "What's that noise?"

"The lights, sir," came the resounding reply.

This happened on numerous occasions, as young teenage boys seemed to find repeating the same thing over and over again as funny as at the first time, until the ingenious Mr Seaton on one occasion, on hearing the buzz, shot over to the light switch and turned them all off. Unfortunately, the buzz did not subside as quickly as the turning off of the lights, to Mr Seaton's triumphant statement, "I told you it was not the lights!"

We were stunned into silence.

What has this got to do with the Fellowships, you may ask. Well, to coin a modern phrase, here's the thing...

I found out that Mr Seaton ran the Christian Union at the school. He held it in his apartment in Carr House, where he was deputy housemaster, and I thought it would be a good opportunity to pop along and cause some mischief there.

Sadly, this was not to be the case, as the first meeting I attended had a certain Mr Bill Chaney speaking, and although I would probably never have associated with anyone who was present there in normal life, I was quite taken by what he had to say. Don't ask me what he said, but I do remember that it was something about him having a 'close to death' experience.

I didn't say a word during his talk, contrary to my plans, and I was also introduced to 'Mrs Seaton' as I will refer to her for now. Alarm bells rang in my head. These were not normal people; there was something about them, and it really did not have anything to do with the talk or praying that went on. I could not put my finger on it. After a few times of me coming to the Christian Union, Mr and Mrs Seaton (I was informed I could call them by their first names, but I was at a public school and he was a teacher) told me about the Sunday meetings, which were also at that point held in Carr House.

I now have to mention my housemaster, Mr John Potter, to whom I must have conveyed my angry self quite evidently since coming to the school. Frequently getting into scraps, and using language unbefitting of a young public school student, he gave me dispensation to attend the meetings although they clashed with 'prep'[76] which I was supposed to do, and in the end he reaped the benefits of his decision, as this angry young man slowly started to become calmer and more under control. He acknowledged this and actively encouraged me to attend.

They say behind every good man is an even better woman. (I am finding that hard to say in these days of equality. Maybe I should raise it with the authorities!) But Mary, as I will now refer to her, was most certainly a true 'help meet'. In short, Tony and in particular Mary, as she took most of the flak from us, opened their homes to a bunch of troubled and maybe a few untroubled teenage boys.

What was the attraction, you may ask. Was it the two- to three-hour meetings every Sunday? Most definitely not! My new liquid crystal watch helped me while away some of the minutes... Was it the fact that I could get out of the school limits for a bit? Most definitely yes!

Now I have to make mention of another couple who had an unusual influence on my continuing to come to the meetings at Carr House – Steven and Sheila Hart. Actually, it was really Sheila. She made amazing cakes. The meeting on Sunday was preceded by a tea, and the cakes were good enough to die for and actually worth sitting through a three-hour meeting for. Such was the life of this public school boy.

You may well suspect that this alone could not be all that made me stay, and you would be right. I felt no natural affinity to many of the people, be they adults or school boys, that attended those initial meetings, but there was definitely something which I did not initially manage to work out or understand. Then it clicked. These people were actually showing a genuine love to me, which I had very little experience of feeling. It was addictive, and I knew it was something that I secretly craved.

And so the journey began, and 'journey' it was and still is, because even to this day it continues. I 'became' a Christian, made some firm friends amongst my peers, and Tony and Mary effectively became my surrogate parents. I met my wife Heather at a Fellowship tea. We have been married for thirty-seven years, have four children, four grandchildren and three daughters-in-

[76] homework

law. We have been active in every church we have attended both in Bristol and now currently in our village in Hampton-in-Arden.

Along the journey, I have spent time in Malawi with three very small children – Jason, Ben and Sam – and I have studied at university full-time with the same three small children and then latterly with Naomi, our only daughter, who was the last of the four.

Have I arrived? The answer has to be no, as I continue on my journey and ask questions and consider new things. Do I belong to Jesus? I would like to think the answer to that is definitively yes.

Had I not become involved with the Fellowships, where would I be now? The answer does not bear contemplation. I am not sure I would even be around. Am I thankful to Tony and Mary? A resounding yes! Am I thankful to the Fellowship and all the meetings and conferences? Again, a resounding yes! Am I thankful to God? How can I not be thankful to Him as He has saved me, using His people? ...

I hope that in some way, what God through His people has done for me, I have in turn managed to pass on to others in a positive and an encouraging way.

This has been shared with much gratitude and thanks from someone who was at a crossroad, and the Fellowships, through Tony and Mary Seaton, guided me onto a path that saved me from some form of destruction.

Perhaps before we continue, it would be fitting to hear from Mary herself.

66 We arrived in Epsom on August 14th, 1972, which coincided with our daughter Jessica's first birthday. We had been given a word by June Claxton from Luke 10:1: *"The Lord ... sent them two by two before His face into every city and place where He Himself was about to go..."* Mr North had also prophesied that I would become a mother of boys who were away from their own mothers. As I had, at that point, only worked with girls, I was somewhat intrigued. Only after Tony's offer for a teaching post at Epsom College did this become more meaningful.

We moved into our spacious accommodation at the college, which had a lovely, large sitting room, and soon began some meetings. We revived the school Christian Union and organised some youth weekends and house-parties. It was a truly fruitful and happy time for us all. A number of these young people became regular members of the fledgling church.

Coinciding with what the Lord was establishing at the college, another opening arose through a mother of one of the boys at the college, Keith Smith, who invited me to take some inter-denominational women's Bible studies in her house. These meetings were hosted by a committee of ladies who were very supportive of the Fellowship, some even joining us for the meetings. Two of these ladies were Rita Cole and Eva Fishley. Another committee lady was Eunice Ellen, a local doctor and member of the local Methodist church. Amazingly, it turned out, whilst in conversation with her, that I had been a friend of one of her daughters at university. The Ellens were a great help, providing us with chairs for the meeting and hiring minibuses for the youth weeks away, and then finally sharing with us that the Lord had shown them that we were to have their house in which to continue the growing work. It was a beautiful, large detached Victorian building, which had in foregone years been owned by the British artist Augustus John. So after seven years at the college, we moved in the May of 1979.

The house had a number of bedrooms, which soon became full of people. We held the growing Sunday school in the large basement and the regular Thursday prayer meetings in the lounge.

We had by this time decided to hire a local Red Cross Hall for the main Sunday meeting; an interim solution whilst Tony began to look for a more permanent building. The events of how we eventually bought the church hall belonging to a local Anglican church is a story all of its own. When the question arose of how we were going to pay for it, we discovered that some of the Fellowship members had been saving for this need for years. On one occasion we needed £1,000, so Tony phoned the bank to secure a loan. Whilst on the phone, I heard a noise in the kitchen. On going to investigate, I found an envelope on the floor – containing £1,000! We never knew who the donor was. Similar events were common in those days.

Soon after moving into St Martin's Avenue, it became obvious that Tony would need to give more time to the church, so he left his full-time teaching post at the college and was very soon fully involved in the building work; re-roofing and extending the new meeting hall. Everyone pulled together wonderfully.

From about 1986/87, the church was expanding in every way. Weddings soon followed, and then children – lots of them – and consequentially, there was a desire to have our own school. The Cornerstone School opened in 1988. As with everything else, we found that the Lord had gone before us preparing for all that would be needed: equipment, teachers, and personnel with much patience and love. A verse from one of Fanny Crosby's well-known hymns echoes this truth.

> All the way my Saviour leads me:
> What have I to ask beside?
> Can I doubt His tender mercy,
> Who through life has been my Guide?
> Heavenly peace, divinest comfort,
> Here by faith in Him to dwell!
> For I know what'er befall me,
> Jesus doeth all things well.

A testimony of love
Lorna Wetherell

❝ I first met Mary Seaton at the school gates when our sons were starting their first year at primary school. When Joseph, their son, came for tea at our home for the first time and asked me why we didn't say grace at mealtimes, I was truly embarrassed and shocked.

The second shock came when my son Andrew asked if he could go to Sunday school in the basement of the Seatons' old Victorian house in Epsom. He started attending and then, later, his younger sister.

At that time, the Epsom Fellowship was made up largely of boys from Epsom College and some other people known to the Seatons of various ages. They met in their home for the weekly prayer meeting on a Thursday evening and at the Red Cross Hall (which housed medical aids and teaching equipment) for Sunday meetings.

Meeting Mary was a pivotal time in my life. I saw in Tony and Mary a couple who truly loved God and who lived the life and didn't just talk about it. Later, when I asked if there was anything for me, Mary invited me to the ladies' midweek prayer meeting, which they held in their kitchen. I remember thinking, "This is a really weird bunch," as they put their hands in the air and spoke out loud in tongues. Coming from a then traditional Church of England church, it was very odd. Every time I went, I said, "I'll never go again!" but God was drawing me and I still kept turning up.

Eventually, I plucked up the courage to go to the Red Cross Hall for an evening meeting. I barged in while the meeting was in full flow, and remember the only seat left was on a commode with a human skeleton in the corner, whom they called George!

When Mary asked me if I would like to go to a baptism at the local Turkish Baths, I found it such a powerful time and cried most of the way through. There was an old lady called Eva Fishley being baptised, and as she came out of the water her face shone. It was then that I fell in love with God. When I went home and told my husband that I wanted to love God with all of my heart, his immediate response was (tongue in cheek), "I don't mind, as long as you don't become religious!"

He became a Christian fifteen years later, but that was another part of God's plan.

Somebody who was also privileged to become an integral part of the early work in Epsom was, at that time, a young, qualified primary school teacher, who later became the headteacher of The Cornerstone School. Here is his account of how the Lord was moving, preparing and establishing this work.

Solid foundations
Grahame Davies

❝ The church was really a loving family, a characteristic that it has maintained over the years. Even those who moved away from Epsom decades ago often still feel close links with the church.

In 1979, the Lord opened up the way for Tony and Mary to move to a very large house in Epsom. Its owner, a member of one of the local churches, had approached Tony and suggested he should buy the house, which was being put on the market. When Tony replied that on his teacher's salary he couldn't possibly afford such a house, the owner offered the house at half the market price and so the purchase was made. God was opening another door of ministry for the Seatons; they opened the house to all in the Fellowship, enabling them to call in at any time, as well as accommodating many people over the years as the Lord led them.

Tony and Mary trusted the Lord to look after the place, so they never locked the back door. On one occasion early on, residents of the old people's home opposite became alarmed when they noticed a man whom they'd never seen before enter the (unlocked) back door. Thinking the house was being burgled, they called the police, who duly arrived and arrested the man, asking him to sit in a police car parked outside in the road. Soon after, another young man walked straight into the house and so the police arrested him as well and put him in a different police vehicle. Finally, a young lady approached the house, knocked on the back door but, receiving no answer, walked away, whereupon the police quizzed her. She confirmed what the two men had been saying about the house being open to church folk and then identified them as being people she knew – and so they were released.

In addition to day visitors, the Seatons had many waifs and strays living with them over the years. Inevitably, Tony became more and more busy with pastoral work in the church, and so he left his post at Epsom College, trusting the Lord for his income.

By 1984, it became clear that the Fellowship would have to move from the Red Cross Hall; there were just too many people attending on Sundays. One of the local Anglican churches was selling its church hall, which, unusually, was located over a quarter of a mile from the church. Tony brought this to the attention of the Fellowship, whereupon a week of prayer was called. Following this, Tony suggested that if each person or couple in the church could give £1,000, it would be possible to raise the £50,000 which was to be offered. So that is what happened, and the Fellowship bought the property despite being outbid by others. (Bear in mind that, at the time, the Fellowship was essentially a group of young people with young families, who had steep financial commitments living in Epsom.) One young couple were led by the Lord to sell their property, pay off their mortgage and put what was left over into the pot. This meant there was enough money not only to buy the property but also to do renovations, including installing central heating and putting on a new roof (a task achieved by the men in the church). Tony and Mary divided their big house so that the couple and family had somewhere to live.

In those early days, a couple of the young men gathered together a group who would go into Epsom town centre to preach on the streets on Saturdays. There was singing, public preaching and one-to-one conversations. On one occasion, a young man who had been listening was invited to the Saturday evening meeting, to which he duly came. He had a criminal background and later he told us that he had actually planned to kill another man that Saturday night – but God intervened.

Having bought the Hall and renovated it, the church decided to purchase a small area of land that was on one side of it. A number of classrooms were built on this for Sunday school. Tony tells the story of how, once all of this was completed, he walked across the road to view it. The thought came to him that the church could not only have a Sunday school, but also a Monday, Tuesday, Wednesday, Thursday, Friday school. This coincided with a number of parents in the Fellowship becoming dissatisfied with their children's schools and wanting a Christian education for them. One of the young teachers in the church was approached as a potential headteacher. Although reluctant at first, because the requests kept coming he spent some days in prayer and fasting, seeking the Lord. Soon after this, the church had a visiting speaker who spoke on his vision for Christian schools. It seemed the Lord was speaking, so once again the church was gathered for a week of prayer. It became clear that God was leading and so the decision was made to plan to open The Cornerstone School and the young man became the headmaster.

Some memoirs from the headmaster

"Once the church had decided to open a school, a governing body was formed and plans began. I was asked what I should be paid. I replied, 'Nothing,' and explained that my vision was to have a 'school of faith' where everyone – pupils, parents and teachers included – would be able to see the faithfulness of God at work. So it became an established principle that those who worked at The Cornerstone School received no reimbursement.

"How did this work in practice? Parents were asked to contribute time to the school each week. This was usually, but not always, the mothers. People gave freely of their time in whatever capacity they could; if they were able to be teachers, they taught. Or people might do administration, act as a class assistant, do some cleaning or any one of the hundreds of jobs it takes to run a school. But there were always a number of school workers who were looking entirely to the Lord for their support, and finding Him ever faithful. Since no one was being paid, school fees were kept at a very low rate indeed. This had the effect that no one ever had to be turned away because of a lack of money. It also meant that there was never a shortage of staff in the school; in fact, at times there were nearly as many staff (almost all part-time, of course) as pupils.

"The Cornerstone School was opened in September 1988 with thirty-five pupils, but the number quickly went up to approximately fifty – which was really the capacity of the building. Initially all the pupils were from Fellowship families, but as spaces became available, other like-minded parents requested that their children should attend too. It was perhaps a sadness that many had to be turned away; despite desire and plans to expand the school, nothing ever gelled in those early days. It seemed as if the Lord was telling us to keep the school small, so that's what we did.

"The initial plan had been to have just a primary school, but there were several parents of secondary aged children in the Fellowship who had fervently requested that their children also be allowed to attend. During planning, Fellowship members had been asked what they might be willing to do to help. The response was overwhelming and, by God's grace, at that time the Fellowship was blessed with many teachers. I quickly realised that with all these teachers it *would* be possible to have a secondary department as well. So when the school started, there were pupils aged from four-and-a-half to fourteen. It was this mix of ages in a small environment where all parents were involved that gave the school one of its distinguishing characteristics: it was like a big family. From the beginning all the children mixed together, at break times especially, and it was delightful to see teenagers helping and playing with the younger ones."

Why have a Christian School?

The simple reason for us was that God clearly led our Fellowship into that work. Why should He do that? Perhaps only eternity will tell the impact that the school had on the lives of those who were involved, but it became clear early on that it was not just the pupils that benefited. No matter that it was small, the school was a huge project and therefore engaged the time and energy of many in the church. This, combined with that fact that so much was at stake, meant that *in practice* people had to lay down their lives for one another. Factions did not form, grievances were quickly put aside, forgiveness and love abounded. Epsom Christian Fellowship never suffered from a split or any similar tensions that sometimes afflict churches.

Lives were being changed among the adults as well as the pupils. Since he had enrolled his children in the school, one non-Christian father was obliged to start attending church – and got saved. He started enthusiastically serving the Lord and went on to do missionary work overseas with his wife. Another father had backslidden long before his children were accepted into the school, though his wife was still a committed Christian. Due to circumstances, it was he, rather than his wife, who came into school every week to help. He had grown disillusioned and cynical at what he had observed in churches that he had attended years before. As he observed the lives of his fellow staff members over several years, he finally had to admit that what they had was *absolutely real*. He came back to the Lord, and subsequently he and his wife left their own jobs in order to come and teach in the school. Since they received no salary, like others before them they proved the faithfulness of God in His daily provision.

Of course, it was the children who received the greatest benefit, and in several different ways. They enjoyed schooling in an environment where they knew they were loved. They learnt in very small classes due to the fact that so many adults gave so much time freely. Daily, they were being taught the word of God and taught that it is all true. They grew up believing that it is normal to believe God and what He says, it is normal to take Him seriously and to seek to obey Him, it is normal to pray, and it is right to believe that Christian morality is not only normal but also the best for people. They achieved academic success above what many might have hoped for; the Lord's hand was on His work. Most went on to study at university, and a disproportionate number achieved masters and even doctoral degrees. There were times when the Lord drew young people to Himself in significant ways and many of these continue to serve the Lord around the world in their adulthood. Many went out on short-term missions and some long-term. It had been the vision for the school to put strong foundations into the lives of the children (hence the school name: Cornerstone), but also to inspire them to want to serve Him with their lives. This has been fulfilled in many cases.

Life in St Martin's Avenue

One never quite knew what each day or even the next minute would bring when living with the Seatons! 'Never a dull moment' would probably be an understatement.

On one occasion, in a major attempt to burn some of the ever-accumulating garden waste, one ever-willing lad had agreed to perform the dutiful task of preparing a large bonfire at the far end of their very large back garden. When it had all been accomplished, and anticipating a truly successful outcome, the bonfire was lit. At the time, everybody was indoors. Then came an urgent cry for help. The fire was out of control. Flames of over fifteen feet were seen leaping into the air. Someone immediately phoned 999.

The fire brigade was quick and responsive, and very soon St Martin's Avenue was a hive of activity (even more than usual). However, there was one major problem: the fire was out of reach of any of the hoses from the front of the house. So option two was hastily implemented, and the firemen raced round to the house whose garden backed onto theirs. Fireman appeared from every angle, and after some considerable time, the flames and black billowing smoke began to subside.

The inhabitants of No. 16 anxiously peered through their back windows, not only relieved to see the fire diminishing apart from some smouldering remains, but amazed to see that the firemen were also celebrating their success. They had found a large banner on which was written "Jesus is Lord" and were dancing round the garden singing, "Jesus wants me for a sunbeam!" News that a rather 'unusual' Christian family lived there was already a well-known fact in the area!

A day or so later, Mary met one of the ladies who also lived in The Avenue.

"Oh," she said, "are you the lady who lives in the house with all the lovely singing?"

"Yes," replied Mary with a smile.

"Well," said the lady again, "the singing is lovely – but please, no more fires!"

Every Saturday morning in Epsom Town Centre, there was a market. Quick to take every opportunity to share the gospel, one of the many talented young men had painstakingly made a portable bookstall which could be easily dismantled and then reassembled, so enabling it to be transported without too much difficulty. It would be used for displaying and selling Christian books, cards and literature in the busy weekend market.

One such Saturday, Mary was still in bed when there came a knock on the front door. Five policemen stood there, looking very spruce and professional.

"We're sorry to bother you, Madam, but it has been reported that some men have been seen leaving your premises under suspicious circumstances."

"Oh, really?" replied Mary, and then quickly explained, "Oh, the men are all taking the books down to the bookstall and then going on to the prayer meeting."

The officer in charge, somewhat bemused, then called out to his awaiting team, "Not needed here, men – all gone to the prayer meeting!"

At one of the far ends of their back garden was a large cedar children's playhouse. From time to time it was used to provide temporary accommodation for someone who was homeless. As has already been alluded to, the many bedrooms of their home were usually in full use with people who had a multiplicity of needs.

During a period when there had been a Luis Palau Evangelistic Crusade, there came yet another knock on their front door. A dear man with an Irish accent spluttered out, "An angel has sent me, lady!" (i.e. Luis Palau!) He was homeless and needing help. He was kindly shown to the playhouse in the garden and allowed to stay there for a few weeks.

These types of scenarios were not only a common occurrence at No. 16, but even The Cornerstone School was not exempt.

The school office was just inside the doors of the hall, immediately on the right. Normally these doors are kept locked for security reasons, as is the door to the office if no-one is there. Mary happened to walk into the office, the door being ajar. As she walked in, she was surprised to see a man crawling around on the floor in front of the safe, the door of which was also open.

In her absolute innocence and usual friendly manner, she said, "Oh, hello, can I help you?"

The man quickly replied, "I'm looking for my coat. I've lost my coat."

"Oh dear," said Mary, "I can't see it here, but I can take you to someone who may be able to help you," and, with that, coiled her arm around his and marched the astounded man into the school hall, looking for the secretary. "Oh, here she is. Now, if you just give her your name, address and a phone number, we can contact you if we find it."

This was all too much for the man, who brusquely extricated himself from Mary's clutches and made a rapid bolt through the main door and disappeared down the main street. One of the ladies helping in the school then turned to Mary and said, "Mary, that was no ordinary man. He was a thief!"

"Oh dear!" said Mary. "Oh *dear!*"

Being a part of a team responsible for the administration of any organisation will always be demanding, whether it be of a secular nature or Christian. Certainly as Christians, who are answerable to the Lord for all that we do and are – our conduct, our relationships and everything else, the challenges are possibly even more exacting.

Being a school secretary and administrator of a Christian school is therefore a position to which one must most definitely be called. The daily challenges, general workload, an ability to be able to respond to numerous and varied needs of the staff, children and also visitors at any one time, coping with the unexpected (such as an unannounced thief in your office!), not to mention the periodic Ofsted inspections, require a very special sort of person.

The following testimony is from one of those 'special people', who faithfully committed herself to all that was needed for over thirty-five years in helping to run The Cornerstone School to such a high standard. As has already been mentioned, nobody received any salary at any point.

However, God is no man's debtor, and He has and will reward, as eternity will surely reveal.

Liberated from the guilt and power of sin
Kathy Bunten

❝ I had been in church all my life and given my heart to Jesus Christ many times. Yet in my mid-teens, I said to the Lord, "I believe You, Lord, but the reality is *the good that I will to do, I do not; but the evil I will not to do, that I practice*[77]. There has to be more to life than this."

Then, in my mid twenties, I heard the testimony of Mr North. It was to have a profound influence on me. I knew this was the reality for which I had been searching many years.

I was married at this time, and we went to a meeting at Rora House, a Christian Fellowship in Liverton, Devon. As the gospel of new birth was preached, I surrendered my life to Jesus. I wanted Him more than anything or anyone else. I was filled with the Holy Spirit, and all that I had believed from my earliest days became real *within* me, and the bondage of sin was broken. This was reality.

The baptism in the Spirit completely changed my life. The first thing I knew was that God was my Father. I had come from Him and now my very nature was changed. Fear was gone. My behaviour towards my husband and family was very different. We joined a church in Bromley, Kent where the same gospel was being preached, and I was built up by the ministry, which was always Christ-centred. My journey of life in the Spirit continued when we moved to Epsom, to join Tony and Mary Seaton and the saints at the Epsom Christian Fellowship. After being in the Fellowship for a year, the church started a school, and I knew that I should give myself to the work. I was the administrator for many years, seeing the Lord's faithfulness in every aspect of the work.

How wonderful Jesus is! How can one put into words what it means to be free; liberated from the guilt and power of sin, to be clean on the inside, to have Father, Son and Holy Spirit living on the inside? Words fail, tears of gratitude flow, and I give thanks to the one who gave everything to give this salvation to me. Thank

[77] Romans 7:19

you to all the laid-down lives of those who brought *this* gospel to me. What a privilege to have lived at such a time as this. What an amazing Saviour we have! What a wonderful gospel to live!

The body of Christ is multifaceted. We are all so different, but all equally important to our heavenly Father. We all have different giftings and abilities. There are many ways in which each member of a fellowship or church can be a part.

This testimony is from yet another utterly faithful member who was responsible for running a monthly mid-week club for the older generation. Like Kathy, she gave herself two hundred percent and demonstrated God's love to these dear people in so many ways. She would bring cushions from her home to soften the seats, regularly visit each one in their homes with a delightful bunch of flowers or small gift, faithfully pray for them, help with lifts to and from the meetings (and anywhere else if need be) and tirelessly give herself to each one. The gospel was always presented in a clear and understandable way; visiting speakers were frequently invited; organized activities and quizzes were arranged that were especially tailored for their age group as well as being great fun; special outings were arranged, garden parties were held in her home, weather permitting; the list is endless!

This sort of life can only be lived if God has first been allowed to work in us, as Margaret shares with us here.

Contentment instead of insecurity; peace instead of fear; joy instead of sadness
Margaret Barrington

❝ As a young mother, looking at the way the world was going, I wondered what the future held for my children. Life is seldom smooth at the best of times, as I found out to my cost when I became seriously ill at the age of forty-seven. My GP sent me to hospital. The consultant prescribed all the medication he had to offer. I felt hopeless as I had been on sick leave from work for over a year and was steadily becoming weaker.

I could see no light at the end of the tunnel. My parents were both ill and I was doing what I could for them within my limitations. Our children were teenagers. Their prospects were not as good as mine had been when I was a teenager. The family unit was not valued by society in the same way as it used to be, and motherhood was very much underrated.

My son Brian was regularly going to the Epsom Christian Fellowship. One day he invited me to go with him to hear a visiting preacher, Andy Hunter. Brian told me that he came from my school in my home town, East Barnet. I accepted this invitation as I had been very happy there. Many of my friends had married and we had a strong old students' association.

Something that Andy said pricked my heart. At the end of the meeting I spoke to him and responded to the message that Jesus Christ could make me whole. I was amazed. I was forty-eight at the time and I had never heard that before.

Sunday meetings were held at the Red Cross Hall in Epsom. Midweek meetings were held at the home of the pastor and his wife, Tony and Mary Seaton, whose lives were, and still are, outstanding. They accepted and loved me unconditionally. Visiting preachers used to come, namely Mr G.W. North, Norman Meeten, Dave Medlock and Andy Hunter. Their lives were very special and different from those of other people.

After about six months of going to the Epsom Christian Fellowship, Andy Hunter, who had been invited back to speak again, spoke about repentance – living to please God rather than ourselves, combining a complete change of direction for our lives with that of saying sorry to God. That day I felt so empty and alone. I sat and cried in a corner, but I listened very carefully to everything that was spoken. Andy said that we had all sinned and fallen short of the glory of God and that we had all gone astray like lost sheep, pleasing ourselves. When I heard this, I knew that this was true. Amazingly, He said that all we had to do to become reconciled to God was to repent.

That morning I really said sorry from the bottom of my heart. Immediately I knew a beautiful stillness that I had never ex-perienced before. It was as if streams of living water had been poured through the inside of my body. I had been washed clean inside. I felt like a new baby in a strange way. I had been given a completely new start to my life. I believe everyone would like a fresh start at some point. There are things we would all like to blot out. It was miraculous. My old nature of worry, guilt, fear, resentment and loneliness had been washed away. In its place is a new nature. I was filled with such a deep love, joy and peace by the Holy Spirit. The old had passed away. I was and am a new creation, fashioned by God. I had no idea that anything so wonderful could happen to me. I received the unsearchable riches found only in Christ Jesus.

My thoughts are quite different from those I used to have. I am not perfect, but I am so grateful not to have my old nature any more. God is still working in me, and when I do trip up, He is always there, loving and forgiving me. I live on a different plane now. I am not hiding from God. Everything is open.

Now I know that heaven, when I die, is a reality. Now I have the love and security I had always wanted but which cannot be found in the world without Jesus Christ. To have a close relationship with the God of the universe has given me a sense of purpose and security about who I am and where I am going.

A graduate from Reading University who joined the Epsom Fellowship in the late '70s shares his memories and thoughts around his time there.

My memories of the Fellowships
Rob Betts writes:

❝ I spent the academic year 1977/78 in Liverpool, where I attended Devonshire Road Fellowship and continued to enjoy blessing in being part of that church. Then I got a job near Epsom in Surrey. I chose Epsom as the place to settle because of the Fellowship there, led at that time by Tony Seaton. Tony and his wife Mary were very much 'house parents' of the church – the church was a real family. For a single person moving to an unfamiliar town, that was an enormous help. It was there in Epsom that I met Carol, and we married in 1990. We moved away to Cambridgeshire in 2003.

One of the features of the Epsom Fellowship was that we regularly had visiting speakers – Mr North, Norman Meeten, Ron Bailey, Dave Medlock, Fred Tomlinson, Dai Patterson, Andy Hunter and others. They supplemented the ministry of members of the church. It was a time of rich biblical ministry. The combination of freedom for any in the gatherings to share, or to use their spiritual gifts, coupled with the solid biblical teaching –

on which the Fellowships as a whole placed great emphasis – was perhaps unusual among the various Charismatic churches that were springing up and growing during the late 1960s through to the 1980s and beyond.

Our times of worship in song and prayer, too, were a significant feature. It was interesting that we in Epsom (and this was widely true of the Fellowships in those days) never had a dedicated worship leader or band. Typically, there was just a piano or keyboard, latterly supplemented by a guitar to accompany us. The worship was guided unobtrusively by one of the elders or someone delegated by them. And despite the freedom for anyone to share, start a hymn or chorus, prophecy, etc., it was noticeable how rare it was for there to be anything 'out of order'. From my perspective, it resembled what the gatherings in the first-century churches seem to have been like as we read about them in the New Testament.

However, looking back, I think there may have been certain areas of need too. An intentional plan to teach believers (especially new believers) systematically through the Bible and in basic Christian doctrines could have been very beneficial as a supplement to the preaching. And the Fellowship movement might well have been helped by a more definite and strategic plan to develop leaders and plant out new churches.

But in conclusion, I remain hugely grateful to God for having been part of the Fellowships over the greater part of three decades. It was a privilege.

Most, if not all, of the Fellowships have known times of great difficulty, disappointment and testing. It is all part of being conformed to Jesus' image.[78] Epsom has been no exception. The most difficult of all, perhaps, was when Tony and Mary came to the front of the hall one Sunday morning and painfully shared how God had been speaking to them quite clearly over some time that it was needful for them to move on. The church fell silent, unable to really take on board the full impact of what they were hearing. Some broke down and cried. Tony graciously phoned those who had not been at the meeting, to let them know personally, rather than to hear the news second-hand from another member. Tony was not only an elder; he was a real father. It had been as

---

[78] See Romans 8:29

painful for him and Mary to break the news as it was for the church to sit in the meeting that morning. Their hearts were broken too, but they had to be obedient and leave the whole thing in the hands of the Lord who loved them and knew what was best for each of His children.

There were two flats that were now on the market in their block. One had been on the market for six months. Tony and Mary's sold in a day! Within a very short time, therefore, they had gone, the Lord not only confirming the rightness of the move but trying to make the parting as easy as was possible. They moved in the May of 2010, after thirty-eight amazingly fruitful years.

Their new home for a time was to be in Suffolk; a large and spacious house in the country, a few miles from Beccles where Mike and Sue Cadman have a small Fellowship, meeting in their own home. They were obviously thrilled at being able to welcome them into their midst.

After four years, God again spoke clearly to them that they were to move on, this time to a quaint little village called St Briavels, on the edge of the Forest of Dean. The main purpose for this move was to be near to one of their sons and his wife, and to have an input into caring for their two very young children, so making it possible for the parents to continue to work until the children were old enough to begin their schooling. They obviously loved this opportunity of seeing so much more of their family, as did the grandchildren, exhausting though it was. During this time, Tony and Mary joined a small Congregational church in the village, meeting some very dear folk.

Once the children began school, the Lord once again began to unfold His next step for their lives. Occasionally, they had been able to travel down to a very small group of Fellowship folk living near Cardiff, who were meeting together in the home of John and Jan Britton. Gradually they knew it was right, now that their 'grandparenting duties' had lessened, to join themselves to this group more permanently. The 'joys' and upheavals of packing up returned with a vengeance, and on Tony's birthday, in July of 2018, the removal vans took to the road once more, this time to a small village in the Vale of Glamorgan, called Ewenny. Interestingly, their new home is called The Nook, the same name as the very first house used by the Manchester Fellowship over fifty years ago.

Tony and Mary continued to pray for them daily. They were regularly invited back to preach and share, and so, in some fatherly and motherly way, they were still able to 'care' for them, albeit from a distance.[79]

[79] Sadly, Tony died not so long ago since writing this.

12

Auchenheath House

New hearts for old

Driving slowly through the Lanarkshire village of Blackwood, turning left at the parish church of Kirkmuirhill, down a very long and windy country lane, and then up again from the valley, one suddenly comes to an open, stone-pillared entrance on a Grade II listed Victorian mansion. Only a small, slate-roofed Gate Lodge on the right of the driveway can be seen from the road. If one continues along the main road for a few more yards, one will come to the small Scottish village of Auchenheath.

Auchenheath House was originally built around 1842, after which it underwent various extensions. With its Jacobean-style library, some stained-glass panelling designed by Stephen Adam, vaulted ceilings and an ornate marble fireplace originally from Hamilton Palace, it is certainly an exceptional building. It stands in approximately twenty-eight acres of ground, although more recently has been considerably reduced resulting from the Forestry Commission reclaiming much of the original land.

Dr Jack Kelly, a highly respected cardiac consultant, and his wife Eileen moved in during the early 1960s and within a short time opened their home for regular Christian conferences, initially inviting speakers involved with the Charismatic renewal movement such as Dennis Clark and Cecil Cousins.

During the early 1970s, the Lord brought them into contact with people from the Fellowships, at a time when there was a significant move of God. Although initially they were in some ways quite wary of what they had heard, Eileen recognised from a conference that she attended in Liverpool that what she had personally witnessed, and that which was being lived out so powerfully, had all the hallmarks of a sovereign work of God. One brother, living at Auchenheath at the time, explains that

"Eileen returned a radiant and transformed woman. Her life and testimony spoke for itself."

They invited Mr North to come and preach, and in 1977 both he and his wife Dolly accepted an invitation to make their home with them, living in the Gate Lodge. He continued to support the eldership for twelve years, although for much of the time he remained committed to an international itinerant ministry.

All those who had regularly travelled over to the many conferences held at the home before Mr North and his wife moved into the lodge were automatically contacted again and invited to their first 'Bible Week' where Mr North would be preaching and ministering. Sadly, and unexpectedly, says Richard Curd, a dear brother involved with the Fellowship there at the time, "it was this event that brought us face to face with the controversy that surrounded Mr North's ministry and the inordinate negativity which emanated from some Christians. No replies were received. This must have been deeply hurtful to both Jack and Eileen, as so many of those who had come before were close friends. Rather than come to hear him for themselves, to make their own judgement, they seemed to prefer to stay at home and criticise."

Thankfully, Mr North came anyway and, as Richard continues, "although we were just a few, we had the most amazing few days of ministry. The presence of God seemed tangible and we were truly transformed. To this day, the overwhelming sense of the love of God remains."

Hungry for God

One of the hallmarks of any real and deep work of God is that there is a genuine longing and heart-cry to know Him in a way not yet experienced, and a willingness and desire – if not an urgency – to abandon everything else, no matter what the cost.

This was certainly true for all those who found themselves drawn to what the Lord was doing at Auchenheath. No distance was too far to travel; no floorboards too hard to sleep on (if needs be); no house duties too demanding, although far from easy. Living in and being a part of the life in a large Victorian mansion standing in so many acres of ground required a givenness and commitment that went far beyond the norm and frequently stretched people to the limit. Many came from across the UK to voluntarily help with the major work that needed their particular skills and expertise, particularly in the early days. Refurbishing such a property, decorating, cleaning, maintaining the lawns and grounds, cultivating the large vegetable plots, rearing chickens, cooking and catering for sometimes over sixty or more over a weekend, laundering... The list was endless of all that was needful on a daily basis. Rising at dawn and often not getting to bed before midnight for those living in was challenging in the extreme. Even those who travelled in for meetings, often from forty or more miles away from Edinburgh and elsewhere, would be prepared for a very long day.

How well I remember those amazing if not hair-raising journeys across country from Edinburgh to Auchenheath along the scenic route of the A70 known by the locals as 'the Lang Whang' (the long way) in Mike Cross's Ford Cortina, usually packed to overflowing! We were desperate to arrive in time for the Sunday morning meeting. We would then return late at night exhausted and bleary-eyed, to crawl into our beds for a few hours' sleep, but thrilled with all that we had been so privileged to have been a part of during the day. As Richard has shared earlier, God was almost tangible and His presence so real. We had hardly been aware of time; the two-and-a-half-hour meeting from 10.30 to around one, with Mr North often preaching for an hour or more, just flew by.

Julie Ray, now married to Len Grates, was one of the many young people who found herself becoming an integral part of the work there.

66 Having heard of Auchenheath House, another home that changed the world, we drove across from Edinburgh each Sunday for a full day, which usually lasted for twelve hours. Nothing was too much. We were spiritually hungry.

I stayed to volunteer at Auchenheath for six years, during which time we experienced many coming to the Lord, being set free and learning how to be a family of God. We were often catering for over sixty at weekends, and people slept like sardines on the floors and anywhere they could find, but they too were hungry for spiritual food. Distance or deep snow were no deterrents!

On one of my weekend visits, I had joined everyone for breakfast one Sunday morning. I couldn't help but notice a young man sitting opposite me on the more than large and very long wooden dining-room table. His face was radiant. Only the evening before, he had been with us for the evening meal but so different. There had been a darkness on his face that was hard and sullen. He spoke little and looked so unhappy. At an opportune moment, I mentioned to someone how different this person seemed from the evening before.

"Oh yes," they answered. "He was born again last night!"

The contrast was surely amazing. His face and whole demeanour had been truly transformed.

Some treasured recollections

Jack and Eileen had big, welcoming hearts for all. Apart from a small sitting room and their bedrooms, the rest of this beautiful home was open for everyone to use quite freely.

One of the favourite areas was the open library area with its Jacobean rafters, an open fireplace and an authentic tartan carpet, surrounded by dark wooden shelves packed with literary gems of every description. Hours would be spent by visitors and friends alike relaxing in the warmth and quietness of this delightful area of 'retreat', although it was part of the main thoroughfare between the front entrance of the house to the left and the large dining room and kitchen to the far right.

Not a few hands laboured tirelessly in the kitchen from early morning till late at night, and the daily menus were amazing. Ask anyone about the 'Auchenheath curries'! It was Scottish hospitality *par excellence*. A very dear friend of Eileen's, Marian, who lived in the house, gently kept an eye on us all and kept us in check, along with Eileen, and graciously supervised all those who came to offer their help, whatever time of day it was. The warmth of the Aga often proved a popular meeting point, especially when the Scottish pancakes were sizzling away on the griddle or the late-night bacon and eggs were on the go!

However, more important than all these culinary delights or the comfort of a beautiful home was the spiritual input and ministry, which has meant so much to so many, and has, at their confession, been totally life-changing.

An opening up of the Scriptures
Willie McNichol

66 I had never heard such a preacher as Mr North before. He preached a very strong holiness / Pentecostal message, all rooted in the new birth of a Christian. He opened up the Bible to me in a completely new way. At last I really began to understand parts

of God's word that had puzzled me before – including the book of Romans. He also opened up to me the life-changing truth of the new covenant – a truth that was to grip my heart and totally transform my life in the years ahead. ... We were experiencing God in a new way. Lives were being transformed. Christians were getting their lives sorted out – myself among them.

Juliana Ray, mother of Julie, who, as mentioned earlier, married Len Grates, also shares her appreciation of Auchenheath.

66 Here was a respected medical consultant, and Eileen his wife, owning a beautiful mansion ... and, instead of keeping it to themselves, had opened it up to people in various states of distress: alcoholics; victims of broken marriages; hippies who had lost any aim in life; and so on. They themselves only occupied one room apart from their bedrooms. The rest of the house – the other bedrooms, the library, the spacious lounge and the dining room – were all at the disposal of those who were their 'guests' and the workers who helped to run the place.[80]

One such hippy was a lad called Mickey Wright, who has now been in eldership for many years, in Lanark, about seven miles from Auchenheath.

66 I arrived at Auchenheath Christian Fellowship in Easter 1976 to attend a conference which was being held there, the speaker being Mr G.W. North. I'd heard about this conference while attending a New Year conference, 1975/76, at Devonshire Road Christian Fellowship in Liverpool. I'd asked if there were any similar Christian Fellowships in Scotland, to which they answered, "Yes." I was given the address and telephone number of Dr Jack Kelly, who was the owner of Auchenheath House, where Auchenheath Christian Fellowship met, and it was suggested that I should get in touch with him and book a place at the conference. This I did, and the end result was that I stayed there for seven years.

Auchenheath Christian Fellowship was a wonderful place. There were about a hundred and twenty people of all ages who met there for Sunday morning worship. At that time many people came from Edinburgh and Glasgow and the surrounding area to

80 See *By Grace Alone;* Juliana Ray; p.173

attend the meetings, and we had a Sunday afternoon meeting rather than an evening one, rounded off with a bacon and egg supper at about 6 pm so that people could leave at a decent hour to get home, due to Edinburgh being forty miles away and Glasgow twenty-five miles away. There was also a mid-week Fellowship meeting for prayer, praise and Bible study on Wednesday evening and a prayer meeting on a Tuesday evening each week. You wouldn't have missed any of these meetings for anything; you were there because God was there.

Auchenheath House, or the 'Big Hoose' as we used to call it, was surrounded by twenty-eight acres of land, part of which were ornamental gardens. There was lots of grass to cut and flower borders to keep weed-free, decorating, fixing the roofs, building walls, plastering, altering rooms etc. and all things that went with looking after a large estate. Life was busy with lots to do, but the working atmosphere was free. There were also several fields which were used for growing vegetables, so there was plenty of work to be done. Of course, maintenance had to be done on the building, but it was good since everyone was of one accord. We were all working for God's glory and the extension of His kingdom.

There were two main families who lived in the house: the Kelly family who owned the house and the McNeill family. Jim McNeill was one of the elders in the Fellowship. There were many women who both worked and lived in the house and some who lived there but worked outside the house. Likewise, the men; some were working in the grounds and were part of the maintenance team and some worked outside the house.

Community living was not easy at times, but that is what it was all about: learning to be one body in Christ, living together, getting all the rough corners knocked off of us. We believed we would spend eternity together, and if we could not live together in harmony while we were here on this earth, what chance would we have in eternity? So we loved one another, denied ourselves and picked up our cross and followed Jesus, preferring others above ourselves. Not easy at times but very, very profitable.

In 1980, I went to Zimbabwe to secure a farm that had been bought for the purpose of starting a Bible school. While I was there in Zimbabwe at Ameva Farm, God spoke to me and told me

He wanted me to build a church in Lanark in Scotland. Lanark is about seven miles from Auchenheath and is the local market town. When I came back from Zimbabwe in 1982, I returned to Auchenheath Christian Fellowship, married my wife Anne who attended there, and in November 1983 we started a work in Lanark. I had spent seven very happy years at Auchenheath, and I can say without any shadow of a doubt that this time was foundational in my Christian life. I had many trials to go through, a few heartaches and painful situations, but it was all in the Lord's wonderful plan. *"...all things work together for good to those who love God, to those who are the called according to His purposes."*[81] I praise God for my years spent at Auchenheath Christian Fellowship, and although the congregation there is now much smaller, the folk from the Fellowship there are still serving the Lord.

Auchenheath House

The Nethanvale

During the late 1970s, a large, disused public house in the village of Auchenheath came onto the market. Eileen Kelly, in particular, but supported by Jack and the other leaders of the Fellowship, saw how this venue could be an effective opportunity for outreach and evangelism, not only to the local community but possibly farther afield too, to the neighbouring villages and towns. Situated on the main Lanark Road, it was also a well-suited stop-off point for a coffee and homemade goody.

[81] Romans 8:28

The Nethanvale, where many years previously Helen Shapiro had often been invited to sing, was much prayed about, and a decision in 1978 was made to buy it. A team of trustees was appointed to oversee the whole project. Their vision was to provide a welcoming café on the ground floor, with the upstairs flat providing a home for Jim and Aileen and their children. Jim, who had sacrificially sold his home in Tollcross in Glasgow, had at that point been invited to live in Auchenheath House with his family as one of the elders, as well as being one of the five trustees of the Nethanvale.

Opposition

An application for planning permission was submitted to the Council, at which point alarm bells began to ring, with much opposition from the villagers and Council alike.

Willie McNichol, who lived with his family in the village at the time and was a member of the Auchenheath Fellowship, takes up the story.

66 There was great opposition – especially from a local councillor. Articles appeared in the local papers claiming that the Fellowship was a commune and that it would attract many undesirable people to the village. Things were really getting out of hand, so I decided to enter the fray. I wrote a long but carefully worded letter to the Chief Planning Officer of the Lanark District Council where I worked, and sent copies of the letter to the two papers who had been running the articles. These letters were published and the following week there were new headlines: "Christian Fellowship defended by villager!" Returning to work the following week, I was greeted by a Christian lady with, "Well, Willie, you have really nailed your colours to the mast!" I certainly had and life in the office was not too easy. However, plans were approved and the 'Nethanvale' came into being!

An enormous amount of work was required: building, renovating, refurbishing and all that was essential to transform an old, dilapidated pub into a café / restaurant, with suitable residential accommodation above. The work in fact extended over a further eleven years before it was ready. Financial pledges and gifts were received, with others volunteering to help and support the work as it unfolded.

The café continued to function for ten years, but unfortunately, due to ill-health of key workers and other problems, it seemed needful to close the venture down. Jim and Aileen, with one of their daughters, continued to live in the first floor flat, and following the death of Jack and Eileen, Auchenheath House was sold and the Fellowship, now much reduced in number, continued to meet on the ground floor, formerly the café. With a small kitchen and some of the tables and chairs still *in situ*, it proved an adequate meeting place where after the meetings people could stay together for a communal lunch and further fellowship. Sadly, Aileen McNeill died in early 2018, leaving just Jim and his daughter Elizabeth in the flat. She was greatly missed.

Eventually it was needful for dear Jim and Elizabeth too to move on to alternate and separate accommodation, more suited to their individual needs. One or two joined Mickey Wright at the New Life Christian Fellowship in Lanark, and others joined local churches in the area.

Lanark Christian Fellowship
Mickey Wright

66 Lanark Christian Fellowship was started in Lanark, Scotland in November 1983. At that time, I felt called to be working in Lanark, and my wife, my daughter and I were duly prayed over and sent out from Auchenheath Fellowship. There were also three others who came with us from Auchenheath Fellowship. I had been asked to come and be the pastor of the then congregation of three members in a small Assemblies of God church, but because I did not feel that I could sign the articles and doctrines of the Assemblies of God, we were soon out on the street. The document they wanted me to sign stated that the initial evidence that the baptism of the Holy Spirit had been received by someone was that they spoke with tongues. I believe that speaking in tongues can be *an* evidence that the baptism has occurred but is not exclusively *the* evidence and that the true evidence that the baptism in the Holy Spirit has occurred in a person is a holy life. This resulted in me not being allowed to be the pastor there.

After meeting for a few weeks in the house of one of the ladies who attended, we then secured the local community Memorial Hall in January of 1984 and started our meetings there. We continued until approximately 1994, when we managed to purchase a rundown building in Duncan's Close, 19a High Street,

Lanark, which we renovated and convened our meetings there. We had a small loan to begin with from an aunt of one of the men in the church to purchase the property, which we paid back quickly. Other than that, God provided all that we needed for the renovation of the building without bank loans or mortgages. We prayed and the money came in. Sometimes there was no money and the work stopped for a period of time, but that served to put us more on our knees and on our faces in prayer until more money was provided. At that time, something that Hudson Taylor, a missionary to China, said was a great blessing to me: "God's work done in God's way does not lack God's supply." I can testify to the truth of that. When we opened our new church building in Lanark, we did not have a penny of debt.

After being the pastor of the church for twenty-four years, I handed it over to the three other elders: Alistair Mackenzie, John Shaw and Peter Smith. Stuart Hastie was at that time a deacon and later became one of the elders. The name of the Lanark Christian Fellowship was then changed to Lanark Community Church. I returned to Auchenheath Christian Fellowship with my family to pray, spend time with God and see what the next step was for me in my walk with God, only to discover that after seven years, God sent me back to Lanark to start a "new, fresh work".

We started that work on Easter Sunday, 2015 in a rented meeting place called The Tollbooth. We called the new work 'New Life Christian Fellowship'. 'The Tollbooth' is the old Scottish name for 'The Jail'. What a wonderful place for the church to meet! Lanarkshire has a long history of the Covenanters, and I counted it a privilege to meet in the very jail where many of the Covenanters had been imprisoned before going to the gallows. I find myself often praying and mingling my prayers with those of the Covenanters that have gone before, in asking God for a mighty revival; as a famous quote says, "The blood of the martyrs is the seed of the church."[82]

Meanwhile Lanark Community Church had been going through changes. Some of the elders had moved on to different places, and another, John Shaw, was now leaving to go to Ireland to help look after his wife Martha's sister who was ill. The remaining elders did not wish to continue the work after John

[82] Tertullian

Shaw had announced he was leaving. John approached my wife and me and asked if we would like to take over the church building. Since the start of New Life Christian Fellowship in Lanark, we had been praying for a place to meet, a place to call our own; and in the wonderful workings of God, the original building we had met in before – Duncan's Close, 19a High Street, Lanark – had become available.

We moved in on the first weekend in October 2016. How wonderful the Lord is, how wonderful His ways are! So I'm full of expectancy that the Lord will build up the church again and save souls and set the captives free for His glory. Amen.

13

Conferences

United in Christ

Unto Him shall the gathering of the people be...[83]

When God brings together a group of His people whose hearts are wide open, with no agenda, expectant and willing for anything that He has purposed for that particular time, wonderful things will happen. There are virtually no limits.

This has certainly been true of all the many conferences within the Fellowships since God first began to move so sovereignly and powerfully in the early 1960s. Numbers were unimportant. Sometimes there were just a few, sometimes many hundreds.

The first gathering together in 1965 at The Longcroft saw only a few. Norman was still a curate in the Anglican church. Testimonies from this time were amazing. On one occasion, two ladies with severe back complaints, not able to stand upright without help, began to sing 'I clasp the hand of Love Divine'[84]. They came to the last verse...

> I take Him for this mortal frame,
> I take my healing through His Name,
> And all His risen life I claim,
> I take – He undertakes.

...and they were both instantaneously healed. God met them both.

The following year, a second conference was held just a short walk down the lane from The Longcroft, in the Barnstondale Centre. Again, God moved in wonderful ways as He subsequently did in High Leigh, a Christian conference centre in Hoddeston, Hertfordshire and then Swanwick.

[83] Genesis 49:10 (KJV)
[84] *Redemption Hymnal*, no. 491

One year on from High Leigh, the College of Education in Derby was hired. By this time, numbers were increasing to several hundred.

John White, who had been an elder at the Rora Christian Fellowship in Devon, shares his memories of the Derby Conference.

66 The Derby Conference was the immediate precursor to the Cliff College conferences, apart from Swanwick. There were many memorable things for me, such as baptisms – including that of Heather and me – in the filthy river Derwent, immediately opposite to the Derby Council Offices. A huge crowd of staff could be seen at every window gazing down on this biblical scene below as well as the police being called!

Norman described the Derwent as a sewer – needing to remove all the scum off the top of the water before proceeding to baptise!

A young Yorkshire farmer's wife had come with her husband who was to be baptised, but she made it clear that she did not want to become involved, standing aloof on the bank of the river. She was immaculately dressed in a beautiful heather-coloured tweed suit together with a very expensive-looking hat. Once all the baptisms had been done, Norman gave opportunity for any others to come forward. He alone can describe what happened next.

66 She just took off! She ran down the bank in all of her attire, with her gold watch firmly attached. After some persuasion, the watch was removed, and she entered the muddy waters of the Derwent to be totally submerged, tweed suit and all!

It reminded him of a similar incident when ministering in Tiverton. A lady had come to watch her son being baptised. As he came up from the water, she exclaimed, "Well, if he can – if the Lord can move someone like him (he is as stubborn as a mule) – it is about time I got myself sorted out!" and she followed him into the water. As Norman has said, we can sometimes be guilty of dragging our feet – sitting tight, pondering, reasoning things out in our minds – rather than simply and spontaneously obeying God and moving on what He is asking of us.

John White continues with another very unforgettable time at Derby.

66 There was one utterly memorable morning meeting. We were all deeply into worship when someone from the back cried out, "Excuse me, Mr North, could we pray now for China?" Mr North, taken by surprise, turned to Norman, knowing that he

would one day visit China, and invited him to pray. Norman got to his feet, then onto his knees, then went flat on his face; groaning, quite unable to put the depth of agony he felt into words. Then Mr North went down too, and like the wind blowing through a field of ripe corn or wheat, people in the hall fell onto their knees one after another until the whole hall was filled with people in agony for people somewhere. I'd never experienced anything like this before, nor have I ever since. Some twelve hours later it was announced by the news media that the Red Guards had been let loose throughout the land of China and terrible things were happening. The Spirit of God had found us, a company of people on the other side of the world, willing to pray "with groanings which cannot be uttered"[85]. God wished to involve His people in His own agony.

For another dear lady, it was a time of great help and blessing.

From darkness to light

I was invited to the conference by a friend who had received ministry from Mr North and had been blessed by the contact. We were planning to go together but at the last minute my friend withdrew from the arrangement, so I decided to go alone, although I did not know a soul and the conference was for over four hundred people.

Prior to going, I had been involved in a very serious road accident in which someone had been killed in our car. As a result of the circumstances, I was sometimes going to another Pentecostal church a little farther away from my own in order to have fellowship with some of the people who had been travelling with me at the time of the accident. On one particular evening, three tongues and interpretations were given one after the other, and I knew that God was speaking to me in a very special way and telling me, amongst other things, that "the vats will overflow". I didn't understand what the Lord was saying, but realised afterwards that it all related to what God was about to do in me and for me at the Derby conference.

When I arrived, I was immediately befriended by a Christian lady, who frequently chatted to me on my way to or from the

[85] Romans 8:26

meetings, so I didn't feel too isolated. I felt loved and accepted in a new way. The first meeting, at which Norman Meeten spoke, left me feeling terrified, as I thought he was preaching sinless perfection, and felt far from that standard in my life. But as the conference proceeded, I was absolutely amazed at the way God frequently spoke by prophecies and interpretation of tongues. I had experienced something of this since my initial conversion, as I belonged to a Pentecostal church where the gifts of the Spirit sometimes operated, but the difference was stark: at this conference, the true character of God was preached, which I had never before appreciated, especially His personal love for me and desire to have a relationship with me. In addition, I realised through the preaching the importance of believing the truth of what God had done for me by His death and resurrection. This sounds very basic, but in the Pentecostal church one felt continually pressurised to be witnessing rather than being led into a truly holy life which would be the best witness of all. I also remember sending my (non-Christian) parents a postcard in which I exclaimed with amazement that "God is in charge of the meetings!" I don't think they appreciated the message, but for me it was a revelation as I had only known the strict control of my pastor over the meetings and, indeed, over the flock itself.

By the end of the week, I was feeling more and more that I should go and ask Mr North to pray with me, which I did on the very last morning. I had been very oppressed by the enemy for a long time because of many things in my background and because of my own sin. As soon as Mr North began to pray with me, I found myself lying across the desk which was between us, as evil spirits were cast out of me.

As time went on, I knew God was calling me to leave my home and parents and to join the Liverpool Fellowship, where I continued to be built up in the truth and to experience the true infilling of the Holy Spirit, and though not perfect, I knew I was now a new creation, delivered from the kingdom of darkness and brought into the kingdom of light.

The summer conferences at Cliff College, Derbyshire

These conferences continued to be 'something else'! For those who had never set foot in such a conference before and had barely known the miracle of true new birth, it was often a difficult place in which to remain. The temptation to turn around and run away was all too real. One such lassie admitted that had she had the money to jump onto the next coach to London, she wouldn't have hesitated. However, because a kind friend had escorted her and others down and paid for all of her expenses, with the promise of returning her home safely in his car at the end, there was no alternative but to stay put.

View of the Cliff College conference centre from the main college

❝ We arrived very late – a carload of rather tired and weary passengers, not to mention the chivalrous driver. We ground to a slow halt outside the conference hall, where a dear man known as 'Dad Moff' greeted us with his ever-attached clipboard and pen. We respectively gave him our names as he studied his long list in front of him. Then, looking at me, he calmly said, "Oh yes – you're in Glory!" I stared at him in disbelief. Was I hearing correctly? I had never felt so far removed from Glory in all of my life! What I hadn't realised at the time was that all the ex-army Nissen huts, now to be our accommodation for the week, had all been named: Love, Joy, Peace, Faith, Glory, to name just a few!

I was duly directed to 'Glory' at the end of this tiring day, with the moon gliding gracefully in and out through the clouds of the night sky. As I gingerly entered the narrow door, rows and rows of iron bunkbeds standing either side of a cold concrete floor greeted me, visible only by several shadeless lightbulbs hanging precariously from the tin roof. I had often heard of the value and benefits of 'missionary training', but this excelled them all. The challenges did not diminish. Each bunk was no more than two and a half feet wide, with a well-used horsehair mattress sinking deeply in the middle above an equally well-used metal spring base, making it feel more like a hammock than a bed. To maintain one's personal hygiene, communal washrooms and toilets awaited us, situated on a slope immediately outside of the exit at the far end of the hut. With no hot water, we had no real problem waking up in the mornings – that is, if we had actually managed to sleep the night before. Thankfully, it was August and not mid-winter. Also, we did have our youth on our side – or just about! Such was my initiation to the summer conferences at Cliff.

Another shock that I encountered was the pure joy and radiance that seemed to emanate from the faces of so many as we had driven into the Centre. I really had never seen Christians so full of the life of God before. I certainly recognised what I was witnessing and silently longed to know that reality too. My Christian experience up to that point had been vastly inferior if not incomparable. In retrospect, I am grateful to see how God had been so gracious and faithful in His dealings with me and in joining me to these Fellowships that have increasingly become so meaningful and precious to me.

The Nissen huts at Cliff College

An event prior to Cliff College conferences organised by the Fellowships

66 When I first attended Cliff College at a conference (organised by Project Evangelism, not the Fellowships) there was a rota for setting the long wooden tables for meals, and on this particular day I was just finishing my task as the meeting started, so I sat at the back of the other people and started listening to a man I had never heard of before: Norman Meeten. He had been invited by Project Evangelism and had travelled from Liverpool, where I think the first expression of a house church was being established, which Norman was leading. He spoke about Christ being *in* you. I remember him taking a glass of water and drinking it, to show that you couldn't see it but you knew it was really inside him. An amazing experience came over me as I watched and listened; God revealed Jesus to me so clearly in Norman that I was absolutely overwhelmed by the revelation and couldn't stop crying – I was completely broken by the presence of Jesus, and I was actually seeing Him. I think this was the beginning of very significant movings of the Holy Spirit in my life and also generally in our generation of young people at the time. Things were happening to many of us, and this continued as the Fellowships began to hold conferences at Cliff in the following years.

Changed Lives
Annie Carrington

66 I first went to Cliff College in 1971, after starting to go to a house church in Newcastle-upon-Tyne. I had been to the Exeter Fellowship in Belmont Road for one weekend during the summer of 1970 and was born again that weekend and really knew a change of heart.

I had committed my life to Christ first in 1966/67 while in my last year at school – a time when others in my school year were all involved in an Evangelical Anglican Youth Fellowship. I then went up to Hull University and was involved in the work of the Christian Union in my hall of residence and in the wider university. I was involved in the organisation of a mission to the university in my final year.

As far as I remember, I went every year till 1978, when I was part of a group of seventeen young people that travelled out to Benin in Nigeria to help the work of the church there during the summer months. I went in response to what I had heard at Cliff College the year before.

By 1970, I had started work, and this was the conference where I had the most opportunity to hear the preaching of G.W. North and Norman Meeten. They were very happy times of worship and prayer and powerful preaching. The accommodation in dormitory-style huts was basic with communal washing facilities, but gave the opportunity to meet and get to know new people and make new Christian friends. The meals were prepared on site in the same building where we heard the speakers. A team of helpers gathered at the back of the building (outside if the weather was fair) to prepare vegetables while the meeting was going on, and after the morning meeting the chairs would be moved to one side to accommodate tables and benches for the midday cooked meal. Another team would do all the washing up by hand – an opportunity for further friendship and fellowship.

It was evident from changed lives that people were coming to the Lord, being ministered to / set free / born again. I had not seen or heard such ministry up to that point in my life, except in a limited way in that first weekend in Exeter and occasionally in the small house group in Newcastle where I went Sunday by Sunday. I discovered what the Bible said all over again. What really drew me was the presence and practice of the love of God. I had been to many denominational churches while at university seeking more of God, and in this particular move of God I found 'something' I had been looking for (and therefore missing elsewhere). I understood what I was reading (and hearing) in the Bible in a new way. Things made sense where I had been puzzled before. This was vital Christianity without religious trappings. During the week, adult baptisms took place in the River Derwent, near Cliff College, by the bridge in Calver.

Drawn by His love
Ann Cliff

66 My first memory of Cliff College Conference is from about 1977. At the time, my husband and I were in a parish in Crewe and had

met up with friends from Longcroft Christian Fellowship on the Wirral. My first recollection was of the love shown and shared between people whom I had never met before but to whom I felt incredibly drawn. I had never experienced this before or the sense of being completely accepted. The first hymn was 'Come O thou traveller unknown' by Charles Wesley, and that had a powerful effect on me. The worship was something else that I had never experienced and it made me very hungry spiritually.

From that time on, it became our habit to attend the conferences at Cliff. We enjoyed 'the year of the mud', which older friends will no doubt remember well. The fellowship on the campsite led Mr North to say, "It's like heaven down there!" God certainly watched over me as I was crossing by the tents near the exit when I encountered a hidden guy rope completely submerged by the mud. I was on my way down to the ground when someone appeared by my side, took hold of me and put me on my feet; when I recovered enough to turn around, there was no one in sight. Angel or brother in the Lord, I do not know, but I was so grateful not to have had a mud bath!

I would need to write a book myself to recount all that became so precious to me over subsequent years!

Baptisms

One of the annual events during these summer conferences was the opportunity to be baptised – in the less than clean and icy waters of the River Derwent that ran through the nearby village of Calver. Apart from the slippery banks, there was also a bridge on the road above that served as an excellent vantage point to witness those upon whom God was moving to obey Him in this very scriptural ordinance.

A baptism in the River Derwent, Calver, Derbyshire

Pete Lock, a dear brother, recalls his baptism, when he attended a conference in Swanwick.

66 I remember very clearly Mr North baptising me in the swimming pool. Due to some physical disabilities, I found it somewhat daunting and was quite frightened.

"Relax, boy," said Mr North in his kindly but firm voice, as he dragged me under the water and nearly drowned me! However, I have survived!

I continued to be a part of the Liverpool Fellowship, although initially I did not join the summer conferences as I was able to become involved in trips abroad with other brothers to behind the Iron Curtain and then to a similar Fellowship in Bammaboda in Sweden where Mr North had been invited to minister.

People came to these conferences from all walks of life. One story has been recalled of how Norman picked up an American hitchhiker who turned up in his 'hippy garb'! However, God truly met with him and some years later he was leading his own Fellowship in Chicago.

A further story is told by Norman of another hitchhiker who he had picked up. His newly acquired passenger then asked him if he was not worried that he could be attacked, or even worse, to which Norman quietly and confidently replied, "I am not alone. There are three other people with me."

The hiker was somewhat scared and stole a look round and commented, "I don't see anybody..."

Norman replied quite simply, "Father, Son and Holy Spirit are all here." Needless to say, no harm came to the driver.

Camp life was basic. There were various options for accommodation. A less expensive possibility was to actually camp out in a nearby campsite near to the conference centre, to where many of the families resorted. There were also more civilised single and double bedrooms in the main college which were made available, as well as the notorious Nissan huts already mentioned. Some chose local bed and breakfasts.

The main and quite large conference hall doubled up as a dining room when chairs from the meeting area were brought through to the trestle tables that were put up for each mealtime. People volunteered to help to prepare and serve meals, wash up, clean toilets, as well as medical staff and nurses being available for any eventuality. Administrative roles were covered by the Liverpool Fellowship, who in later years transferred these commitments to a committee. It is also on record that the caretaker of the college was born again as a result of witnessing the godly behaviour of those attending the conferences, and especially as he saw their willingness to 'go the second mile' and to take on the more menial tasks. The life of God was certainly evident in so many.

Commitment to serve
Bryn and Sue Vaughan

❝ We first went to the summer conference held at Cliff College, Derbyshire in 1974, having been greatly encouraged by our friend Hazel Manton (now Hazel Lock).

We were immediately blessed by the ministry and depth of the preaching of the word, and the worship and fellowship were wonderful.

We returned again, only this time joining the campers in a nearby farmer's field. I enjoyed helping with the practical work, such as digging a hole in the field to accommodate a large septic tank, generously given to us by John Gibbons. The fellowship that we had as we worked together was a precious experience.

One year John Valentine was given an opportunity to share about a Bible School which he was wanting to set up in Zimbabwe, having already been involved in missionary work at Benin Bible School in Nigeria. He spoke powerfully from John's Gospel on resurrection life and laying down one's own life. The secret, he said, was to lay your life down, then God will give it back, and then you lay it down again. He then talked about the project which he had first shared with Mr North. An appeal was made for men who were willing to go, to stand. I stood up with many others. This was followed by an appeal for women who were also prepared to join the men to stand. My wife Sue stood up with many other ladies. Wow – what a blessing! A final appeal was made for financial support. Together we pledged the money from some savings we had made for our fuel bills, which in those days were paid every three months.

A few years later I went to Zimbabwe with a small team led by Ron White, to help with the building of the Bible school and student accommodation. Several years later, in 1993, Sue went to visit and to 'spy out the land' and help in any way possible.

Eventually, after Sue had prayed much, God's call came in 1995 to fulfill the commitment we had made. I taught in Ameva Secondary School, and Sue started the crèche and looked after the first aid.

We returned home in 1998 but have been back several times since on various work parties with Jim Bailey. I have also helped with the teaching of some Bible modules on the BTCP (Bible Training Centre for Pastors) course, with Sue running a health clinic.

The commitment to go originated from the early days of the conferences, and this was fulfilled many times over as we laid our lives down to serve.

Sometimes a hush would come over the meetings and then there might be several tongues followed by interpretations and sometimes prophecies too. At times it would seem as if we were transported into eternity where time was no more, and Mr North, if leading the meeting, would say gravely, "Beloved, the spirit of prophecy is here – we could go on all night[86]."

At other times, dramatic events would take place; evil spirits might manifest themselves or people might go forward to be prayed for and were often delivered there and then, publicly. Once, a man who had been mentally ill for some time clambered directly over chairs which were in front of him, rather than using the aisles, and, as a result, caused quite a stir in his eagerness to respond to the word that had been preached.

There was also much careful exposition of the Scriptures, including the teaching on ladies wearing a head covering, and I remember Mr North saying, with humour, that he would wear three hats if he were a woman, such was the importance he put upon this act and the honour he considered it to be, to be obedient to the teaching in the Bible. Few ladies at the time attended the meetings without covering their heads, such was the impact this had on us.

[86] or morning / afternoon, as the case may be

With God, nothing shall be impossible

Norman Meeten

66 One of the most outstanding things I can remember about the Cliff conference concerned a young man called Peter Horsburgh. His sister used to go to the Liverpool Fellowship, before moving to Leominster. His father designed some of the most beautiful and distinguished buildings still standing in Liverpool today. Tragically, he committed suicide whilst Peter was still a young boy. This resulted in him having frequent mental breakdowns and becoming totally insane.

I had been asked by his sister to visit him in Ludlow where he was living with his mother. I went. There was no communication at all. I felt so helpless.

"Lord," I prayed, "what do I do?" I prayed for him, but nothing seemed to happen.

Then the Lord said to me, "Take him home and nurse him as your own child, and I will give you your wages."

We brought him home to The Longcroft. I used to take him out for walks. He was a grown fellow by this time. He would hold my hand. It didn't bother me what some people would think. I was simply being obedient to what God had asked me to do.

One year we took him to the Cliff conference. It was a nightmare. We eventually arrived, at which point I asked John Valentine if he would look after him as I was involved in the ministry. On the Tuesday morning, I looked up and saw Peter coming forward in the meeting. He looked absolutely wild, completely insane. His hair was standing on end. He had a beard which he had tried to shave, which resulted in him chopping pieces out of his face!

That evening Mr North ministered on Jericho. As he finished, he said, "Nothing has ever been accomplished of that magnitude from one single shout, either before or since." Then he said, "SHOUT!"

I have never heard people shout like that. Anyone coming into the hall would think we were all insane. There was a lady sitting on the back row, obviously refined and very cultured. The thought that came to me was, "Either this is the end for her or the beginning for her!" She actually came to me afterwards and said, "This is the first time in my life that I have felt normal."

Amidst all the shouting, I suddenly heard a shout that could be heard above all the other shouts. I looked up to see this young man Peter literally running through the crowd, pushing people out of his way, up to the front where Mr North and I were standing. Mr North turned to John Valentine and simply said, "Go and put him to bed." The next morning Peter got up as sane as anyone!

That sort of thing didn't happen occasionally. It was something that we actually anticipated and expected and believed the Lord for.

We need to do this again and again, because there are people with needs today who need emancipation, who need deliverance, who need to be set free and to be healed.

Moving on

As numbers continued to increase each year, it was becoming evident that a new venue for the summer conferences was going to be needed. Various options were considered until it was agreed to accept the offer of the Rora Fellowship in Devon to use their grounds, the main reason being financial. As Norman said, "One of the things that has always concerned me is that we don't eliminate the ordinary man, woman or family. If prices are raised, it means that one is left with an upper middle-class company of people which excludes the working groups with lesser incomes."

After approximately fifteen years at Cliff, therefore, the Fellowships bade farewell to the Derbyshire Peak District and the muddy waters of the Derwent, and relocated to the rolling hills of Devon and to Liverton, on the edge of Dartmoor. The large conference hall was now replaced by hired marquees to house the main meetings and the various children's groups. The challenges of camping continued and the English weather continued to be predictably English!

For a further twenty-eight years, Rora became synonymous with the summer conference. For many, it was difficult not to look back to those very special and unique times at Cliff when God had moved so powerfully and sovereignly. For others, the various changes that were gradually introduced were seen as a positive move forward. The latter part of most mornings was divided into various seminars on specific Christian topics and current issues of interest. A team of trustees was appointed to oversee the week's activities and agenda. Bouncy castles, cream teas and barbeques were programmed to add a 'holiday' flavour to the week. Evening meetings were shortened and the luring smell of hot chips would waft through the doors of the tent as the meetings closed each evening – a real hit with the young people, if not with some of the slightly older age group too!

The main marquee at Rora

One thing that remained was the Missionary Day each Wednesday, when those working abroad who had flown in for the summer were able to share their hearts and bring everybody into a greater awareness of the very challenging demands and needs of the foreign fields with which they were faced daily. Not a few people can testify that it was during these missionary days that God clearly spoke to them to obey His call and to go in obedience and lay down their lives for His gospel.

Another move

In 2018, the summer conference moved its venue again, this time to a more central part of the country, to Quinta – a Christian conference centre near Oswestry in Shropshire. More indoor accommodation was available, with the added attraction of a sports hall and swimming pool.

As only two conferences have been experienced at the time of writing, it is obviously very early days, but from those who went, it was felt to be a very good and enjoyable week.

Other conferences

In the earlier days, the Exeter Fellowship, having moved from Belmont Road to the Chapel at Westgate, began an annual Exeter Bible Week at which Mr North was the main preacher. Many from other Fellowships around the country joined with them, and this continued for many years, proving a profitable and valuable time of teaching and ministry.

Cloverley Hall
Les and Vicki Wheeldon

❝ The conference at Cloverley began with a vision to have an opportunity for inspirational in-depth Bible teaching coupled with prayer and worship. It has proved that there is a thirst for the word, and the conference has quite often filled the centre at Cloverley Hall. It has been a particular blessing to see the ministries of Blaesius, Larry Hill, Matthew Chilvers and Mary Seaton have such a deep and lasting impact on lives. God has moved and people have been built up. God has also graciously moved in power to set people free and enable them to deepen their walk with God.

Apart from weekend conferences that happened almost weekly in the beginning, according to Norman, there was also an annual New Year conference hosted by the Devonshire Road Christian Fellowship in Liverpool, which continued through to 2018. As the numbers increased, various venues were used, finally being convened at the Christian Fellowship School. Guest speakers were often invited for the weekend as well as our own elders and leaders, who all shared the ministry together.

As much as time spent alone with God cannot be underestimated, so, as a result of these times, the coming together of God's people, His Bride, whether only a few in number or in many hundreds, are times that will bring much blessing. Jesus Himself has said:

> *"For where two or three are gathered together in My name, I am there in the midst of them."*[87]

It has also been noted that at the birth of the church on the Day of Pentecost, the disciples had been gathering together for prayer and worship for many days, resulting in the pouring out of the Holy Spirit.

---

[87] Matthew 18:20

*Mr North leading a time of worship, with Norman Meeten;
summer conference, Rora, 1991*

From what has been shared by many in this chapter, and elsewhere, these times of meeting together in conferences have proved to be life-changing experiences and where the Lord has moved so sovereignly to meet specific needs and to speak to hearts in special ways. When godly preachers filled with the Holy Spirit minister the word of God in power, authority and love, and where His people are open and hungry, there God will command His blessing to be poured out. Amen.

14

Special Features of the Fellowships

Biblical principles

In many ways, each church and Christian denomination is special. Each has its own characteristics and individuality.

The Greek word for 'church' means simply 'a gathering', and therefore when the term 'fellowship' or 'church' is mentioned here, we are simply talking about the people who are part of that gathering. There are no denominations with God. Those who are truly born of His Spirit[88] and in whom Christ lives are part of His church. There will be members of His body found in every denomination worldwide.

God showed Norman very clearly that 'church' was fundamentally not going to meetings; church was *living*, and wherever and whenever possible, it was within the context of a normal home within which people met. They shared together, they ate together, they lived together, as well as meeting for prayer and worship, preaching and teaching.

This was, and is, costly for those whose homes had been opened up and made available for this purpose. They never quite knew who would be knocking on their door, possibly needing a bed for the night or a meal. Many of the youngsters in Liverpool 8 didn't have a home or know the luxury of a regular meal each day or have a change of clothing. Physically, emotionally, mentally and spiritually they were bereft and very needy, but as God began to work through the lives of those who had willingly laid down their lives for each one, so God began to move and the Holy Spirit poured Himself out. People's lives were transformed and needs met – most miraculously.

Many of the Fellowships in more recent years, for logistical or other reasons, have chosen to own or hire a separate building in which to meet, not only on Sundays but also during the week. Others still enjoy and

[88] See John 3:3,5-8

function within a home environment, be it small or large. Most, if not all, have 'house groups' meeting during the week in the homes of church members, so providing a more personal and informal time together and usually incorporating opportunities for Bible study and discussion. There is certainly much to be said for those who are still able to function as a church within a home environment.

Plurality of eldership

The Fellowships have always been encouraged to follow the scriptural teaching of plurality of eldership wherever possible. Not all were able to implement this, particularly initially. Those who did often found differences in their outworking, with one elder sometimes seen as the more senior and the others accepting a 'lesser' role, rather than all equally working together as a unified team. As any church will surely admit, being responsible for such a gathering is demanding, requiring much godly wisdom, maturity and a clear understanding of the word of God. It has therefore been felt that seeing these qualities outworked and implemented was, and is, best known when the duties and functions of the eldership are shared between godly men who have the same heart, share the same vision, are united together in His Spirit and are able to minister not only to each other but to each member of His body and to those who are being joined to His church.

It needs to be said that in the very early days of the Fellowships, with in some ways only a limited experience of the things of the Spirit, there was a certain amount of carnality, and mistakes were made unwittingly. We have had to learn and to discern that which is of God and that which is simply of the flesh. Many will remember so well that when Mr North was leading a time of worship and prayer, if a 'prophecy' or 'tongue' was being given which he thought was not right, he would kindly but firmly ask that person to stop and would explain why. On other occasions, not infrequently, a line of a hymn or chorus would be changed if it was thought that it was not in line with the new covenant teaching in Scripture. He was always encouraging us to 'speak truth to ourselves', for which we were grateful. We felt safe.

Many churches today have more than one leader and there will be many different models in their outworking. With others there may be one actual minister or priest but who will be supported by a team of those who will be responsible for the overseeing of different functions and/or age groups within their church setting.

No hierarchy

It has always been seen as important that each Fellowship or church be self-governing. There is no hierarchal structure, no one person or even a group of people who have any dictatorial authority over another. The eldership within each Fellowship will take full responsibility for their own particular church. They may find it helpful on occasions to seek help or advice from other ministering brethren, but in the end the responsibility lies within themselves as to how to proceed in any given situation or particular need. Authority, when wrongly understood outside of its biblical boundaries, can cause untold distress and havoc, and should never be entertained. Each member is ultimately answerable to God in the way he or she conducts themselves and will be helped to take responsibility for their own life and walk with God.

Body ministry

There has always been a clear appreciation and acceptance, as seen in Paul's first letter to the Corinthians,[89] that each member of His body is as important as the other, and we have been encouraged to take an active part within the life of the church, whether that be within or without the context of a meeting and times of worship. Each will have received some specific gifting or ability that, when exercised in a sensitive and godly fashion, will be able to encourage and edify the whole body. Many of us may have felt that we fall very far short of any ability to be of any help at all, but there have always been those who have spoken that 'word in season' to our hearts and expressed their gratitude for something that we may have seen as so insignificant.

Leading a meeting within the role of eldership will always require those who are able to discern truth from error and on occasions even the demonic, and how grateful we have been for this! It has also given other members confidence, as we too may have been unsure of particular issues, and it has been the same Holy Spirit who has put that check within our own hearts that something was amiss. The need to lead a meeting in this way may not be easy, particularly for the younger and less experienced

---

[89] chapter 12 in particular

elder, but it is all part of the body being *"fitly joined together"*[90], each member functioning in that into which he has been called and exercising the gift that God has seen fit to impart.

Leadership outside of the meetings will also bring with it many demands and pressures, but we all need to be aware that although the hearts of those in leadership will always be more than willing to help when help is needed, we must not take advantage or be continually taking up their time, or make them our first port of call.

The life of the Fellowships, and the godly leadership that has ensued, has always been so precious and such a joy to be a part of. Being an integral member of His family on earth, sharing in each other's joys and sorrows, experiencing God's love in practical ways on a daily basis cannot be underestimated. Laying down our lives for each other, praying together, worshipping together, being available to just be a help means everything to those who have known this ongoing work of God, however small a part we have been able to play.

Encouragement to move in the gifts of the Spirit

As important and as helpful as these spiritual gifts are, as listed in 1 Corinthians 12, Fellowships have always persuaded members to first look to the Lord and to seek Him before ever seeking His gifts. These gifts will spontaneously be known as a natural outworking of loving Him and giving ourselves to Him, whether that be in a meeting or in our everyday lives. He is the one who initiates, not us. He may well put a desire within our hearts to receive a particular gift or to function in a particular way, but if our priorities are misguided and wrongly focused, no gift or ministry will be of any value. How grateful we have all been for our elders and leaders, who have helped us to look to the Lord primarily, to seek the Giver, not the gifts, and to allow His love and His life within us to be outworked by His Spirit. If we *"have not love"*, as Paul says in 1 Corinthians 13,[91] then everything else counts as nothing.

Sound biblical teaching

A whole volume of books could be written to cover the revelatory teaching that has so faithfully been expounded to us over the years, and in fact, many already have. The individual testimonies already covered in

[90] Ephesians 4:16, KJV
[91] e.g. verse 1

the preceding chapters bear record to this fact. So many of us had previously been members of other churches and denominations, becoming disillusioned and falling short of all that has always been on God's heart for us all. Our one cry had been, "Surely there must be more to the Christian life than this?" but not knowing what it was or how to get there. We then not only heard the Scriptures being taught in a way never known before, but witnessed the transformed lives being lived out before us. They were truly a demonstration of the biblical truths that we were hearing. These lives have challenged, and still challenge, us so much. They have truly ministered *"the whole counsel of God"*[92], and lives have been transformed and filled ever since.

Lacking Nothing
Hugh Burney

❝ My first contact with the Fellowships was in 1977, when some people from a church in Middlesborough arranged a trip to hear Mr North preach at a church in Bradford. Some of us also went to a summer conference that year held in the grounds of Cliff College in Derbyshire, and I learnt more about these particular Fellowships that were meeting around the country. From then on, when I was looking for a move, my priority was to be near to one of these Fellowships.

The key word in the first message I heard Mr North preach was "nothing". I found that both in his and other Fellowships, there was much encouragement to believe that God could do a complete work in my life. James 1:4 says, *"Let patience have its perfect work, so that you may be perfect and complete, lacking nothing."*

I remember someone at university quoting Roman 7:25: *"So then, with the mind I myself serve the law of God, but with the flesh, the law of sin."* A lot of people accept that sin is an inescapable part of human nature and that we can't do very much about it. However, in the next chapter, Paul writes, *"...the law of the Spirit of life in Christ Jesus has made us free from the law of sin and death."*[93] This was the message that Mr North and the Fellowships preached, and it was wonderful to hear a positive message of victory.

[92] Acts 20:27
[93] Romans 8:2

I found the open worship in the meetings encouraging too, as it meant that even I could have a chance to participate.[94]

One book which describes different churches speaks about the Fellowships as a "Pentecostal Holiness movement". I think that is similar to saying that they are a move of the Holy Spirit!

We need to keep looking to Him to keep us in the Way.[95]

A real church

66 I first came to a Christian Fellowship meeting at the age of seventeen. Although I was already a Christian, during one of the meetings God brought me to what I understand now to be a genuine conviction of sin. I found myself sobbing and crying to God for deliverance from sin and to know Him in my depths. It was a life-changing, person-changing experience.

As well as the meetings, which were rich in worship, prayer and prophecy, a big influence in my life at that time was the love and acceptance for all that was shown by the church. The 'open house' of the leaders was an amazing demonstration of this love of God. The young Christians were really taught by their example.

To me, the Fellowship movement is a real church.

The cross

Central to the life and ministry of the Fellowships have always been the cross and scriptural holiness, for it is not really possible to separate the two.

Many of us may have had a general understanding of what the Lord Jesus Christ accomplished for us at Calvary. We frequently heard as churchgoers that Jesus died on the cross to save us from our sin and that if we believe in Him and ask Him to forgive us of our sin, then He will freely give us eternal life and save us from the penalty of sin, which ultimately is spiritual death and eternal separation from God. These things are all true and scriptural and a sound basis upon which to begin our walk as a Christian. It is clear and simple, to which a young child can respond, as did Norman when he was only four and Mr North when he was just three. It is the heart upon which God looks, and whether a young

---

[94] See 1 Corinthians 14:26
[95] See Acts 19:23

child or an older person, if we are sincere and truly see our need, then God is faithful to His word and to His promises.

It has, however, been a life-changing revelation for so many of us, since we first heard the gospel, to begin to realise just what true new birth is all about – and *must* be all about. Jesus Himself used that same phrase – *"You must be born again"*[96] – and then went on to explain, initially to Nicodemus and now to us, how this can be.

To be truly born of His Spirit, the cross must be allowed to do its ever-eternal work within the very depths of us, as we deliberately choose to die to our old nature and all that would seek to keep it alive. We have been helped to see that when Christ died, we died; our old nature of sin was buried with Him, and when He was raised so miraculously from the grave, we rose with him – into all that He now is. Paul says that as we reckon ourselves dead but alive in Him,[97] so we are changed and conformed into all that He has desired us to be. His nature becomes ours. In some ways this is a lifelong process, but it cannot begin till we have truly been 'born from above'.

When Jesus cried out from the cross, *"It is finished!"*[98], He was proclaiming to us all the most wonderful and amazing accomplishment that the world had and has ever heard. He had gloriously fulfilled, in His Father's perfect timing, that for which He had been sent. We need never be slaves to sin and ourselves ever again. He had paid the ultimate price, and undeserving though all of us are, by His grace we can live and walk in that same resurrection ascended life here and now, as we allow the work of His cross to become a reality within us.

It has been such a privilege and help to see the truth of all this shine out from so many whose lives we have been brought into contact with – a demonstration to each of us that it is true and possible and that it works. I think it would be true to say that not many in the Fellowships ever heard or witnessed these things in our earlier days, but having seen the transformed life being lived out before us, so the teaching and preaching confirmed what we were witnessing and we were hungry to know it for ourselves.

[96] John 3:7
[97] See Romans 6:11
[98] John 19:30

Holiness

Pursue holiness, without which no-one will see the Lord.[99]

Holiness simply means being separated or set apart for God, and as we learn to allow the power of the cross to work within us, so we find ourselves separated from sin, from the world and all that would ensnare and hinder us. Lives will simply but powerfully express the holiness of God.

There is a purity of heart and spirit that, in a very special way, emanates in unmistakable ways to those around. It's tangible. This is accompanied by a quiet and peaceful spirit and with a joy and love that are certainly not in any way manufactured.

This purity of heart and spirit will always have a very practical outworking. We have been separated from the world and all that that entails, and therefore we have often been exhorted to demonstrate this by the way we live, by the way we dress, by the way we speak and conduct ourselves, by the music we listen to and in every aspect of our daily lives. Our one aim is to glorify God in whatever we do and for Christ to be known.

One baptism

There is one body and one Spirit, just as you were called in one hope of your calling; one Lord, one faith, one baptism.[100]

Scriptural truths are virtually inexhaustible in their depth, as those to whom God has gifted to expound the word of God to us have testified. In his booklet *The Generation of Jesus Christ*, G.W. North says this:

> There is always a vast amount more in it than just that which meets the ear or eye. Deep below deep lies under the surface of the mighty ocean that at first strikes the eye with its greys or greens or blues of reflected light, or tosses its foamy whiteness on the head of some curling wave tumbling into a sandy cove – and so it is with the precious Book...

The purpose here, therefore, is to simply provide the very briefest of summaries of this truth that lies embedded as an integral part within the life and ministry of the Fellowships.

[99] Hebrews 12:14b
[100] Ephesians 4:4,5

True new birth – that is, those who have been "born from above" and have the kingdom of God being expressed and known within them – is clearly seen from Scripture as being synonymous with this "one baptism". We have been immersed into all that God is, and God in essence has been immersed into us. All of His attributes – His very nature, his life, His authority, His Spirit, His love and all that He is – can now be experientially known on a daily, moment by moment basis. Truly, *"old things have passed away ... all things have become new"*[101]. Paul says that we are *"complete in Him"*[102].

Wonderfully, this was first depicted through the account of Noah's ark.[103] Later on, a further picture is seen as Moses led the children of Israel miraculously through the Red Sea, escaping the Egyptians.[104] God's fulfilment of these truths, when His timing had fully come, was on the Day of Pentecost, when God poured out His Spirit and the church was born.[105] Hence the stark contrast between the failure and despondency of all the disciples before this and their total transformation from the Day of Pentecost onwards. They had, as Ezekiel had prophesied hundreds of years beforehand, come into a completely new life and had been changed from within.

> I will give you a *new* heart and put a *new* Spirit within you; I will take the heart of stone out of your flesh and give you a heart of flesh. I will put My Spirit within you and *cause* you to walk in My statutes, and *you will* keep My judgments and do them. *Then* you *shall* dwell in the land. You *shall* be My people, and I will be your God...[106]

One of Charles Wesley's hymns puts it like this:

True pleasures abound
In the rapturous sound,
And whoever hath found it hath paradise found.
My Jesus to know,
And feel His blood flow,
'tis life everlasting, 'tis heaven below.

[101] 2 Corinthians 5:17
[102] Colossians 2:10
[103] See Genesis 6-8
[104] See Exodus 14:13-31
[105] See Acts 2
[106] Ezekiel 36:26-28 (emphasis added)

> My cup it runs o'er,
> I have comfort and power,
> I have pardon – what can a poor sinner have more?
> He can have a new heart,
> So as never to start
> From Thy paths: he may be in the world as Thou art.

Mr North wrote:

> Having thus been born of God, and finding this same nature
> within us, we now belong to the generation of Jesus Christ.
> Being now made sons by regeneration, we must in all things
> be made like unto the Son. This must be our sole reason for
> living, for no lesser reason is acceptable to our Father. The
> Holy Ghost, who has come forth from the Father through the
> Son, is under command to accomplish this very thing. His
> work is to glorify Jesus by reproducing His nature and
> personality in each of God's other sons. Jesus Christ is the Seed
> accepted for a generation, and each one of that generation is
> demonstrably of Him – clearly and firmly marked out of God
> as belonging to the generation of Jesus Christ.[107]

New Testament ordinances

Some would say that there are three distinct ordinances laid out by God
for His church; they are water baptism, communion and head covering.
Others see two.

There is certainly no disagreement regarding the first two, although
the Anglican church in particular would argue for infant baptism by
sprinkling. Concerning head covering, there are various opinions, but as
the Fellowships began to emerge, there was much teaching on this, and
therefore this needs to be included, especially as still today there are not
a few who feel this to be important.

Water baptism

Many churches believe strongly that when somebody becomes a
Christian and truly believes in Christ and has accepted Him as their
personal Saviour and Lord, there is a scriptural obligation to be baptised

[107] *The Generation of Jesus Christ;* G.W. North

in water by immersion. Jesus Himself taught His disciples to *"Go therefore and make disciples of all nations, baptising them in the name of the Father and of the Son and of the Holy Spirit, teaching them to observe all things that I have commanded you..."*[108]

This and the other ordinances are simply an outward expression and demonstration of a spiritual work that God has first done within the believer. Being baptised does not save a person. They are testifying to the fact that God has saved them and that they wish to openly witness to this fact by being obedient to His commandments, of which this is one.

It is not only the Baptist churches and the Fellowships that specifically teach this; many other denominations do too. Interestingly, even some Anglican churches have come to see this as important, although they are in the minority. Here is one lady's testimony, who is very much an Anglican and attended York Minster.

Baptism – never too late, and why now?
Pat Henshaw

" On 29th April, 2018 I was baptised by full immersion, and confirmed, at my home church, St Michael le Belfrey Church of England, York.

Baptism by full immersion is a regular occurrence at the Belfrey, both indoors and, in more clement weather, ever with a view to witness, outdoors. Five other adults, all young and new to the faith, were baptised with me.

What is perhaps unusual about my experience is that I had been a Christian for many years, dedicated as an infant and received as a young adult Christian into membership of our family church.

The decision to be baptised was not easy. Much of the struggle struck at the heart of my identity. Was the church I had attended as a child not good enough? Was I, by association, not good enough? Would I betray my roots if I were baptised – roots that I valued as good and strong? Was my standing with the Lord compromised? Or was it all just a matter of different churches doing things differently and this not really impacting on the most important thing: my relationship with the Lord?

---

[108] Matthew 28:19-20

One cannot attend the Belfrey for long without being brought face to face with baptism by full immersion. It is a regular, natural feature of church life – and such a joyous happening, usually celebrating new life in Christ and stamping the hallmark 'Christian' on a person. Yet there I was, sitting in the congregation, genuinely rejoicing with others but not having experienced this myself. I began to feel uncomfortable and that something was missing. Shouldn't I be baptised? But I rationalised to myself that I had gone through the equivalent experience many years ago in my own family church. It was just a different way of doing things.

However, baptism loomed larger and larger in my thoughts. I first talked about it informally with one of my Longcroft friends. She was very clear about the biblical basis of baptism, and spoke of the experience of a relative of hers who, a lifelong Christian and church member, had been baptised by full immersion later in life. She struck a beautiful balance between urging me that baptism was something I should seek the Lord's will on, yet enabling me gently to work this through with Him. There was no pressure, but the significance of baptism was made clear.

On a subsequent visit to The Longcroft, I raised the issue again, this time with the person in whose home I was staying. Again, there was very clear, loving guidance and a more direct urging to take this step. ...

Yet, as all this was happening, loyalty to my family church and a feeling of anger were bubbling away. I was wrestling and far from peace.

Things came to a head when, on my return from a China trip early in 2018, I went to the Wirral for debriefing. I was asked whether I would speak to the Longcroft women's group – on any topic the Lord laid on my heart. I found myself speaking of our identity as Christians. Wriggle as I might, I found no escape from including the centrality of baptism to this. Outwardly speaking to the women of The Longcroft, I became indubitably aware that I was listening to God as He spoke unequivocally to me.

The account of Jesus' baptism in Matthew 3:13-17 said all I needed to hear. Jesus lined up with people engaging in, yes, a religious ritual – confessing to the mess in their own hearts and lives, and wanting to be washed clean. He did not need to do this but still joined people in their own acknowledged mess. Why? So that we can join *Him* in *His* family. ...

As I concluded my talk to the Longcroft women, I told them that God had been speaking to me about something He wanted me to do and that I must take action. I didn't share with them what that was though. Returning home to York, I resisted all temptation to dissemble or delay. At the first opportunity, and a little emotionally, I spoke with the vicar of the Belfrey, who said, "I think we should get that put straight. Don't worry; it's all right. And the Bishop is coming in a fortnight's time, so we'll go for baptism and confirmation then." ...

There followed two weeks of the most intense inner turmoil – but I knew that this was to be resisted as the attack of a furious enemy, enraged that I was doing the Lord's will and making a public declaration of faith. I approached baptism with mixed feelings, heightened emotionalism and feeling under par physically. Yet my perspective had changed. Rather than fixating on what might or might not have happened in the past, I focused on what the Lord wanted me to do *now*. Instead of viewing it as a betrayal of the good in my past, I looked to what God was saying to *me, through the Scriptures, now.* ...

It was an amazing service, with six baptisms and over fifty confirmations. I was thrilled that I could welcome my Fellowship friends to *my* church, and I know that they were much blessed by the service. They were particularly impressed by how those who had been baptised and/or confirmed spontaneously gathered in small groups with arms around each other (in the manner of a football team before a match!) and prayed with and for each other.

Something particularly interesting happened as we were baptised: we were immersed three times, in the name of the Father, and the Son, and the Holy Spirit. I had seen our Belfrey curate, who was in the baptismal pool doing the immersing, lead many baptisms, and immersion had been only once. However, the Bishop insisted it be three times. We were well and truly immersed and washed. Thinking about it subsequently, I found significance in this, in that God had been speaking with me about His triune nature and encouraging me to come into a fuller, more balanced experience of each of Father, Son and Holy Spirit. Being immersed three times seemed to emphasize this.

The waters of baptism demonstrate burial and resurrection. The believer first identifies with the death and burial of Christ – as someone who has died to his old life and to sin and subsequently been raised by Him into His new life.

> *We were therefore buried with him through baptism into death in order that, just as Christ was raised from the dead through the glory of the Father, we too may live a new life. For if we have been united with him in a death like his, we will certainly also be united with him in a resurrection like his. For we know that our old self was crucified with him so that the body ruled by sin might be done away with, that we should no longer be slaves to sin – because anyone who has died has been set free from sin.*[109]

Paul, in his letter to the Galatians, speaks about being *"crucified with Christ"*[110], and that it is no longer he that lives, but Christ who lives in him.

Communion

As someone has said, spiritual "baptism and communion are companion truths and belong together".

> The Communion is both the reason for and the ultimate goal of (spiritual) Baptism. The Baptism was designed by God to be a personal crisis; the beginning of spiritual life: the communion is the state into which the spiritual Baptism grants his immediate entrance; it is the end in view. The Baptism is the Alpha, the Communion is the Omega.[111]

In the context of the church, the fellowship and communion known between those who have truly been born again, whether that be just between two individuals or within the wider body, is something that can only be given by the Holy Spirit. *"Deep calls unto deep,"* as David expresses in Psalm 42:7, although in a slightly different setting. It is a

---

[109] Romans 6:4-7
[110] Galatians 2:20
[111] *Communion;* G.W. North

result of being made one with God and therefore with our fellow brothers and sisters.

As with baptism, therefore, celebrating that which is often called 'the Lord's supper', or the 'breaking of bread' or 'communion,' is an outward expression of a much deeper and inner spiritual reality.

> In this simple meal properly understood lies the true basis of all spiritual sacrifices. Although by it we primarily show His death till He come, by it also we show forth our own death till He come. It is the simplest yet profoundest manifestation of both Christ's and the Church's universal sacrifice; doing this we proclaim that we, as He, are a broken body – a breaking body and yet a whole body. ... He did it in prospect; we do it in retrospect.[112]

We participate in this because the Lord Jesus Christ instigated it.[113] He wanted His church to be continually mindful and understanding of (as much as we are able) His sacrifice, death and burial, and the shedding of His blood, that would by His grace alone enable us to be one with Him and a part of His kingdom. It is certainly a precious time that we take seriously, out of a pure heart and out of our deep love for Christ and His church. In fact, we are reminded by Paul, in his first letter to the Corinthian church, that this must not be done in an unworthy manner, and that if there is any known sin within the believer, then we must first make restitution and restore fellowship before participating.[114] Those leading this time may sometimes remind us of the importance of this, as well as encouraging those who may not yet know the Lord personally to pass the bread and wine by and not to participate.

> By the act of eating and drinking the communion, a man is testifying of his own fitness to be a member of the Body of Christ. He is saying that he is worthy to do this because he is living in present communion with Christ. He does not come to the feast to be made a member of Christ thereby, neither does he come in order to have himself restored to life in Christ and communion with his fellow-members. He comes to testify that he is helping to build up the Body of Christ, in communion or common-union with all the saints; otherwise

[112] *Communion;* G.W. North
[113] See Luke 22:19,20
[114] See 1 Corinthians 11:27-34

participation is in vain. Worse still, continued eating and drinking is destructive to self and obstructive to others.[115]

Head covering

Although there may be an unspoken sense of importance of this associated with some Christians in some of the denominations, it may be out of a sense of duty and an adherence to an ongoing practice and culture without understanding or appreciating its full significance. On the other hand, it would seem that there are those within the Fellowships who at one point seemed more than happy to accept this but no longer hold such views. It is certainly something that is of a very personal nature, and no elder would normally insist on ladies covering their heads or, for that matter, for a man to uncover his head, should they choose not to follow this practice. On some occasions, however, it has been known for those praying for someone on a specific issue to ask that person to cover their head. If and when questions arise as to why it is felt to be important, those who are part of the eldership team, as well as any other member, will quite readily share their biblical understanding of this. It will then be up to the individual to seek God for themselves.

As this is something that has been very much a part of the Fellowships, particularly at their onset, it has been felt that it is a subject that needs to be included, not least because there still are many who see it as important, not in any legal sense or duty, but because it is a joy and a genuine heart response to what the Lord has shown them.

Delighting to do His will
Sandra Brown

66 I became a Christian in my late thirties when, through a series of events, I began to seek the Lord. Not having a church background, I visited several churches over the course of a few months, seeking for something I didn't understand at the time.

Attending my first Fellowship meeting, I sensed the presence of the Lord and immediately knew this was my spiritual home. I was warmly welcomed by the people, encouraged and challenged by the ministry, and often touched by the love of God during the worship.

[115] *Communion;* G.W. North

However, I found the practice of head coverings strange. Why do women want to cover their heads when worshipping the Lord? I decided I didn't like the custom and felt I didn't want to conform.

After several months, the Lord started to speak to me about head coverings and I read the appropriate scriptures. A covering on a woman's head is used as an illustration of the order of headship and the authority of God. A woman's submission to God's delegated authority over her is an example to the angels. I pondered over these scriptures for a few weeks but failed to do anything about them.

Several weeks later, during my lunch break, I walked to the local shopping mall, and taking a shortcut through Marks and Spencer's, I noticed a beret. It was priced at £6.99.

I said to the Lord, "If this had been 99p, I might have bought it."

The very next day, taking my usual lunchtime route, I cut through the same shop and there, to my great surprise, was the beret for 99p!

"OK, Lord," I said, "you win!"

Almost thirty years later, I still wear a head covering in submission to the Lord, because I love Him and delight to do His will."

Christ my head
Liz Rumsey

66 When we began as a family to visit the summer conference at Rora in the 1980s, it was not a problem for me to wear a covering (like most of the ladies at the time) because I often wore a scarf to keep my long hair tidy. At our first brief visit to Rora, my impression of the preacher (Norman Meeten) was that this man was like Paul the apostle. It made such an impression on us that we returned to conferences when we could, and I came to believe what was written in 1 Corinthians 11:1-16 about covering my head. I found Mr North's booklet *Sign of Authority* very helpful in opening up my understanding of the importance of what head covering represents before the heavenlies (angels in particular) as well as being a declaration on earth to those around me that I agree and

sit under God's order of things – Christ my head and my covering in life.

Although the subject isn't discussed very much, even among ladies, Paul, who never wasted his words, clearly believed that these sixteen verses in 1 Corinthians 11 were important and needed to be taken seriously.

A sign of authority

A situation arose some years ago when a dear lassie in great spiritual need was accompanied by a friend to seek help from an elder and his wife. Time was initially spent sharing and talking through some of the issues that were troubling her. Before praying, all three of the ladies covered their heads, simply out of a genuine personal conviction. As they prayed, it became apparent that there was need for specific deliverance and they began to pray accordingly. At this point, completely involuntarily, the lassie being prayed for suddenly grabbed her head scarf, pulled it viciously off her head, and flung it to the ground and stamped on it with an expression on her face that was both alarming and almost venomous and full of anger. The demonic powers within had been challenged and rebuked and could not stand the spiritual authority being shown and demonstrated against them.

Although her friend had not needed any persuasion of the importance of head covering, it certainly confirmed to her more than ever that there are very real reasons why God has included this specific passage in Scripture concerning head covering[116] in relation to prayer and worship. It may not be fully understood or appreciated as to its full significance, but it is a way of showing our obedience and love to our Lord and wanting to show our heart's submission to Him, and a sign to the angels in recognition of His ultimate authority in our lives. It is a joy and privilege, as it is for the men to *not* cover their heads.

This was not an isolated incident. It was a frequent occurrence.

Obedience to Scripture
Angela Webster-Gardiner

66 My experience relating to head-covering began before I was a Christian, when I was randomly looking through some books in

---

[116] i.e. 1 Corinthians 11:3-16

a bookshop and saw the title *Head-covering*. I was surprised at my reaction, which was almost one of revulsion.

Sometime later, I realised it was scriptural, along with baptism and communion (or the 'breaking of bread'), topics which to a non-Christian have little meaning but are deeply meaningful to those of us who have accepted the Lord Jesus as our wonderful Saviour. The relevant scripture in 1 Corinthians 11 explains how this is a *"sign of authority"*[117] and that it is also a sign to the angels who are watching and learning from us.

Nowadays the Lord prompts me, particularly when a serious issue arises in a time of prayer, to cover my head. I am also mindful that it is important not to be disrespectful to my head, the Lord Jesus Christ. *"But every woman who prays or prophesies with her head uncovered dishonours her head..."*[118]

It is also important that men should pray with their heads uncovered. It was against all the customs of the time and still is in many cultures.

An outcome of unexpected blessing
Ann Cliff

66 I came into contact with the Fellowships in 1977. I noticed that all the ladies wore head coverings but really didn't question this very much as I had previously been in churches where hats were worn as a matter of course by ladies. I just accepted the tradition, but as I progressed in my Christian walk, I realised there was more to it than I had formerly realised. The scripture in 1 Corinthians 11 gave me the reasons but which even now I don't fully understand. However, as I believe it is God's word and He does not change his mind, I accept it. Also, given the fact that at a recent discussion at church our elders were in agreement with the practice but said there was no pressure on people, that too was a reason for me to continue.

However, one of the greatest reasons for me was some years ago when a good friend, who is now with the Lord, shared with me the following. She was not in the habit of covering her head in church, so it was quite telling when she related this happening to me. A friend of hers was a leader in a church in Manchester. It

[117] Verse 10 (AMP)
[118] Verse 5

was a community church. One of the ladies had been praying and was challenged to ask the other ladies if they would cover their heads in worship as she had felt convinced about this by the Lord. Much to her surprise, they agreed, and what happened was really wonderful. In the following days and weeks, people came to the Lord; people were delivered of various problems; women who had difficulty conceiving became pregnant; sick people were healed and the church was mightily blessed – all this information from a lady who didn't believe it was necessary! There is no doubt that my friend was not 'spinning a tale', as she had no reason to do so and was always true to the Lord. It seems a very small thing in the light of all that blessing to wear a head covering.

Honouring God
Maggie Worsley

❝ To wear a head covering is a voluntary decision. Prayer is not demanded of us but rises to God in gratitude for His mercy towards us. Some prefer to pray kneeling – it's the heart attitude. In the same way, to wear a head covering implies obedience. I consider that it is necessary if I wish to honour God.

Since Adam's fall, man has veered from the course that God desires for us. *"Has God ... said...?"*[119] To wear a head covering simply shows obedience to 1 Corinthians 11 to keep the ordinances.

On a personal note, to wear a head covering, for me, is not only about public meetings, for there is a communing with God all of the time. How we long to find ourselves under the shadow of His wing!

Fred Tomlinson, an elder of a Fellowship in Abbotsford, Canada, has kindly given his permission for us to include his biblical understanding of this, which he has written in Appendix 2 at the end of this book. A much more detailed appreciation of the subject, entitled *A Sign of Authority*, has been written by Mr North, which can be downloaded from Ron Bailey's website, biblebase.com.

As has been said, this is a personal thing, and every Christian will need to seek God for themselves, both men and women, as to what their response should be before Him.

[119] Genesis 3:1

Hymns of Eternal Truth

This hymnbook is unique to the Fellowships, in which there are a hundred and twenty of Wesley's hymns, many of which are well known by most churches, and some of which may be less familiar. The differences are twofold. Firstly, they include many more of the original verses often not included in other hymnbooks, hence its nickname, 'hymns of eternal length'! Secondly, many have been set to alternate tunes which are believed to be more suited to the words being sung. They are much loved, particularly by those who were part of the Fellowships in their earlier days, and express so meaningfully the longings and worship within a believer's heart.

It was compiled in the 1960s, when the Fellowships first came into being, and held a very special place within the meetings and times of worship and praise. An accompanying hymnbook was, and still is, the *Redemption Hymnal*, used also by the Pentecostal and other churches, along with a more modern collection of hymns, songs and choruses, *Songs of Fellowship*. The use of all three provide a wonderful and wide selection of hymns and songs, suitable for all age groups.

Perhaps the best way to describe the 'blue hymnbook' (so-called because of its blue cover) is by sharing with you what so succinctly has been expressed in its Preface:

> Here is a selection of the incomparable poems of the Wesley brothers, the poetry of which is as sublime as it is heavenly, and breathes from the Eternal Spirit who inspired their hearts. In this realm they have no betters and few, if any, equals.
>
> This book is a collection of long-loved and new-found truth, 'treasures new and old', offered to lovers of Jesus our Lord.
>
> Throughout the land hearts cry out for the realities herein set forth, and these hymns give expression to the unspeakable yearnings within in a manner which beautiful poetry and utmost piety unaided cannot accomplish, for many have produced such hymns but have failed of that 'something' that so permeates the writings of the Wesleys as to place them in a class above all others.

The difference surely lies in the fact that these hymns were born in revival, and come from the Spirit of Life then breathing through the land.

Our Lord gave them to His Church, and wherever souls long for language of the Spirit these hymns will be sung by all so blessed as to know them.

Could heart-cries be formed and framed in better words than these, or man declare his faith more gloriously?

Within the hearts of those who were a part of the Fellowships in their beginning, the 'blue hymnbook' holds a very special place. Singing these hymns within the context of a powerful move of God as was known then, and still today, is something that can never be forgotten or erased.

Missionary outreach

Resulting from the spread of the Fellowships throughout the UK from the 1960s, the work has continued to grow to over seventy countries worldwide.

There has always been a strong emphasis on the importance of reaching out, not only to our immediate neighbours, families and community but farther afield to all nations globally. It has often been said that we should only stay at home if we have to. The Gospels teach clearly that we are to *"Go into all the world..."*[120]. As God confirms His call to each of His children, so He has promised to equip, to go before, to provide for every need, and to bring forth His fruit in and through the lives of others. We sow the seed; God brings forth the fruit.

For those who cannot go, they nevertheless can equally be a part of His work abroad; firstly, by praying and interceding for not only those He specifically lays on our hearts but also those for whom we have promised to pray. Many people find a notebook helpful to keep the memory operational. There are also the weekly church prayer meetings as well as other times set aside regularly when groups come together specifically to pray for those known to them working abroad; usually under extreme circumstances and having much need. It is always a joy to feel a part of the work in this way if we cannot go. So often it has been known by those on the foreign field when people at home have prayed.

[120] Mark 16:15

Circumstances have suddenly changed; needs have been met; prayer has been answered, and often miraculously.

Some of the Fellowships have found it helpful to have a world map on the wall of their meeting room, with photos of those known to them working abroad and connecting them to their specific countries.

'Avail' is a missionary trust run by various elders of the Fellowships, whereby support is given not only by prayer and financially but, when possible, by visiting those abroad, where they can then minister on a more personal level into their specific situations and needs, providing spiritual, pastoral, emotional and practical support to mission workers in partnership with their churches. It is therefore a work that is not specifically related just to the Fellowships but has a much wider implication. Their aim is to "serve those who serve", from all churches and denominations. Missionaries abroad may often feel quite isolated, and therefore communication from those at home by various means has meant so much and continues to do so.

Another specific Fellowship initiative is the 'Forget Me Not' child sponsorship scheme, which has made such a difference to children abroad living in poverty and in need of basic health care and education. Many children have been saved from hunger, illness and even death by the scheme.

It has always been encouraging to receive and listen to those working abroad when they have returned home on furlough or for a time of rest and change. Prayer updates, newsletters, e-mails and even the occasional phone call all have a very valid place, but meeting and personally sharing with them when they come home or are visiting is even more precious and helpful, for them as well as for the home church. It has often been the means, too, of encouraging those at home to become involved by short-term visits to many of the countries represented, and often by the young people giving up their school or college holidays to team up and engage with the work abroad in some small measure. Opportunities are many, and they have come back to us full of enthusiasm and with a greater understanding of the many different countries and lifestyles encountered. In 2018, ten different countries were visited by members of the Longcroft church alone.

Hospitality

The practice of hospitality, not only within the Fellowships but in all cultures, faiths and denominations, has been a much-valued exercise, providing real opportunities for friendship, fellowship, outreach, support and encouragement for all involved, whether we are those who are able to share our homes and churches with others, or whether we have been invited out. Both are important and have their place.

The forms in which this can be done are numerous, most often being on a very informal basis. Those who are familiar with the house churches will no doubt have appreciated the ongoing gatherings around the lounge fire or sitting together at mealtimes sharing and talking about our lives and experiences, joys and sorrows, or whatever, usually following the morning meeting. It can also provide an unthreatening way of reaching out and befriending those who may not be familiar with a church or Christian setting; this often being the means of meeting much need, not only spiritually but also physically and emotionally. Those who are not in a house church setting will also have been able to offer hospitality from their own homes as well as using the church for particular social functions. Every Christian home is invaluable, and so many have known the ongoing joy and blessing of sharing it with others, whether that be on a one-to-one basis or several people together, not only for a 'cuppa' but for many and varied 'culinary delights', however simple. An added bonus is being able to provide accommodation, so often needed by those travelling for longer distances, or missionaries and Christian workers from abroad.

It would probably be true to say that those who live on their own, without the support of a family, children or grandchildren, are particularly appreciative for the company that hospitality provides, whether it be within their own home or in that of others. When the body of Christ functions together in this way, it is a precious thing. It is interesting to note that Peter the apostle, within the context of being encouraged to demonstrate *"fervent love for one another"*[121], writes, *"Be hospitable to one another without grumbling."*[122] He also writes to the Christians in Rome *"distributing to the needs of the saints, given to hospitality"*[123]. It is surely a privilege to share what God has given to us

---

[121] 1 Peter 4:8
[122] 1 Peter 4:9
[123] Romans 12:13

with others in this way, which brings with it a real joy. Not a few people will have the testimony that it was simply over a friendly chat and a cup of coffee that they were first drawn to know the love of God for themselves.

Living by faith

There has always been a strong leaning within the Fellowships (not only amongst those within the role of eldership and leadership, but also others) for trusting the Lord to meet all needs, should God lead in this way, particularly in the realm of finance. Their desire to commit themselves to the work of the church will have been such that they were willing to leave their secular work of employment and to give themselves completely to the needs of the body, both at a local level and also more widely, as the Lord has led.

It certainly would not be too difficult to write a book sharing the many wonderful stories of how God has been so faithful in meeting the needs of those who have trusted Him in this way, receiving no income from any other source other than from God Himself, and not making their personal needs known in any way. Testimonies already shared in earlier chapters bear record of just how miraculously God provided for buildings and resources of every description.

One of the first things that God spoke into Norman's heart was that he was not to make any mention to anyone concerning any of his needs but only to God alone, and as he obeyed the scripture to *"seek first His kingdom and His righteousness"*[124], God would honour His promise to provide for everything needful. Norman's testimony has consistently been over the years that God has been utterly faithful above all that he would have ever envisaged or even sought. He has often said he could write a book on this alone, and that he has seen God sovereignly provide so bountifully for all that he has ever needed, as well as having been given substantial funding for those abroad to whom he ministers several times each year, without ever mentioning anything to anyone – no fundraising, no requests, no publicity of any description.

As Hudson Taylor, whom God used to found the China Inland Mission (now the Overseas Missionary Fellowship) said, he too learnt to "move men to God by prayer alone". This will have had much wider connotations, but it included all of his financial needs. It was once asked

---

[124] Matthew 6:33 (paraphrase)

of an elder in Epsom by the local MP, "Do you still get little brown envelopes being put through your door at midnight?" to which the reply was given, "Yes, sir!" What a testimony to those who don't yet know the Saviour!

For some elders, leaders and many others, God has not led them to live in this way. It is not wrong to be employed or even to be an employer. Each one will know in his own heart what is right for them.

What a joy and what a privilege to have such godly men and women in our midst and to witness their lives in this way. It is a daily challenge to us all.

Conclusion

How can one conclude a story that is still ongoing and that must continue on until the Lord returns?

In the Gospel of John, we read that *"unless a grain of wheat falls into the ground and dies, it remains alone; but if it dies, it produces much [fruit]"*[125].

All that has been shared within these pages has surely shown the fruit that has resulted from each life of a saint who chose to fall into the ground and become as nothing so that God could become everything and bring forth His fruit and reproduce His life within the lives of so many. The leaves of the tree were, and still are, being used for the healing of the nations.[126]

How grateful we have been for all those who have faithfully shared with us the *"unsearchable riches of Christ"*[127] as they gave themselves to His word without limit, allowing the Holy Spirit to inwardly reveal the things of God, initially to their own hearts so that they in turn could expound these unrivalled truths to us. They have truly been life-changing. Academic studies may have their place, degrees or diplomas in theology may have proved of some value, but nothing is comparable to allowing the Holy Spirit to be our teacher and to open up the Scriptures to our hearts in a way that is rarely found in any textbook.

Being a part of the true body of Christ – having the same heart, the same vision, the same understanding of His word, the same fellowship in His Spirit one between another that rises so spontaneously from within us, even with those we may never have previously known – is indeed very precious and so real.

From these many and varied testimonies, we can see that the body of Christ is made up of very ordinary people who in God's sight are all equal. He is no respecter of persons. He shows no partiality.[128] No-one has been put on a pedestal. They may have different functions and different giftings, but that is all. We are simply those who, by His grace, have been saved and washed in His blood that He so sacrificially poured out for us at Calvary to redeem us and sever us from the power and

---

[125] John 12:24; the word 'fruit' comes from the NKJV footnote
[126] Revelation 22:2
[127] Ephesians 3:8
[128] Acts 10:24

consequences of sin. Each have walked, or are walking, in the path which God has chosen for them, and each are equally valued and precious. They have come from different countries, different cultures and different denominations or none, but in Christ we are all one.

Not a few have, over these past months, if not years, expressed their conviction that this remarkable story of how God moved so sovereignly in the early 1960s, and which has increasingly spread throughout the UK and abroad, should be retold and committed to paper.

May all who have read this be encouraged and quickened to embrace these scriptural truths in a way perhaps not yet known or experienced in their fullness. May God give us all eyes to see and ears to hear with that new heart that cannot help but say, "Yes, Lord, do it again!"

APPENDIX 1

Additional Testimonies

Recollections
Dick Hussey

66 My recollections date back to before the Fellowships started; firstly to Bradford, where Mr North was ministering prior to his subsequent move to Kent.

I attended one of the earliest conferences in Liverpool, in 1965, where I met Dave Wetherly, along with Norman Meeten. I can only describe it as a baptism of love and holiness. The fire of God came.

I had been working with the Argentine Airlines in London but was transferred to Manchester. After staying at The Longcroft for six months, whilst Mr North was living in the lodge, we moved to Macclesfield in May 1966, which was equal distance between Manchester and Liverpool. We went to the Fellowship in Queens Road where Norman was ministering. For a time, we met in Friends House, home to the Quakers, but soon returned to Queens Road as the presence of God seemed so absent within that context. A similar thing happened when we used the Chinese church in Liverpool, due to our own meeting room being too small for the numbers, but this was also short-lived.

One of the distinctive features of the Fellowships, resulting from experiences just described, is that it was believed that the real church – His body – should live and meet in real homes. This, in fact, can be seen in the Scriptures. The early church met in homes.

Mr North was the key minister by this time but worked very closely with Norman, who had begun to move out from his Anglican roots and was deeply involved with the young people of Liverpool, providing a secure and loving home to which they knew they would be welcomed and loved. The lives and ministry of both Mr North and Norman were so enriching and so life-changing. Although I had been saved in Argentina at the age of fifteen and knew a 'baptism of fire', it was through the ministry of Mr North that this truly came forth. The revelation of the Scriptures was wonderful, which so benefited and enriched me, particularly when I was preaching in Spain. It was quite rare and has never left me.

Every good work of God has to be tested, and we certainly went through times of severe testing. As a result of this, it was realised that there was a great need for plural leadership and eldership, and Mr North appointed Norman, Dave Wetherly, Ken Moffat and me to fulfill these roles.

The work continued to grow at Devy Road, and Mr North was much in demand, moving to Exeter where he had been invited to oversee the work there. One of the most precious things at this time was the love and unity between us all, as we worked, lived and ministered together in a work that was so supernaturally of God.

The time then came when Norman was asked to relocate to The Longcroft, and I became involved in what God was doing in Spain. Two other elders were appointed – Fred Tomlinson and John Valentine. The vision that God first gave to Norman – of leaves "like a maple in autumn" first falling into a glowing heap, which, after burning for a time, were caught up by the wind into a canopy over the globe and then settled throughout the nations – was being fulfilled and outworked. Fellowship people were going to be allowed to burn together in love and then scattered over the earth by the wind of the Spirit. God was moving, we were being scattered – to reproduce, both in the UK and abroad.

Set apart for Him
Dave Wetherly

66 I was raised in London until the age of twelve and was indeed very poor because they were hard days. I was not academically brilliant, but reading became my way of escape – often to America! Yet I feel, to this day, the inestimable, unspeakable charm of Jesus who loved me through others, my Sunday school teacher especially.

The poverty where we lived in Streatham was not a disadvantage to me. It made me appreciative of everything, for the little things seem so valuable; but it did make me feel the 'odd man out' at times, and I could not learn at school because of fear of the teachers. Then my parents were given an amazing opportunity to get me into a very good school in or near Farningham. I shall never know who paid for me all those eight years.

As well as enjoying the life there, I learnt an excellent trade as a carpenter and joiner, although no good at other studies, and found joy in the grain of wood, which I have never lost. However, being a wicked young lad, I was very opposed to spiritual things, although we were blessed with the gospel each Lord's Day and some of the staff were the personification of the truth and sweetness of Jesus.

I was about eighteen when one Sunday somebody came down from Cambridge University to speak to three hundred of us boys in the school chapel and twelve of our senior boys were soundly saved. It took the place by storm, and later some of these fellows became missionaries.

At twenty years of age, at a boys' camp, I heard a young American's testimony (he also was at Cambridge) and after two years of obstinate refusal of such great salvation, I went back to the school and, kneeling down on the dormitory floor, I gave myself to God, overwhelmed by such love.

Coinciding with such a momentous change in my life was the beginning of the second world war, which changed so many lives. I was called up, and after six months in the Royal Artillery, I was drafted out to work on a government firm to repair bombed houses during the Battle of Britain.

I never cease to praise God for keeping me clean and pure in the army. I was certainly the 'odd man out', but the thrill of preaching to the men was always exciting. Then the Ministry of Works sent six hundred of us to Liverpool, where there was such devastation and thousands were killed. Although death was on every hand, life was so full of meaning. Every weekend I crossed the Mersey to attend the Bible school in Birkenhead, and I became so taken up with the glorious thrill of God.

There, in that place, I met the deep, irresistible challenge. I, the 'odd man out', the useless scholar, had found grace in the eyes of

God, who wanted me to serve Him! One move, one act of the will, no other interest but Jesus and the souls of men; it was a heart revival of will and spirit. I knew deep within the thrill of being called; me, just a kid from the streets of London.

God then told me He had called me into His eternal purposes but that to fulfill His calling I must come out of the army. I was seconded out for eighteen months with thousands of others, but with the evacuation of Dunkirk we were all recalled, and now I was to know not only the call of God but the privilege of the sufferings of the cross. What He had done sovereignly, now I was to do willingly and of my own volition. That meant prison, prison, prison for refusing to fight – but, oh, the honour of prison life and the unspeakable thrill of doing His will and now having fellowship with Joseph, Daniel, Jeremiah, Peter, John, Paul and myriads of others! I knew that it was no stigma but the honour of the cross.

I was 'awarded' six months in civil prisons, and Winchester, Dorset and Wandsworth were to be my new schools, where I was to learn the hidden mysteries concerning my future. Eventually I was released from prison and the army, whereupon I began to prepare myself for missionary work, but one day I was brought to a standstill, realising that the Lord was saying to me, "You are not to go to Bible school but to live and work on a farm."

I was dumbfounded and unnerved. Why, I thought, I was better off in prison! Patiently God waited. His love gradually melted my pride and prejudice, until I finally came to the place where I was prepared to let Him have His way in my life. I detested farm work; it was so against the grain (having worked all my life with wood!) and I hated the soil.

During the eight years I was on the farm, a church was formed and another brother on the farm, who was a Christian pacifist and a lecturer from a Swiss university, became the leader. The farmer and his whole family were saved; the Lord moved mightily. The village green became an open arena for God and my preaching ground. The farm became an international centre, for we had German prisoners and refugees from the borders of Russia, Hungary and Romania, and many were finding Christ on our farm.

One of the outstanding happenings at that time was when a crowd often went to hear a certain Mr G.W. North in 1950 at an old, corrugated-iron church, and I heard God speaking in a most glorious way from that young Baptist minister, as he was then.

Fifteen years later, at a conference in the Wirral, Cheshire, he, led by the Holy Ghost, called me out from my mother, my home and my job to go and serve God for ever. My mother, bless her, let me go – and how much she sacrificed when she gave me over to God, only He knew, for she depended on me. Bless her generous heart and love for God!

In 1965, having now left the soil and the timber, I was led to join Norman Meeten, who had been called to work in Liverpool among the drug addicts and alcoholics.

God had spoken to me as a young man of twenty-two from Isaiah 43:5-6: *"I will bring your descendants from the east, and gather you from the west; I will say to the north, 'Give them up!' And to the south, 'Do not keep them back!'"*

Not only were souls saved and filled with the Holy Spirit, but a church was brought into being through Norman and Mr North.

Now the gospel was changing men and enlarging me. My first missionary adventure was with two young men from the church on a visit to Greenland. From Liverpool I went to work at The Longcroft for a time, and then in 1978, the Lord graciously moved me on, to further His purposes and designs for my life, to work with Terry and the Fellowship here in Eltham.

At an elders' conference in 1978/80, the Lord called me into foreign itinerary work, but still using Eltham Green as my base, and discovering the necessity and value of each member in the church and their loving fellowship, although often thousands of miles away from home.

So I can say as a fact that God's ways are perfect. I wanted to be a missionary in the Belgian Congo, now Zaire. How much more the Lord has in store for us than our puny minds can comprehend!

Nearly fifty years have elapsed, and for me, the profound call of God on my life has brought such deep eternal rewards with unspeakable delight, in spite of the severity of the huge responsibility that it bears with it. My life is caught up with the calling of God and the salvation of souls.

I view the Lamb in His own light
Whom angels dimly see,
And gaze transported at the sight
Through all eternity.

My recollections of the early days – Liverpool
John Wood (Walsall)

❝ Keith Kelly and I met at Richmond Baptist Church, Breck Road, Anfield in 1960. We were thirteen and twelve respectively. Richmond was a vibrant church with a large congregation, and we were very blessed and learnt much in those days.

By 1965, I was living in Maghull and attending Maghull Baptist, but was still regularly back in Anfield and in contact with Keith. We began to be aware of the need for something more in our lives. Keith and I, with a few other young men, met together and prayed in a little upper room at Richmond (room 5). During this period, Norman was invited to speak at Maghull Baptist. I think this was probably at the instigation of Mrs Joan Porter, an 'ancient' (in our eyes!) forty-eight-year-old lady who was a great supporter of Norman.

I thought Norman was wonderful when he spoke in the morning but thought Mr North was rubbish when he spoke in the evening. I did tell him this years later, much to his amusement!

We were now meeting from house to house in Anfield and Maghull. All of us were young people. I think the oldest was twenty-one; most of us were sixteen to eighteen.

One Tuesday, in February 1966, I rode home to Maghull after our prayer meeting and was soundly baptised in the Holy Ghost at my bedside.

I was not the first nor the last of our group to be baptised in the Spirit; most of us came through in a very short period of time. Some of us had visited 137 Queens Road, The House, but none of us at this time attended regularly.

It wasn't until October of that year that I was able to commit myself to attending Queens Road as a proper church. Even though we had originally seen it as a sort of English version of Teen Challenge, I believed quite early on that this was a new expression of New Testament Christianity. The loving welcome was the thing that hit you when you entered the house.

One of our friends was the son of a police inspector, who came along to see what was going on. After Dave Wetherly had given the young lad a bear hug, he was satisfied that his son was not going to come to any harm! The meeting was so full that the first-floor meeting room was rammed and people sat up and down the stairs and in the adjacent bedroom, forcing the speaker to stand on the landing. They were good, primitive days. Mr North now made sense to me and Norman was such an instrument of God's love to us all. The enemy was also at work, but suffice it to say that the Lord eventually gave the victory.

It is all about revelation
Martha Shaw

66 Revelation brings newness, total newness. That was what the revival for us was like, and it was all happening to us individually in different ways.

It was the opening up of our minds.

As Derrick Harrison said to us, "God is doing *a new thing.*" Well, if God was going to take this revelation to a complete conclusion in my life, it would certainly need to be a new thing. *The cost did not matter!*

The early symptoms were showing in my life of a serious mental breakdown, so thoughts about this spiritual revelation were only shared with a few select friends – because one could be, and certainly was, misunderstood.

When it was settled in my mind that this move of God in Chestnut Road, Moseley, Birmingham was the real thing, then whatever course it took us, we decided then and there that we were 'candidates'.

After I prayed in the meeting, a lady called Hilary said to me, "Martha, *you* prayed what we want..."

The Comforter, the Holy Ghost, was coming to us. We were coming out of the set religion of the Brethren Church, which had been an excellent beginning to a good quality of life. Now we were in meetings when you could *feel* the cool breeze of the Holy Spirit blowing in the room.

Nobody had any money – or very little.

'Revelation' is the key word in all of this. It takes you 'out of the box'. It was liberty, but as the years went on, *we only had the liberty to do God's will.* It was psychologically scary but very safe. Meetings with Mr North and Norman Meeten were *safe.* We had been told in our youth that we must "go in for it". Now I know what 'it' was. Another exhortation from the same person in bygone days had been, "It is the day of the individual. Get it yourself!" We therefore needed to come to God as a single person – no attachment of any kind.

The message from these men flowed and flowed, and we drank and drank. In all parts of the country, from Exeter to Glasgow and to County Armagh in Northern Ireland and all places in between, our Austin 1300 did many, many miles!

We slept and slept – the sleep of the peace of God in our hearts, on and on – in the Spirit of God.

Moving on with God
Martin and Helen Thorman

66 We were part of the Exeter Fellowship from August 1968 (the month and year that we were married) until we moved to Reading in 1976. We knew Bob and Nora Love, John Williams, Peter and Joy Palmer, Paul and Di Moss, Mr North and Norman Meeten, among many others. We lived first in Tiverton and then in Wellington, Somerset during those years. We loved being a part of the Fellowship in Exeter under the loving care of Bob and Nora Love, with excellent teaching times from Mr North, Norman and others. From 1976 to 1979 we were part of the Earley Christian Fellowship, Reading, under the leadership of Dave and Yvonne Medlock.

In both of these Fellowships there was much encouragement to move in the spiritual gifts and for men to develop teaching and preaching skills. As a result of this, after consulting with Mr North about Martin's call to full-time ministry, Martin was asked to become the pastor of the Blackhorse Christian Fellowship, Mangotsfield, Bristol, an unusual move, as it was then an FIEC[129] church. After two or three years in leadership there, Chris and Shirley French joined us for a while before they moved to Leeds. We had much fun and fellowship with them.

[129] Free Independent Evangelical Church

In about 1986 we moved to Nottingham for Martin to join the leadership of Carlton Christian Fellowship, where Keith Greener and Charlie Swan were elders. Dave and Judith Raistrick had just left to move to leadership elsewhere. Within a year or two of us living in Carlton, Nottingham, both Keith and Charlie left with their wives because of job opportunities. Martin was left as the sole elder until Derek and Carol Camfield moved to Nottingham and Steve Grimm also became an elder.

In 1992, the Lord called us to China. We spent one year in Mainland China and then fourteen years in Hong Kong. During those years, Martin was in a mostly pastoral and administrative role, visiting English-speaking Christians who were ministering in China. During our years in Hong Kong, we joined a large international church which was part of the American Assemblies of God. In our last two years there, Martin was a pastor on the staff of that church. We would probably still have been there had it not been for the life-threatening illness of our son-in-law, which caused us to see that the Lord was calling us back to the UK in 2007. The Lord healed our son-in-law of cancer – praise the Lord! – since when we have been living in Northampton where we are now part of a very lively Anglican church.

Our links with the Fellowships have become less obvious since living in China and Hong Kong. Nevertheless, we highly value the godly Bible teaching and training we received over the years in the Fellowships, and treasure our friendships with many of the saints whom we met over the years, both in the UK and abroad.

Purchasing Epsom Christian Fellowship's church building
Angela Webster-Gardiner

66 The local Anglican church in Epsom, Christ Church, was selling its damp and redundant church hall in 1983. They were wanting to build a new hall closer to their church.

The vicar had been approached by Tony Seaton, but initially Tony was turned down, as the vicar believed that his new independent Christian Fellowship was a cult! Their PCC (Parish Church Council) had voted to sell to the highest bidder, which at that point was the Odd Fellows Society.

Amazingly, my husband Graham, endeavouring to board an already overpacked commuter train carriage, found himself in the one empty seat available, next to the organist of Christ Church, Peter Lyle. As they chatted, Peter made it clear that he was unhappy about their current offer, wanting their hall to be purchased by Christians. There was just one week to go before the PCC would confirm their acceptance for the Odd Fellows' offer. He urged Graham to persuade Tony to raise his offer.

Increasingly, on his journey to the office that morning, God spoke to Graham and prompted him quite clearly to be willing to substantially help with the extra finance, although not knowing how. As soon as he arrived in the office, he phoned Tony and told him he would give the amount that God had required of him and to thereby raise his offer. Tony immediately called a prayer meeting and for a week of prayer and fasting, resulting in the money pouring in from all the members' savings accounts, jewellery and all else besides! One family put their flat on the market, trusting that the Lord would provide an alternative place to live – which turned out to be with Tony and Mary, who decided to convert some of their rooms in their rambling large and old house.

Wonderfully, the offer was able to be matched, Tony not wanting to outbid the secular group but giving the Anglicans a true choice to sell to Christians. His offer was accepted, following which a member of the PCC resigned and joined the Fellowship, finding himself, just one week after the purchase, on the roof of the hall with Graham, Tony and others de-weeding the gutters and repointing the Bell Tower! Graham and the former PCC member, also named Tony, were from that time onwards seen as the 'free gift' that came with the purchase!

My introduction to the Fellowships
Paul Bach

❝ Growing up in a small village in Kent, I was thoroughly committed to the Anglican church – Sunday school pupil, then Sunday school teacher and Scripture Union leader, and with attendance at every possible service and event. I cannot put a date on a 'conversion', but I certainly avoided the world and developed some relationship with God. At eighteen I went to the University of Keele, where I initially benefited from the Christian Union but really lost my way in the second year.

Back from summer holiday at my parents' home and desperate for a touch from God, I cried out to Him while walking along a country lane and saw a small notice pinned to a telegraph pole: "Gospel Meeting with George Tarleton". At first I paid it very little attention as I was due to return to university. Then, to my amazement, I realised that the meeting was the next evening and in my own church!

I duly went along, listened enraptured, and when the call came to stand in response, I found myself immediately on my feet, despite the self-consciousness of being in the middle of the front row. Such a meeting was a complete departure for my church, and when a few days later I met one of the movers behind it and told him what a great blessing I had found it, he replied that he thought I probably had as I was the first one on my feet!

Back at university, I soon found that a friend of mine was getting great blessing from visiting a house church which his girlfriend had discovered while studying in Bradford. After declining many invitations to go with him, I eventually gave in and made the long journey by public transport over on Friday night and back on Sunday afternoon.

Sherborne Road was full to bursting with young people hungry for the renewal of the early '70s. I made that long journey many times at weekends and holidays, and came away every time on an amazing spiritual high. Scores of students from Keele did the same over the next two years as the word got around and as they saw the evidence of changed lives.

After graduating from Keele, I went to Aberystwyth for teacher training. To my surprise, I learnt from Sherborne that G.W. North and Norman Meeten had supported a little fellowship there in the seafront hotel of Gerallt James and his wife; and so, together with five other students, I stayed that year in one of his cold, crumbling, damp attic rooms, and got to meet many passing visitors – the Storeys, Meetens, Dave Wetherly and many holidaying from Devonshire Road Fellowship.

Towards the end of that year in Aberystwyth, I started to apply for jobs and was called for an interview in *Sefton.* Two things surprised me about this: I had no recollection of applying for the job and I had no idea where Sefton was! I guess the Lord knew what He was doing though, as I got the job just outside

Liverpool and was able to join the Devonshire Road Fellowship, which of course I was by then very aware of. I had entered the life and vibrancy of the Fellowships, where I have now been for close to fifty years.

The Fellowships and their impact
Len Grates

66 It was in 1967, when I was fifteen years old, that John Valentine, who went to the same Anglican church in Bootle, invited me to a conference in Swanwick, Derbyshire, where I heard a white-haired gentleman (Mr G.W. North) and another man with a beard (Norman Meeten) preach messages with such power that I had never heard before. It was here that I first met Dave Wetherly, Andy Hutchings, Peter Moffat, Phil Williamson and others who would later become close and dear friends. Something had been planted in my heart.

A few years later, whilst in the police force, I was invited to another meeting by Louie Orchard, who invited me to a meeting every time she saw me on duty on a school crossing! After eighteen months of her persistence, I went to a meeting in her home where Ken Moffat was speaking. That evening, on my knees in my bedroom, I was filled with the Holy Spirit.

I started attending a Fellowship in Devonshire Road, Toxteth, in Liverpool. Within six months I left the police force, as I knew that the Lord had been calling me to serve Him. I was twenty-two at the time. At Dave Wetherly's suggestion, I was invited to work in the Auchenheath Fellowship in Lanarkshire, Scotland for six months under Dr Jack Kelly and his wife Eileen. Little did I know that this would be my home base for almost five years.

I had been asked by John Valentine to join him and Phil Williamson in helping establish a Bible school in Benin City, Nigeria under Benson Idahosa, which we did in 1975. Keith and Christine Kelly joined us a couple of months later. After nine months, Dr Jack Kelly asked if I would consider returning to Auchenheath. I felt that this was the right thing to do. I continued to work in the house and grounds for the coming months. On one journey, whilst driving Mr North to Auchenheath, I shared a vision I had of an army reaching both our nation and many other nations, and suggested a national men's conference, which he got excited about and agreed to support. In 1976, the first national men's conference was held in Birmingham Central Hall with about three hundred men in attendance.

It was also at Auchenheath that I proposed to Julie Ray, who four years later became my wife (Norman married us) and who is still amazing and my best friend today.

In 1977, on one of Norman Meeten's visits to Auchenheath, he invited me to join him on a three-month trip to India, Afghanistan and Nepal. I said yes without hesitation! I travelled with Norman to carry his bags, serve him and to learn. It was a truly humbling and amazing time for which I am truly grateful; even today, almost forty years later, I have travelled to India and Nepal a further three times with Norman, but have also accompanied Ron Bailey, Andy Hutchings and Andy Hunter over subsequent years. I am aware of how privileged I was for those blessed times. Norman and Jenny Meeten have remained faithful and dear friends over all these years.

In 1978, I left Auchenheath, having been invited by Paul and Lesley Evans to help at Devonshire Road Fellowship, Liverpool. Again, I was being given a wonderful opportunity to work with some very special people. In 1979, on returning from one of the Indian trips, Paul Evans approached me and informed me that whilst I was away, the church had decided they wanted to invite me to become an elder alongside Paul. I accepted and was prayed into eldership in January 1980 by Paul, John Valentine (who was home at the time from Africa) and Mr North. I was twenty-eight. Later that year, I married Julie and began working as a team.

It was a privilege to work alongside Paul and Lesley in leadership. Over the next couple of years, we saw the blessing of God in so many areas. The Lord spoke to us about opening a bookshop. One day, whilst I was in the town centre praying about a city centre witness, I went into a Christian bookshop and asked if they knew of any property that may be available. The manager told me they were moving and gave me the contact details of the owner. It turned out to be owned by a charitable trust. The end of the story is that we took over the trust and 'Contact Books' was born, later to be renamed 'Gladstones' after the name of the Trust Deed. The bookshop is still a blessing to the City of Liverpool.

It was around the same time that Phil Williamson came to visit Paul and me and shared the vision to start a Christian school. We immediately saw that this was a God-given vision and mission, and got behind Phil one hundred per cent. We offered the basement of 16 Devonshire Road as a venue for the school. The Fellowship also got behind the vision and worked to transform the basement into a school. The Christian Fellowship School (CFS) was birthed with around eighteen pupils. Phil Williamson was the headmaster, and Carol Jerman and Barbara Lord were teachers, with other volunteer teachers including my wife Julie teaching French and me as deputy head. The school continues to thrive today, although Phil was promoted to Glory a few years ago.

Paul and Lesley moved on to Walsall in 1983. We continued to see Devonshire Road Fellowship grow in numbers over the coming years, which necessitated us moving into a school for our morning meetings.

In 1986, the Lord spoke to Julie and me about planting a new church in Liverpool city centre, and in 1987 'City Church' was birthed with about forty-five people from Devonshire Road who also had the same vision. It was a difficult time coming to terms with the Lord's leading, but we got there in the end. Our time of leading the City Church with Jim and Jean Hamilton, Frank and Anne Cook, and Ken and Ruth Brew was also very special. We saw God do amazing things in the city which in itself would fill a book!

During our time in City Church, God began to speak to us about training English teachers for mission. After taking a group of fifteen to Hungary in 1994 for a summer language camp, we returned, seeing the opportunities in Eastern Europe for mission, using the teaching of English to this end. Through a series of divine appointments, I met some folk in Bournemouth with whom I shared the vision. In 1996, we launched the 'International Training Network' (ITN), training TEFL/TESOL[130] courses, leading to an internationally recognised qualification. This five-week course equipped those called for mission to go anywhere. Since those small beginnings, we have trained over a thousand

[130] Teaching English as a Foreign Language / Teaching English as a Second Language

teachers, many of whom are serving abroad. Again, a book could be written on the testimonies of many of these teachers.

In 1999, another work grew out of these courses. This was the 'International Care Network' (ICN), working with asylum seekers and refugees. At one point we were employing eighteen full-time staff. We had Government departments and local authorities asking us for advice!

In 2000, we felt the Lord leading us to begin a new house church in our home. 'Gateway' was born and has been a wonderful blessing to us over these past years. It became a house of prayer for the nations.

I believe everything that has happened to us can be linked back to the vision God gave to Norman Meeten in the very early days of the Fellowships, about the "leaves of the trees" being for "the healing of the nations"[131]. It has been, and still is, a privilege to be one of those leaves.

Saved for his glory
Keith and Christine Kelly

66 Our dear brother Norman Meeten had a word from the Lord at the beginning of the Fellowship in Liverpool, that those who found life through the work would be as the leaves of the tree in Revelation, who would be scattered worldwide, taking the word of life. Here is our story of how God allowed us to be like those leaves, scattered by the wind and carried on the river of life to reach the nations with the love of our Lord Jesus Christ.

The Lord in His providence introduced me (Keith) to 137 Queens Road, Liverpool at about the end of 1965, going into 1966. In the Lord's plan, a group of us had attended Richmond Baptist Church, which was only about half a mile away from Queens Road, but then we discovered this new work which people were calling 'Revival House'.

My first impressions were of an atmosphere of love and grace. A white-haired man, Mr North, was speaking at the front of a crowded upper room. It was like water to thirsty souls. We sensed the love and power of other dear brothers like Norman Meeten, plus a host of others.

---

[131] Revelation 22:2

I had already turned to Jesus just a few years before, when I was fourteen, at the local Baptist church in Anfield, Liverpool, but Queens Road appeared on the scene at an enormously opportune moment in my life.

Oh, what a debt of gratitude I owe to the Lord and to the saints who faithfully ministered God's love to me and prayed me into His life! How wonderful it was to lose my fears, sorrows and depressions! How incredible it was to experience new life in the Holy Spirit!

I became a junior newspaper reporter with the *Bootle Times Herald*, then a school teacher, and began sharing wherever I could about what the Lord had done for me. We also began to travel, first to France and Spain in an old ambulance with our friend John Valentine, then to eastern Europe, taking love and Bibles to the communist nations of East Germany, Poland, Hungary, Romania and the USSR.

This whetted our appetites, and so with my friend Phil Williamson, we saved up our money and went out again to the nations of Ghana, Nigeria, Kenya, Jordon, Israel, Lebanon and Cyprus. The little crumbs we had devoured at Queens Road, and subsequently at 14 Devonshire Road, we discovered had become loaves of bread for the nations.

When we returned to the UK in 1972, the Lord gave me a wonderful wife, Christine. Then, after a year of marriage, we went off to Africa again, taking the word of life to the nations. All that we had received in Liverpool and at summer conferences we were able to carry to the hungry world. Doors opened to preach on television, in football stadiums, towns and villages, from a base in Benin City, Nigeria. They even made me pastor of the thousand-strong Lyaro Church of God Mission! Christine was my choir mistress! Her choir was known as the Super Choir and they even were able to sing on television.

The Lord kept opening doors to the nations, such as Nigeria, Zimbabwe and Malawi. One thing leads to another, for whilst in Africa, opportunities came to write Christian columns for thousands of people in Malawi and Zimbabwe in *The Daily Times of Malawi*, *The Police Magazine* and *The Farmers Monthly*. I was also allowed to broadcast to many, many people in Malawi on the radio. Malawi had a million radio sets. Opportunities also came along to teach at four Bible colleges in three different nations, sharing the word of life.

In the UK we bought a big gospel tent and reached many of our own population. We saw a young Sikh girl aged about fourteen find Christ at one of our tent missions in Potternewton Park in Leeds, in about 1980. I had a letter from her recently, thanking us for introducing her to this wonderful life. She is now a QC and one of the top judges in our land, and married to the grandson of the famous missionary Norman Grubb. Praise God for fruit that remains!

We were helped by great brothers like John Valentine and Mickey Wright. The gospel went out to Rastafarians, West Indians, prostitutes, homosexuals and many others. Doesn't our great God love His creation!

We were able to reach many nations by our tent missions in England, Scotland, Wales and the Isle of Man, as well as in Sweden, France, Portugal and even Zimbabwe. I must emphasise that it was the life we received in those early days that gave us the power and the motivation to reach out to so many. We planted churches in Ghana, Portugal, Leeds and Liverpool. How God loves to use the weak and naturally insignificant vessels because it's *"Not by might nor by power, but by My Spirit' says the LORD..."*[132]

In the last few years, we have had wonderful opportunities to preach and to paint the gospel on sketch-boards at street corners and school assemblies, reaching our own multiethnic and multicultural nation.

My dear wife has pioneered English classes, so reaching over eighty different countries and ethnic groups in Greater Manchester in the last twelve years, seeing Bangladeshis, Russians and Iranians coming to Jesus. Currently we are teaching and training believers from a Muslim background from Iran (the fastest growing evangelical church in the world at the moment) and we are beginning to reach out into the Syrian community in Salford, teaching English, using our Bible stories.

How those leaves keep blowing and flowing out across the globe! What the Lord did in those early days was like a Krakatoa volcanic eruption. The tremors can still be felt today. Praise God!

[132] Zechariah 4:6

Norman's Healing

After many, many years of excruciating pain, God sovereignly and miraculously intervened and wonderfully healed Norman of a long-standing back problem. Prior to this, over the years, he had frequently been prayed for, been anointed with oil, had hands laid on him, and there had been much fasting and prayer; all to no avail, it would seem, but God had heard and saw and knew. We let Norman himself take up his story, which he has shared with many ever since. This was taped at a brother's conference in Birmingham in October 2017.

❝ Probably the most significant word that the Lord has spoken to me in recent days is the word that has given me new life; not just spiritually but physically – literally. Over thirty years ago now, I had a horrendous accident in the Amazon and tore a place in my back which could not be rectified. For years I have lived on very strong painkillers that kept it slightly under the surface and made life just about bearable, but not comfortable.

Then four years ago, in Delhi, I woke up and I thought someone was pouring acid down my arm. I couldn't move my arms; I couldn't turn my head. Surgery followed, and I was told by the surgeon that the top five vertebrae in my spine were causing the problem but, because of their proximity to the brain, they could only operate on the two middle discs, which he did. This alleviated the pain to some extent, but then it gradually got worse and worse. I was given two root blockers. One lasted for six weeks, the other for two.

It was soon realised that this could not be continued indefinitely, so the decision was made to operate again. This time, they would operate from the front, as accessing the spine from the back could prove seriously problematic, the danger being that should the slightest mistake be made, I would lose my voice and be paralysed from the neck down. Very exciting!

It was all arranged to have it done at the Walton Centre in Liverpool – a fantastic hospital. The surgeon was a delightful man – an Indian. Most of my connections with the medical world have been Indian. I was asked to ring the hospital, which I did, but was told, "Sorry, sir – no bed!" I put the phone down. Ten minutes later, the phone went again and this time they said, "Yes, sir – there is a bed!" I packed my bags, got to the front door and the phone went again. "Sorry, sir, it was a mistake. There is no bed; ring tomorrow!"

'Tomorrow' was a Sunday, so I went to the meeting at The Longcroft in the morning. After the meeting, I rang the hospital, to be told, "Sir, tomorrow is a bank holiday. There is no surgery tomorrow. Sorry, it is all a big, big mistake!"

My wife replied, "I hope that your medical expertise is greater than your administrative!" That's my wife!

By now I didn't have any more time. I was going to Sicily for two weeks and then I would go back to Nepal and India, and I wouldn't be back home again until the middle of December. It was therefore arranged that I should go back to the hospital in January.

In the December, about three years ago, I woke up. I was in Delhi. My daily reading that morning was from Jeremiah 17.

Now, I had given up – completely given up. I had come to the realisation that I would suffer pain for the rest of my life and exist on painkillers. Thousands of people have prayed for me, for which I am eternally grateful, with gallons of oil poured over me, but nothing happened. It was not that I didn't want it to happen, but nothing *had* happened.

Jeremiah 17:14 says, *"Heal me, Lord, and I shall be healed."* And I was instantly healed. Then, In Isaiah 38:15 it says, *"He has both spoken to me, and He Himself has done it."*

Sometimes people still ask my wife, "How is Norman?"

I say to her, "Don't listen to the lies of the devil. He has done it!"

I knew I had heard the word of the Lord that morning. I hadn't been looking. There are thousands of verses in the Bible relating to healing, but I knew that morning that there was power behind the word to accomplish what God had said. The word was quickened, not only to my understanding but to my experience.

Jenny asked me how God had done it. In John's Gospel it says, Father speaks the word and Jesus does the work. Amen. He did. All the glory to Him!

I feel I have been given a new lease of life. Bless the Lord, and I am going on! People say to me, *"You are eighty-four and you are crazy enough to keep going off to India..."* I will go as long as the Lord gives me grace and strength to continue. I can only wait upon the Lord.

APPENDIX 2

What About Head Covering?

Fred Tomlinson

❝ The path to radical obedience to God's word has always been the road less travelled. The broader, easy-going way, where men do that which is right in their own eyes, continues to be the preferred choice.

Many things don't make sense

In order to accurately comprehend the message of Scripture, we must resist the temptation to read it through the lens of common sense, personal preferences and popular opinions. The God who inspired the sacred text said of Himself, *"For as the heavens are higher than the earth, so are My ways higher than your ways, and My thoughts than your thoughts."*[133]

R.C. Sproul notes, "It does concern me ... that the custom of the woman's covering her head ... did not pass away until we saw a cultural revolt against the authority of the husband over the wife, not just in the home or in the church but in the whole of culture. It frightens me that we're taking our cue not from the Scriptures but from the culture or the fashions."[134]

Undeniably, the most damaging opposition to the practice of head covering is society's surge toward gender equality. When God created man and woman, he designed them as equals in value and worth, yet with distinct gender differences. These complex features would enable them to be a complement to each other. To this end, God assigned a structure of roles, functions and responsibilities. Should there be a failure to recognise and endorse

---

[133] Isaiah 55:9
[134] *Hard Sayings;* R.C. Sproul; p.138

these category distinctions, any teaching on the topic of head-covering will appear meaningless, if not offensive.

First Corinthians, chapter eleven

Under the heading 'ordinances', Paul occupies the entire chapter with two issues – head-covering and the Lord's Supper. Both functions, along with water baptism, were ordained to be preserved and practised in the churches. Their purpose is to symbolically portray, and keep fresh in the minds of Christian believers, the spiritual issues they represent. These incredibly simple practices can appear irrelevant in today's sophisticated age, but God's view of their importance is highlighted powerfully by the consequences of destroying the symbolism of the Lord's Supper.[135] They did this by their divisions and their absence of care for one another.

Just sixteen verses

The first sixteen verses of this chapter contain the only instructive reference in the New Testament to the practice of head-covering. Some claim this signals its relative unimportance, but such reasoning is soundly weakened by the fact that the only *apostolic* instruction for practising the Lord's Supper is also limited to this same chapter. Did any evangelical assembly abandon the practice of communion based on this argument?

Many satisfy themselves that Paul was dealing with a cultural issue that is irrelevant to Christians today. But one thing is beyond debate: the apostle left no stone unturned in order to convince his readers that head-covering was a required practice in the Christian assemblies. It was certainly not a casual suggestion that could be easily missed.

Paul's life had been spent in an Orthodox Jewish context, where both men and women covered their heads (something not legislated in the Law of Moses). Some believe he was either imposing a Jewish practice upon the new Gentile converts, or working around a current social issue. What we know for certain is that this epistle was addressed to the church at Corinth, a sophisticated multicultural city – awash with customs and traditions. But nothing in these sixteen verses suggests Paul was

---

[135] See verses 27 and 29

attempting to either promote or impose a Jewish practice. Quite the opposite is true. Using a common everyday practice, he applied to it a protocol and a significance that was entirely new.

The outward and the inward

The outward protocol specified how head-covering should be practised in the local churches. It was both simple and uncomplicated. The men were to remove any head-covering they were wearing, and the women were to cover their heads for the occasion.

The new invisible and symbolic significance can be summarised in one word: headship. Opposing voices are quick to point out that the word 'headship' never appears in the Bible. Some will label it an invention of male chauvinism. However, while it is true the word itself is not used, the concept of headship is certainly biblical and is in plain view for those willing to see it. Actually, it is a concept with a very long history, predating human existence and reaching into the mystery of the eternal government and administration of God.

In the third verse, Paul identifies headship in three separate relationships: *"the head of every man is Christ"*, *"the head of the woman is the man"* and *"the head of Christ is God"*. The third of these categories is the most difficult to comprehend, since it references the unfathomable mystery of the incarnation. The word 'Christ' Paul uses here is a title ascribed to Jesus, the Son of God, who is identified as being in substance one with His Father and *"the brightness of His glory and the express image of His person"*[136]. This verse along with Philippians 2:6 leave us in no doubt that the Son of God is eternally coequal with His Father. Yet for the purpose of redemption, He presented Himself as subordinate to His Father and was obedient to Him in all things, even to the furthest extent – *"the death of the cross"*[137]. This statement very clearly teaches that headship neither presupposes superiority nor inferiority. On the contrary, it is a structure of relationship or function within the context of equality, and focuses on the issues of responsibility and accountability. Recall this principle being expressed in the garden of Eden. Eve first took

[136] Hebrews 1:3
[137] Philippians 2:8

the forbidden fruit, but every subsequent reference to that event names Adam as responsible for the act.

The tradition of men removing their cap when entering a place of worship or during public prayer has become a virtually uncontested tradition. In the event that the average man was to be asked for a reason for his practice, it is likely the best answer might identify it as a token of respect. Very few would have any idea of it being biblically mandated, or of symbolising deep spiritual principles. According to the apostle's teaching in this chapter, a Christian man must not appear before the Lord with his head covered,[138] for in doing so, he is guilty of symbolically concealing Christ – man's spiritual head – thus dishonouring Him.[139]

At its basic level, a Christian woman wearing a veil signals her acceptance of the divinely ordained order. However, the practice includes even richer significance – consider Paul's letter to the Ephesians where the Christian man represents Christ; the woman (wife) represents the church – Christ's bride.[140] Verse 23 compares the headship of the man to that of Christ being the head of the church.

Maybe the police can help

Should a woman knowingly, or deliberately, refuse to cover her head, she signifies her rejection of authority – not merely that of man, but far more importantly, that which belongs to God. A simple illustration will help explain this principle. When a vehicle pulls over in response to a police officer's direction, the driver is responding to the authority of the officer. However, a higher authority has delegated that authority to the officer. Therefore, as the driver obeys the officer, he is, by extension, submitting himself to the government that delegated the officer's authority. So it is for the Christian woman; in recognising and submitting to God's delegated authority, she simultaneously submits herself to the overarching authority of God.

Paul, in yet a further break with Jewish tradition, proceeds to open the door to women's participation in ministry within the

---

[138] See verses 4 and 7
[139] See verse 4
[140] See Ephesians 5:21-33

church, specifically referencing prayer and prophecy. The Authorised Version refers to the covering she wears during this ministry as *"power on her head"[141]*. Here the word 'power' is a translation of the Greek word *exousia* and is quite misleading. Several other versions have preferred the word 'authority', thus identifying head-covering as *"a symbol of authority"* – an outward sign or symbol that declares her inward submission to the divinely instituted structure of authority.

Twin issues – glory and covering

In the sixth verse, Paul makes a statement which, if taken literally, appears almost outrageous, namely, *"Let her be shorn."* Is he advocating such a procedure be performed in the churches? Surely, he is not. Rather, with this startling metaphor, he is affirming the gravity of the subject matter he is presenting.

The woman's long hair is identified here as a feature of her personal glory.[142] By concealing that glory, she proclaims her deference to the Lord and her acceptance of His scheme of headship. Beyond this, her action and demeanour provide a model for the entire assembly gathered in the Lord's holy presence.

One of the most common counterarguments to a woman wearing a veil is that her hair itself is sufficient covering. But this is a meritless claim, lacking even basic logic. Think carefully: if this were the case, every male worshipper would be required to shave his head. As noted, a man must not have his head covered when he comes before the Lord. It is true that a woman's hair is referred to as a covering, but Paul's deliberate use of a particular Greek word in verse fifteen is noteworthy. It implies hair being thrown around. This is in contrast to the word used in the sixth verse, which denotes 'to cover completely'.

Contrary to popular teaching, prostitutes didn't have their heads shaved as a result of their trade. In Paul's day, the primary reason for women to have shaved heads was in order to shame a married woman found guilty of adultery. Records also reveal that it was not unknown for some to crop their hair (maybe similar to popular styles today) as a token of mourning. Either way, the force of Paul's illustration is that a woman is shamed who appears

[141] Verse 10 (KJV)
[142] See verse 15

before men either shorn or shaven. The application of this powerful metaphor is unmistakable.

Angels watching

In the tenth verse, Paul reinforces his instruction with the words, *"because of the angels"*. This statement benefits greatly from a parallel reading of Isaiah 6:2, where angelic beings cover themselves entirely in the presence of the enthroned King of Glory. By appealing to the witness of angels, Paul virtually eliminates the argument that head-covering was a practice belonging exclusively to an ancient cultural tradition.

Evidently, angels are present as witnesses when the assembly gathers for worship. This is certainly confirmed in Paul's letter to Timothy, where he wrote, *"I charge thee before God, and the Lord Jesus Christ, and the elect angels, that thou observe these things."*[143] There can be no doubt that angels, standing in the presence of Almighty God, possess a vivid understanding of the concepts of authority, submission and obedience. Are they perplexed at the insubordination of men and women who have been redeemed by the blood of the King of Glory? Is it possible they recall the disobedient multitude of their own company, who found no place for repentance? But rather than witnessing insubordination, God's desire continues to be that the angelic hosts will witness His many-faceted wisdom – through the church![144]

It is likely that many women practising head-covering do so merely out of tradition. By the same token, it is virtually certain that men who remove their hats before entering a Christian meeting have not the faintest thought or understanding of the teaching contained in these sixteen verses. If the practice is less than an act of a conscious and deliberate obedience to the word of God, it is reduced to a legalistic tradition, with no spiritual merit. Sadly, many who once covered their heads have surrendered their privilege, evidently preferring to worship as they please.

---

[143] 1 Timothy 5:21 (KJV)
[144] See Ephesians 3:10

<u>Just ignore it!</u>

The final verse[145] in this section has caused much confusion. Some seem convinced that the inspired apostle was saying, "If this thoroughly argued passage is a problem for anyone, just ignore it!" That would be an absurd treatment of the word of God. The same apostle reminded Timothy that *"All Scripture is God-breathed... "[146]* The true meaning is obvious: it is contentiousness, not head-covering, that is not customary in the churches of God.

Wherever true worshippers bow in His holy presence, whether praying or prophesying, every man's head should be uncovered and every woman's head should be veiled. *"Unto him be glory in the church by Christ Jesus throughout all ages, world without end. Amen. "[147]*

---

[145] Verse 16
[146] 2 Timothy 3:16 (AMP)
[147] Ephesians 3:21 (KJV)

APPENDIX 3

Tributes

A tribute to Mr G.W. North
Fred Tomlinson

" The year 1966 was very significant for my family. Several relatives did the unthinkable: they broke ranks with the Brethren Assembly and started attending meetings in Liverpool at a place known simply as The House. All were passionate about what they had found. My brother, the instigator of the breakaway, pressed Sheila and me to join them. In spite of considerable reservations, we eventually decided to go and check what all the fuss was about. Little did we realise how that decision would impact our entire lives and those of countless others in the years to come – but that's another story!

Mr G.W. North
"Many learn the words;
few learn the song"

We had heard about the main speaker, a Mr George Walter North, but when we heard him preach, we were captivated with a sense of the love of God and the prophetic spontaneity of his delivery. At the close of the meeting, we were left with the undeniable impression that we had been exposed to the word of God – and its power and challenge.

Mr North preached a lot about the love of God, but it was so much more than his words. Love emanated from him. While paying him tribute at a particular event, Dr Jack Kelly recalled the months of travelling together in India where they shared a wide range of life's experiences. He climaxed his memories with, "I am able to tell you that Wally's life is better even than his preaching." How true!

For over three decades, my wife Sheila and I had the joy of sharing many precious occasions with Mr North. Initially our knowledge of him was limited to sitting in his meetings – watching and listening. At the close of one meeting, he came over to me and said, "Fred, you just sit in these meetings and soak it all up like blotting paper." He was so right. I recall that seeing his little Mini Traveller upon arriving at the meeting locations filled my heart with anticipation. I can honestly say that I never went home disappointed. There was certainly no famine of the word of God in those days!

Mr North often shared the Lord's wisdom with me in private. In one instance this resulted in a career change that was pivotal in the direction of my life. On another occasion, Sheila and I were sharing breakfast with Mr and Mrs North, when he said, "At some point you must break out of the cycle that revolves around money, and get into a cycle that revolves around Jesus." We received that as the word of God and acted upon it. Our participation in the ministry today can be traced back to that conversation. My appointment into eldership elevated my involvement with Mr North to a new level; discussions and debates became richer, and my relationship with him deepened. The man I esteemed so highly as a preacher had become one of my dearest friends.

In January 1974, I shared with him that I had been invited to move to Ontario, Canada. Although uncertain of his response, I could not have been more surprised. He said "Well, Fred, it was my intention to chat with you this weekend to ask you if you would be interested in relocating to Cyprus." He had recently made his first visit there and felt that Sheila and I might be of use in a particular situation. However, having heard of the invitation to Canada, he suggested that I visit and 'spy out the land'. I did, and later that year our family immigrated to Canada.

In 1976, Mr and Mrs North came to visit us for a period of six weeks. As I carried their cases into the house, he said, "You know, there are people in England who think you are getting a rather large slice of the cake!" We certainly were – they were weeks we shall never forget.

On their first full day in Canada, we chatted as we walked along a lakeshore. I had been enthusiastically sharing how I believed that if the word of God was fully preached in the meetings, there would be no need for private counselling and ministry. It had seemed to me that a lot of time was wasted in that practice. No sooner had the words fallen from my lips, than he swung around and pinned me against a tree, saying, "You're wrong, Fred. You will never see a true New Testament church established without the ministry of deliverance." This, he went on to say, would usually take place outside the context of the meeting. Then he added, "While I'm here with you, ministering to your people, you join me." My resulting observation demolished my earlier theory and replaced it with a new paradigm.

Another pearl of wisdom came as we were chatting about the upcoming meetings. I suggested that I might reach out to a person who had been upset and left the church some weeks earlier. "Fred," he said, "whatever you do, never attempt to bring back those whom God has put out." That statement would often regulate my natural inclinations during the ensuing decades of pastoral ministry.

During the same visit, Sheila and I counted the repeated circuits Mr North and I made around our large driveway, as he, with his fatherly arm around me, counselled and encouraged my heart in the things of the Lord and His ministry.

On a different note, the question of how Mr North should be addressed was a topic of perennial discussion. His attitude on the subject was old school. He believed it proper, particularly for younger people, to show respect by using the term 'mister'. He once took Dave Wetherly to one side and tenderly reprimanded him, "It's not right for these young folks to call you Dave; they should call you Mr Wetherly." Dave could never bring himself to request such a change – he was 'Dave' to the end.

While travelling with him in the United States, I discovered that this was a much bigger deal. I heard young leaders addressing him as 'George' – something virtually no-one ventured to say back in the United Kingdom.

Perhaps the most interesting moment took place in a southern part of the US. The brother unlocking the building in preparation for the meeting welcomed us with a hearty, "Hi, I'm Willy!"

There was a pause, then Mr North responded with equal vigour. "Hello, Willy. I'm Wally!"

Willy had no idea of the threshold of UK convention he had just crossed! I am sure my inward response showed on my face, but only Mr North would have identified its cause!

Many years ago, Mr North was enjoying some relaxation with our family. Our daughter Wendy was a little girl and was pretending to take orders for meals in a restaurant. Sheila and I glanced at each other as she asked him the million-dollar question: "What is your name?"

"G.W. North," he replied.

She figured the initial 'G' stood for 'George', but since she was making no progress in determining the significance of the 'W', she exclaimed, "It must stand for Washington – George Washington North!"

On a particular trip to St Catherines, Ontario, Mr North preached in a series of meetings which I recall as being unusually powerful. Back in our home in Stouffville, I noticed him leaning on the kitchen counter writing on a piece of paper. He straightened up, turned around and handed me a cheque. It was the cheque he had received for his preaching. He had endorsed it. He said, "There you are, Fred. Here is your fare to Cyprus." I was staggered. It seemed almost too sacred for me to use. However, he insisted, and in due course I made the trip to Cyprus. I know the Lord made that visit special for me and I believe for others also.

Years later, responding to a gift that our church had mailed to him, Mr North wrote back, "The Holy Spirit is the Spirit of generosity, and when He fills a life, He makes that life generous too." In so many ways, he was a wonderful example of that generosity.

In subsequent years, Mr North made many visits to us and to the churches where we have served. Each occasion was special in one way or another. He was always a pleasure to have in our home – so spiritual, yet so natural. Shortly after the close of one meeting in the barn next door to us, he returned to our house and made himself comfortable. Sometime later, we arrived home, along with a man and his wife who were also our guests that night. Once in the house, I noticed the couple standing and staring into the living room. Intrigued, I walked to where they were standing. There, stretched out on the couch, was the man who had preached so powerfully in the meeting. Now, unaware of his spectators, he was engrossed in one of our boy's annuals! The bewildered couple were struggling to process the scene – he was human after all!

In spite of the obvious confidence with which he preached, my personal observation was that he found confrontational situations to be extremely upsetting. It was my privilege to have him request my company on several such occasions. One situation, which I will never forget, affected him physically in a very distressing manner. Before travelling to a preaching engagement in the Midwestern United States, he was made aware that a powerful individual intended to confront him. Immediately prior to that interview, he developed a terribly painful case of shingles, affecting his face and mouth. As a result, that meeting never took place.

The flight back to our home in Ontario was not easy for him. The weather was bitterly cold, but peering through the glass portion of our front door, we could see the blazing log fire which Sheila had prepared for his arrival. His favourite chair was pulled close. As the door opened, our family Alsatian dog welcomed us both. I can still see the painful smile on Mr North's precious face, which shingles had made so raw. Within days he was on his way home to the UK. That was the only occasion when Sheila and I were relieved to see our dear friend leave.

Like so many others, Sheila and I have a wealth of stories that have arisen from our times with Mr North. He was one of our dearest friends and was like a father to Sheila and me, and a kindly grandfather to our children. Whether reading and praying at the breakfast table, giving us advice on some complex church matter, scooping down ice-cream, or riding pillion on my motorcycle, tantalising me with, "You'll never scare me boy!" he was a pleasure to be with.

Although he was some thirty years senior to us, we never thought of this man as old; he made aging attractive! My teenage brother was deeply impressed with the life he saw in Mr North and once said, "Fred, I can't wait to grow old!"

His ministry

The early 1960s was a time of extreme turmoil and unrest in the United Kingdom. Young and old alike were desperately searching for reality and meaning in life; several issues transpired to create this extraordinary crisis. These included the sexual revolution and the use of illicit drugs, but by far the most serious factor was that Christianity had degenerated into a severely weakened state and had virtually lost its prophetic voice.

It was against this backdrop that the Lord began expanding Mr North's ministry. Other ministering brethren were becoming prominent, but this man was uniquely prepared by the Lord to carry an essential message for that period in time. This was reminiscent of Esther, who was providentially promoted to become the Queen of Persia during a time of terrible crisis.[148]

Although he strongly resisted the title of apostle, both Mr North's calling and stature were unmistakably apostolic. One of his arguments against accepting that designation was that he had never founded a church. While that remains debatable, one fact is indisputable: God used him to bring into being an entire movement – a movement that continues to have great influence around the world. Numerous men and women serving in Christian ministry can trace their spiritual roots back to the ministry of Mr North.

The distinctiveness of his ministry can be credited to many things, but one anecdote from his early life is very enlightening. Each student in the Bible class he attended was required to write an essay on the Ephesian epistle. Mr North's initial impulse was to open a commentary on the epistle. Instead, he repeatedly reread the epistle until close to the due date. At that point, he wrote his essay. Evidently, his classmates took the easier route, which left Mr North's article unique, and he received the award.

That action was destined to characterise his ministry for the rest of his life. In a very real way, he was taught of God. His library was virtually non-existent, and he showed no interest in browsing around Christian bookshops. His preaching was revelatory in content and spontaneous in style. His messages had

148 See Esther 4:14

little or no framework. He preached what God gave him in the moment, and he did it with consistently powerful results.

One memorable occasion highlights this practice. Beginning by reading in the third epistle of John, he interrupted the reading to talk a little. Soon his comments blended into a most profound prophecy. Finally, and almost indistinguishably, his words became a prayer that was bathed in extraordinary passion. I can't say how others were affected, but that progression of ministry and outpouring of his heart was so inspired by the Holy Ghost that I was overcome and lay face down in tears.

"Waiting on the Lord" was one of Mr North's common expressions. He had discovered the spiritual secret of retreating into the Lord's presence. Only infrequently did he talk of his experiences in that holy place, but we can be certain that the clarity of his life and the power of his ministry were the product of what transpired there.

During one of his fatherly chats, Mr North reminded me, "We only have one message, but it's amazing how many different ways we can say it." Although his ministry was incredibly rich, there was a sense in which he really did have just one message – it was not a new message; in fact, it was a very old message. It was the message of the early apostles. It was a foundational message – the promise of a new birth; a radically transformed life, utterly liberated from the dominion of sin and lived by the power of the indwelling Holy Spirit. Mr North knew that all attempts to live a Christian life without this foundation would invite frustration and certain failure. Little wonder he was heard to say that if he were ever to be a local pastor again, he would preach the new birth message at least once every month.

The authority he exercised was also recognised by the realm of demonic spirits. A clash between the kingdoms of light and darkness was not uncommon in his meetings. Some people made a hasty retreat from the premises, while others would make their way to the front in order to find deliverance. Demonic screams of one sort or another were not uncommon in many of the meetings. Often in private sessions, evil spirits were confronted and cast out. Mr North would not use the common phrase "in Jesus' name"; instead, just the words "Get out!" were enough to cause deeply entrenched spirits to be exposed and expelled. He lived in Jesus' name!

When it fell to him to lead a meeting, he was so obviously in his element. It would be easy to credit the richness of those sessions to his natural abilities, namely his knowledge of music and his melodic voice. However, his greatest asset was his ability to worship. He never made the mistake of imagining worship could be taught, but he succeeded in inspiring hearts in numberless congregations.

In the early 1970s, the first conference for elders from around England took place. It was convened at Rora House in Devon and took place over three days. It was a most memorable event for many reasons. One of the topics discussed focused on the future of the Fellowships as a movement. I vividly recall my profound sadness when I heard Mr North say, "In all likelihood, history will repeat itself and this movement will eventually become reduced to a mere monument." The pros and cons of such a hypothesis can be debated, but it is tragic how quickly a man and the message God used in such a superlative way can be forgotten – even disregarded. How quickly another generation arises *"which knew not the LORD, nor ... the works which he had done"[149]*.

The black-and-white, radical, sometimes blunt manner of Mr North didn't please everyone. There were those who misunderstood him, misrepresented him, even disliked him, but no sincere observer and listener could deny that he lived and preached Jesus, and in so doing, he truly lifted up a standard for the people.

For several decades, my mother had a picture on her wall. Superimposed over a pastoral scene was a classic quotation of Mr North that read, "Many learn the words; few learn the song." Here was a man who learnt the song, and he learnt it well. But better yet – he helped us to learn it too.

---

[149] Judges 2:10 (KJV)

A memorial to Dave Wetherly

Fred Tomlinson

Dave Wetherly

❝ David Wetherly experienced a disadvantaged introduction to life. He was conceived out of wedlock; his mother, whom he loved and diligently cared for, attempted to abort him while still in her womb, and he never knew his father. He was raised in an orphanage, yet his funeral was attended by hundreds who gathered to bid him farewell. We knew many more hundreds around the world who would have dearly loved to have attended. By the Lord's grace, he was a "brand snatched from the burning".

The invitation to publicly reflect on the life of Dave Wetherly was a high honour, but it carried with it an almost impossible challenge. I felt myself a beggar as I attempted to describe a man whose identity dwarfs every adjective available to me.

Dave was a man unlike any man I have ever known. Concerning my personal spiritual life, he provided an essential key that allowed me to discover a deeper, richer experience of Christ's indwelling. He had been a constant inspiration, and one of my dearest friends. From that memorable day in the summer of 1966 when I first met him, until the last occasion in his presence a few weeks before his death, he never failed to excite and sharpen my love for the Lord Jesus. I owe to him a debt I can never calculate. One of my friends described the same sentiments this way: "When I first met Dave up close and in person, I was stretched and expanded beyond what I knew (or thought I knew) about love and acceptance."

A common trait of Dave was to use the word 'our' in that quaint British way – *our* John, or *our* Pete, or *our* Sheila; but if this endearing term should be applied to anyone, then surely it would be to Dave Wetherly himself, because in the truest sense of the word, he was *our* Dave. He belonged to us all – equally. Although he succeeded in making each of us feel as though we were his greatest friend, it would have been the height of folly to imagine that we held a monopoly on his friendship. He was our Dave, and with his great heart he gave himself to us and loved us unconditionally – every last one of us.

In virtually every area of his life, he was the epitome of extravagance, ranging from his expressions of affection and appreciation down to the style of his handwriting. Working with him in eldership and living in the same house for four years allowed me to observe this at close range.

He was possessed with a fervent love for Jesus and was an enormous asset in every meeting graced with his presence. Could we ever forget his characteristic praying and prophesying?

He was constantly vigilant to maintain a testimony of moral purity and never allowed himself to be found in a compromising situation.

He chose to live a remarkably simple life and seemed drawn to the tiniest quarters available.

He had no time for small talk or anything that would waste his precious time.

He would never be found speaking ill of anybody, no matter what the circumstances.

He didn't represent 'a position' or 'an opinion'. He was committed to unity and harmony.

He succeeded in avoiding trouble and division; somehow, he was above those things and bigger than them. Doubtless this fact was reflected in the very diverse gathering at his funeral.

I believe that, to a man, we would agree that Dave Wetherly was one of the biggest men any of us have encountered in the journey of our lives. Like the apostle Paul, he was faithful to the faith, faithful to the fight and faithful to the finish. As an elderly man in a hospital bed, drifting in and out of consciousness, without a trace of murmur or complaint, he never ceased to express the sweetness of Jesus. Little wonder that for many days his friends eagerly volunteered to sit with him, hold his precious hands and assure him he was not alone. But perhaps the greatest tribute to his unfading witness was paid by an unknown nurse who, minutes after his departure, laid a rose upon the body of this saintly man of God – that said it all!

A tribute to Pat Coombs
Gill Silver

Pat Coombs

❝ I first met Pat sometime during the 1990s, whilst I was visiting a friend in Exeter. Pat was living with Susanne in Hamlin Lane, when they were both an integral part of the Exeter Christian Fellowship (now known as Westgate). It was a precious time and the beginning of a long and lasting friendship. I loved visiting her. She was always so welcoming and so genuinely interested in what was happening, how things were going, what you were doing, and we'd chat away with such ease and a genuine oneness of heart that only God can give. It was such a privilege to be able to share our lives together, unburden ourselves, pray together and to know a real fellowship of kindred spirits in Christ.

Following her move to Milborne Port, I continued to visit regularly, as did Susanne, who had also moved to the same village. She would always have such a lovely smile, and her face lit up as you walked through the door of her sheltered accommodation. Despite her increasing and quite serious medical problems, she chose to rise above all her limitations and value every visit made.

Pat, to all who knew her, was that very special friend that was the result of, and came from, her close walk and obedience to her Lord and Saviour whom she loved so much. None of us are anything in ourselves, as she would be the first to admit, but when we belong to Christ and have been truly born of His Spirit, then friendships take on a depth of love with which nothing else can compare, and which is totally spontaneous and immediate.

It has truly been such a privilege to have known her, and how wonderful to know that there will be a time when we will truly meet again, in and for eternity! What a time that will be: forever together, His body, in the kingdom of God; never to part again.

Those who were privileged to have known Pat – and it *was* a real privilege – are all of one heart. She radiated the love and peace of God and welcomed you with open arms; with always a smile on her face, no matter how difficult her circumstances may have been. She was a joy to be with, and those who shared her faith would know a real oneness with her spirit and would share precious times of fellowship together.

Pat was the dear saint who sat quietly at a typewriter for hours, days, weeks and years, with a few friends in Exeter, typing out, pre computer days, all of Mr North's books and leaflets.

Firstly, let us look back into her earlier days and see so clearly the overruling sovereignty of God in her life and how He wonderfully prepared her for all that He had planned for her life.

Sarah Duckworth, a niece, writes:

66 Pat was born on June 19th, 1921 in a small, picturesque south Somerset village called Milborne Port, a few miles from Sherborne. She was the youngest of six children, her father owning the High Street bakery. Their home was always a hive of activity, and over the years a number of the family worked together in the business.

On occasions, Pat would muse over the fact that she had had a near miss when she was still a baby. Having been put to sleep in her parents' bedroom, she just couldn't settle, so she was brought downstairs. A few minutes later, the contents of the loft collapsed into the bedroom, covering the cot she had so recently vacated.

Following her school years, she began some clerical work for a while before being drafted into the ATS (Auxillary Territorial Service) and posted to various parts of the country. Following the war, with a new focus, she embarked on her general nurses' training and midwifery.

Pat came to know the Lord in her early thirties through a Billy Graham Crusade in 1953. In 1958, she went to the Sudan to work as a nurse in an American Mission School in Khartoum North. She loved it, and after a time, recognising her skills, the governors asked her if she would be willing to teach English Literature, together with the Bible, to which she agreed, for the next twelve years.

The political atmosphere changed during her time there, and by 1970 all the foreign missionaries were required to leave the country. Many of the people she had lived with there became firm friends.

Pat returned to Milborne Port, for what turned out to be a six-year stay. Settling back into life in England again, with its many changes, wasn't an easy transition, but she was needed to help run the family home for her brother Marten, following the death of her mother just a few weeks after her return. In conjunction with helping with running her family home, she also reacquainted herself with her nursing and worked as a district nurse, travelling around in her much-loved Morris Traveler. I amusingly recall the story of Pat running out of petrol on one occasion; Pat was seen filling her tank with the emergency supply, fed in by a funnel and tubing that was normally used to give enemas!

It was during this period that Pat was introduced to a new House Fellowship in Exeter and, when able, would get into her car on a Sunday morning and travel down. This proved to be her real spiritual food. Eventually she was to move to Exeter in the October of 1977, proving to be a time of much joy and friendship.

Richard Curd takes up the story:

66 On moving to Exeter, Pat attended the Exeter Christian Fellowship which by that time had moved out of Belmont Road where Mr North had been one of the leaders and moved into The Old Chapel in Bartholomew Street. The input of the teaching and ministry of Mr North and others had undoubtedly been the main influence in Pat's life, even before her move, and was instrumental in preparing her for the work that God had called her to do.

Pat wanted to get the messages of Mr North into print. I believe she began by transcribing one or two of his audio messages. He had already begun to write down his inspirational thoughts, and it was Pat who had it on her heart to type them out. His writing was near illegible and minute, but she had a gift to read them. Not only did she type them out, but she began to have them printed.

This was costly. I believe it was with the help of Peter Richards that she began to print them off herself. She used a duplicating machine. Only those who lived at that time would know what that was! In the light of today's technology, it was very primitive, and the resulting print looked very amateurish, but it was an economic means of getting the messages out, which was appreciated by many. The vision was that once his writings had been printed, they could then be sold, but they were made available free of charge. Pat financed this herself throughout all the years that she continued to print and produce his writings. This was a true work of faith. Never was money asked for. I cannot remember how many years she worked on this project, but it was for at least ten years and the money always came in.

My part in helping Pat came when the church leader removed me from the work that he had appointed me to do. I was therefore available for new things. Peter Richards suggested that I could help Pat with the in-house printing which he had helped to establish. With Pat and Peter, I learnt the art of printing and collating and binding books. The publishing work was carried out on the ground floor of Belmont Road in the room where the meetings used to take place during the days when Bob and Nora Love and Mr North were resident. It was now a plain, colourless room, furnished with a desk for Pat to type on, a table with the printing machine, and other tables where the individual pages of the books were set out in page numbers and from which they were collated.

Many happy hours were spent in chatting and quite often discussing the contents of the books. Some of Mr North's expressions or phrases were incomprehensible! We tried to understand them in order to simplify them by altering punctuation or even one or two words. These were then returned to Mr North. He always checked the typed manuscripts. Almost without exception, they were returned with the alterations changed back to his original wording. We decided that it would need to be up to the reader to work out what he was saying!

Once the *gratis* nature of the books became known, the books flew, especially to the African continent. We received a lot of post requesting them. Occasionally we had positive feedback! We were happy to believe that his books would be helpful in grounding many in good, biblical teaching.

The time came when the work had to vacate Belmont Road. For a time, we used a small room in John Amer's business premises, but the lack of space and time meant that we had to use a High Street printer to produce the books, which added to the expense of production. The work was then moved to Hamlin Lane, where Pat and Susanne lived, where weekly meetings to discuss and monitor its progress continued, and where it eventually came to its completion some years later. It was probably in the late '80s or early '90s that Pat laid the work to rest, but the influence of those books no doubt continues.

I should also have mentioned that John Corcoran was also so helpful in all of this work. He was a great asset and advocate in all that we did.

John Corcoran

❝ If memory serves me right, I gave up employment in 1982 to help Pat produce the writings of Mr North. Peter and Richard were also involved before me. Phil and Jenny Glover had purchased 23 and 25 Belmont Road, and they gave me some room in the basement, formerly the Fellowship House's laundry room, to store the books we produced. Initially the books and other writings were done by hand, but this was before I became involved. Pat produced the typewritten pages on a Gestetner Paper Stencil, and then multiple copies were run off from this primitive machine. Pamphlets were made up from this and distributed. Everything was done on a no-charge basis. The many original manuscripts were in Pat's possession, and she typed every book that was produced onto a stencil. Several copy stencils will have been needed to reproduce copies of the pages that could not have been produced with just one stencil. I believe that Richard was responsible for despatch and correspondence, Peter Richards having moved from Exeter. Most of the original pamphlets have been reprinted, such as *A Sign of Authority*, *Initial Evidence*, *Communion*, *The Altar* and many others. They are now found on the website hosted by Ron Bailey, biblebase.com.

At some point, the original method of printing stopped, and it was then that the first book, *One Baptism*, was commissioned from a printing company in nearby Crediton, by Peter Richards. I remember driving back from Crediton with Peter and several thousand books – ten thousand approximately, which made the suspension of the van sway!

It was after this that I became involved, and it became necessary to find another means of producing these books. Fortunately, I discovered that there was a book-producing company in Exeter which was able to produce a small number of books when the machines were not being used for more profitable work.

As donations mounted up, it became possible to produce further books. Another Exeter company specialised in shorter books, and many titles were produced by them. It was very much a subsistence operation, and whilst it would have been welcomed to produce a more attractive and expensive cover to the books and pamphlets, we attached more importance to the distribution of the content, which we valued so much.

It became necessary to move the stock of books from Belmont Road, and they were distributed around various Fellowships and contacts overseas, with a small stock remaining in The Old Chapel building, now known as Westgate.

Everything that was published was typed by Pat Coombs, initially on her manual typewriter, but latterly on a word processor which Clem Fisher advised us to purchase. Pat was seriously allergic to computers and this was an acceptable compromise! Manuscripts, or CRC (Camera Ready Copy), were made on ordinary quality paper; the different printing companies made up a hard disc from the CRC to use in their machinery.

For most of her time in Exeter, Pat lived with Susanne, a friend from the Fellowship, to whom God had clearly spoken, asking her to offer Pat a permanent home with her. This was a wonderful provision, recognised to be entirely of Him.

Susanne, who had become such a close and treasured friend, concludes this tribute.

66 Eventually it became clear to Pat and me that we were to leave Exeter and to go to Milborne Port, which was the place of her birth. Pat was offered a warden-controlled bungalow, and we moved in 1996, much to the delight of her brother, who was a near neighbour. The Lord provided me with an attractive terraced cottage very near to Pat in the same village.

She found the new circumstances difficult at first, as for many years she had been living and working amongst Christians only. However, she loved her bungalow and she became an active member of the Milborne Port Christian Fellowship, running a small Bible study group in her home for a period.

Pat's health slowly deteriorated over the years, to the point when full-time nursing care became needful. She moved to a nursing home in Sherborne in October 2011, where the staff grew to love her and recognised her Christian faith.

After a period of protracted weakness, the Lord took Pat home, on 29th July, 2016, shortly after her ninety-fifth birthday. As with so many saints of God who have gone through with Him to the end, we will never realise her full legacy for Christ. But there certainly is one.

A tribute to Bob and Norah Love
Their daughter, Sue Heathcote

❝ My mother was the youngest of seven children. She was born in Cawnpore (as it was then) in India in 1916, as were her parents and her father's family, going back to the 1780s. Her mother's father went to India from Derbyshire about the time of the Indian mutiny. Mum's first family members in India were Dutch indigo planters and manufacturers, who were born in Aleppo, and before that came from Europe. Tracing my mother's history back even further, to the 1500s, it has been recorded that they were Anabaptists / Mennonite and Remonstrands, who had to flee from religious persecution.

Bob and Norah Love

She and her brothers and sisters were in boarding school in Naini Tal. Her father worked on the Indian railways. Her oldest brother had to work to help my grandparents pay for Mum to go to school. I know that they found this difficult to come to terms with. Her brothers and sisters said she was spoilt by her father. Close relatives were aware that she was very spoilt by Grandad in particular. He was a morose man and could be very critical. He converted to Seventh Day Adventism, due to the influence of his eldest son. My grandmother was not in favour of this, but the family who were living at home joined the Adventists.

Naini Tal lay in the foothills of the Himalayas and was a three-day train journey from where they lived, so for nine months of the year the children never saw their parents. Both boys and girls were in Naina Tal at separate schools, so Mum was able to see her brothers from time to time. Boarding school started when she was seven years old. She and her youngest sister Ida were both very sporty and entered the Olympic trials for the 1936 Berlin Games. She was not selected, but Ida was, although she could not pursue this due to financial constraints.

Dad's father was a hundred per cent Scottish and an architect by profession. After he was married, he moved to Fleet in Hampshire, where Dad was born in 1913. His father had designed many of the homes built for retired Army Officers in 'The Blue Triangle', an area around Fleet and Aldershot.

Dad's parents had met in St Alban's. He had one older sister who had lived throughout her life in Fleet. She was also a nurse and has told me that she remembers a plaque in the operating theatre of the local hospital in honour of her father, who had designed the hospital. In true Scottish style, Christian names as well as surnames of the family continue to be passed on from generation to generation.

During the Depression, Dad was offered a job in the Mercantile Bank of India (apparently because he could swim and play water polo!). He opted for overseas service, was posted to India and met my mother in Bombay, where he had been posted. At the onset of the second world war, he joined the army in India.

My mother and her sister Ida commenced their general nurses' training in St Georges' Hospital in Bombay. My parents, I am told, first met at a cocktail party! They were instantly attracted to each other, their eyes meeting across the room, although some have suggested that this may just have been romantic imagination! They were very friendly, outgoing people and loved socialising; they regularly danced at the Taj Mahal Hotel amongst other places. They both loved dancing. Their relationship continued to blossom and they were married in Poona, earlier than they had intended as the war started and Dad joined up.

Dad was captured in Libya and eventually taken to a prisoner of war camp in Germany, from where he was eventually released after a couple of years and returned to England. My mother made her way to England for the first time. They lived with my paternal grandmother in Fleet. After a few months, Dad returned to work for the Bank in Ceylon, and Mum followed on.

We lived in several countries: India, Pakistan, Ceylon, Singapore, Australia and Hong Kong. I remember a very happy life.

We all came to England several times before we finally settled here in 1956. They were holiday visits to see the family in England. If not in England, we visited Australia to see Mum's mother, brothers and sisters.

From being very worldly, with lots of parties and lots of fun, living around the world, we came to live in England. My parents' lifestyle changed considerably over a few years. Having less money also meant less of the luxuries we had known before – no car or telephone. As my sister and I were not spoilt, we did not really notice it.

I found living in England very difficult. I hated it! I found people very insular, and as they did not seem to believe anything that I shared with them of my life abroad, I stayed silent. Only years later was I able to talk about my life abroad which I had so loved and appreciated.

My family's friends were from all races and colours: Chinese, Malay, American, European, Australian, as well as British. I enjoyed mixing with all races of people, which people in England did not do then. My parents treated all people equally. I only remember attending church once or twice as a child, but when we came to live in England, Mum decided we were to attend church each week, which we did. Early on, Mum became a Christian and taught a Sunday school class. Over time we all became Christians, attending our Anglican church.

There seemed to be a move of the Holy Spirit generally in England during the early '60s, and people were hungry to know more of God and to experience the Holy Spirit in their lives. Even though we attended the local Anglican church, we used to visit Pentecostal churches and went to hear various preachers. I remember my parents holding prayer meetings in our home for those, mainly from the Anglican church, who were seeking to be filled with the Holy Spirit. This would have been in the early 1960s. Many were saved and filled with the Spirit at this time, as well as being baptised by immersion. Mum and Dad were baptised in Frensham Pond. Unfortunately, due to their conviction of their need to be baptised by immersion, they were denounced by their vicar from the pulpit as heretics. He could accept the gift of speaking in tongues but not water baptism. Thankfully, their relationship with the vicar was restored before he and Dad died.

Having had to leave the Anglican church, they attended a local Baptist church where other Anglican friends had gone.

I do not know why my parents came to the West Country. They started off living on a farm with friends in south Devon. From there, after a year or two, they moved to Exeter. They met with various young Christians in the teacher training college and university, and were soon reaching out to the young lads with nothing much to do in Exeter.

I was not living with my parents when they moved to the South West, so only visited them. Things changed gradually, and soon there were people with all sorts of problems coming to live with them and being helped. I was used to our home having people in it as both my parents were always very friendly and sociable.

When I was married, I lived with my family in and around Exeter as well as abroad. Dad was always aware that we needed them as much as they needed us. Strangely, Mum shared with me years later that she wished that she had sat with my father in meetings instead of a few rows away. I have no idea why she did that. I always thought it odd.

My parents were well suited and trained for their life in Exeter, even before they were saved, in reaching out to people; showing friendship; entertaining; mixing with everybody unconditionally, no matter what their race or background. Later, after Dad died, Mum moved to Worthing in her seventies, to help Peter and Jane Richards in the work there for several years. Eventually she was to return to Exeter and spent her final eleven years with us.

My memories of Bob and Nora Love
Anne Simkins

66 John and I moved to Exeter in August 1974 from Walsall with our two young boys aged three-and-a-half and eighteen months. In pursuing what we felt was a call to Nepal, John approached

Mr North about possibly, for a month, joining part of his upcoming visit to south Asia by way of 'spying out the land'. At a planning gathering for their trip in Eddie Horner's hotel in Burford, Mr North suggested to John that he would join him and Dr Jack Kelly for the whole of the six-month visit, which would be to both Nepal and India. Bernard Hull later joined the team too.

Going for six months would mean John leaving his job as a GP and us leaving our rented flat in Walsall. Bob Love was at that same gathering and welcomed us to move to their home at Belmont Road in Exeter for this period.

So we moved. We had two rooms at the top of 23 Belmont Road (affectionately known as 'the big house') and shared in the life of the household and the Fellowship that gathered there. For us, it was both a provision and a privilege. For me, during the months that John was away, it was a very special time. I learnt so much from being part of the day-to-day life of the household and the example of Bob and Nora. Their welcoming heart, love and wisdom for all who came to No. 23 was an inspiration and education.

It was quite a mixed company. Many people passed through the house for many different reasons. I was able to be in nearly all the meetings as they were in the house. Bob led the meetings with a quiet authority and so wisely, and it was a time of much blessing.

Living in a community setting with two young boys (and many stairs!) had its challenges, especially as I was also expecting our third baby. It must also have been a challenge for Bob and Norah to have children in the house, but if so, they never showed it. Everyone in the household and the church were very kind to me and the boys. Hazel Hull, who lived at No. 25, was also expecting a baby while Bernard was away, and our little boys had fun together. Norah kept the house beautifully, and I learnt many tips from watching her create lovely fresh flower arrangements each weekend. Those months were somewhat frustrating for Bob, as he was having to be careful with diet and activities on medical advice; not easy for one so big-hearted! However, when the drains blocked, which was a regular occurrence, he still insisted on being the one to go down and do the clearing.

The travellers returned after five months of journeying in Nepal and all over India. For John, it was an instructive and informative time, and for us both, an experience which would shape the future course of our lives. It was clear though that there was no obvious way for us to move overseas at that time. There had been one possible short-term placement in Nepal, but it seemed inappropriate in the end. So we began to consider our future. In his study, Bob had big maps both of the UK and the world, with pins marking places where Fellowships were developing and where people were serving the Lord. There were many opportunities, and Bob's heart was to see the gospel and blessing spread widely.

In May 1975, our daughter Jo was born; one of three or four babies born in the Fellowship within a month or so. A month later, the household and all the Fellowship were deeply saddened at the sudden passing of Bob from a heart attack. The grace and dignity with which dear Norah bore her loss, and that within the context of an extended household, is something that made a lasting impression on me.

Things opened up for us to move to Nottingham, to join the few who had begun a Fellowship meeting there – one of the pins on Bob's map. We moved in September 1975.

Our year in Exeter was significant for us in many ways. The link with southeast Asia began, and still continues. The example and encouragement of Bob and Norah was very important to us, and we kept in contact with Norah over the years until she died. When we returned to live in Exeter in 1984 (again to live in No. 23 until we found our own house), Norah was living in Worthing. I had the joy of staying with her on at least one occasion when I went to Worthing to share about the work and craft of the Nepal Leprosy Trust.

She always maintained a prayerful interest in India. In the years after she returned to Exeter to live with her daughter Sue, she and Sue were part of our monthly prayer group for India until only months before she died. She wonderfully remembered names and places of all those we prayed for. These included people that John visited and contacts of Mike and Sue and others in the group. It was fascinating in the context of these prayer times to discover more about Norah's own links with India where she grew up and married Bob. She had clearly been part of the social scene in India in the days of the British Raj – as came out in presentations at her funeral.

It was a privilege to have known both Bob and Norah.

A personal tribute to Norman Meeten
David Vine

❝ I first met Norman in September 1969, so I knew him for more than fifty years.

I had been baptised in the Spirit in my home town of Eastbourne in East Sussex, a link with Norman who was from West Sussex. He often referred to this when we were together.

Six months or so later, I arrived in Liverpool to study at the university. There I found a few students in the Christian Union who had had a similar experience to me in the same year. They took me along to The

Norman Meeten

House, the affectionate name for the church where they were meeting, and I was able to enjoy discovering life in the Spirit with many other young men and women.

The church was characterised by vibrant worship, dynamic preaching, love and the gifts of the Spirit.

I had been brought up in a Brethren church under regular ministry of the word, but I had never heard preaching as I heard it then. One particular memory was of Norman speaking for two hours at a small meeting of less than ten students. This was the norm at those meetings – if you will excuse the pun!

Norman and Jenny moved to The Longcroft in the early '70s, and Ann and I followed before we were married in 1974 and became part of the very small group developing there.

Norman played a significant part in my spiritual growth. He was like a father to me, helping me in the early steps of my movement into ministry and eldership. During those forty plus years or so that we worked together, I found him absolutely consistent in his life and ministry.

He was a lover of men and women primarily. He was less concerned about preaching to people as he was about loving them. When he did preach, he was unconcerned about numbers, happy to share with the many or the few alike.

He was supportive, humble, willing to give way to a younger man and fatherlike in his care.

I have been privileged to have had a number of key men who have been role models to me in life, but Norman would be among the very most influential.

A tribute to my 'Dad'
Rajesh Kumar

66 It was in 1976, at the age of ten (and now I am fifty-six), when I was in grade six in my school, I met 'Dad' and 'Mum' with their three sons through a very godly lady named Aunty Hester Withy. She too is now with the Lord. In those days I could not communicate in English, therefore Aunty Hester, since she could read, write and speak good Hindi, used to be my mouthpiece. However, after a few months she moved and went to live in another city, and unfortunately I lost contact with her. I had to depend on my own limited ability to read, write and talk in English.

Mum, Dad and their three sons stayed with Aunty Hester Withy for three months in Mussoorie, and therefore I was able to see them every day and played with their sons every evening after school. During their stay, the birthday of their eldest son, John, was celebrated; they very graciously invited me and my younger sister to join the party. I think we had a lot of fun, without conversing much in English. We laughed when we saw them laughing and ate when they ate! For three months, I played much football and cricket with their three boys.

My little heart was so touched and moved by Mum and Dad's love and care. Love itself is such a strong language, which needs no other tongue for further explanation; I could not understand English but could fully understand the language of love and its warmth. Today I am where I am because of the great miraculous power of the love of God shown and revealed through His only son, Jesus Christ the Lord, and later through Mum and Dad and others; it's their love that drew me near to Mum and Dad. Now, looking back, I can see the plan of God in His love for my own life.

Thank you, dear Mum and Dad, for allowing me to address you as 'Mum' and 'Dad', because you both have loved me and my family so very much and have demonstrated it in variety of ways. Even though I met Mum only a few times, yet she has always loved me and my family. But I was able to meet Dad after 1999, and later on, at his request, I was able to be his travelling companion. Dad was a dad to me but also a guru[150], from whom I learnt how to love and care for people with a pure and clean heart, and never to be selfish; no matter how great my personal need would be, always sharing with others must be my priority. He was such an expositor of God's word, teaching without notes, yet everything in accordance with God's word and accurate in time. Dad lived by faith and proved God's faithfulness. He used to say, "By *His* faith." Matthew 6:33 was one of his favourite verses. Dad, your one great desire was to put God first, no matter what. You were never afraid of sharing the good news. Dad's other favourite verse was Galatians 6:3, where Paul said, *"If a man thinks he is something when he is nothing, he deceives himself."*[151] Paul's life was such an inspiration to Dad and always motivated him.

For about twenty years I did not meet Dad, but every month we used to send a letter. In his letter he always quoted Matthew 6:33 at the end of his writing. I did not understand its meaning then, but now I do, because later when I heard Dad sharing his own testimony, I came to know that the Lord had spoken to him from the same verse three times in the course of ten days. Dad said, "Even though I had nothing, I never doubted God, and He took care of my own personal needs and the needs of my family as well as provided for other good and noble works with which I had been involved."

Simplicity was another virtue in Dad. He often said, "If the Son of God could live the way He lived here on earth, why can't we? Why should we spend all and everything on ourselves when there is so much need out there in the world?" I can testify that Dad hardly spent any money on himself; his heart always went

[150] teacher
[151] Paraphrase

out to others and helped them generously. Wherever Dad stayed during his travel for the Lord's work, he always contributed generously toward his boarding and food. He never became a burden on the brothers.

Fear was never seen or found in Dad. I once asked him, "Dad, are you not afraid or scared to sit with me on my two-wheeler?"

His response was, "My son, if I get afraid or get gripped by the fear, I wouldn't be able to do what the Lord had assigned me to do, and then I would have to sit at home and twiddle my thumbs! We need to learn to trust the Lord, be wise and diligent, not giving a foothold to Satan. And once you have committed your life into the hands of the Lord, then it is His responsibility to take care of you, no matter where you are on the face of the earth."

No one has ever loved me as did my Dad. He always said, *"Do not owe anyone anything, but love them."[152]* My Dad lived what he taught and preached to others. His life and his words matched; he was always so transparent, consistent, honest, kind and compassionate, hardworking and passionate for the Lord and His people. His life through my perspective was like an open book that anybody could read inside out; because what he said, he was, and what he was, he said. For me he was Christ[153] and *"Even as He..."[154]* This was the phrase I had heard Dad say repetitively many years ago when I was just ten years old and would listen to him preach the word, sitting in the back row in a church hall. This was the only English phrase I could understand, and the rest was through his love and care as the years advanced.

Through Dad's love and warm fellowship, I always got inspired to compose songs. Driving on a two-wheeler, sitting with me and holding tight, he so inspired me that the Lord used to give me songs. I have no idea how I have been able to receive the lyrics and melodies along with the words. Most of the songs the Lord gave me were during my time spent with Dad, riding on an old, rusty two-wheeler or sitting listening to him teaching, sharing God's word or while even interpreting for him. For my sake, each time I would interpret for him, he used new English words – he

[152] Romans 13:8 (paraphrase)
[153] See Galatians 4:14
[154] 1 John 1:7 (paraphrase)

would slowly whisper their meanings, and I used to write them down right there on a piece of paper hidden in my Bible – so that I could learn them and increase my vocabulary. I had no difficulty in understanding his English; in fact, I knew what his next sentence would be. On many occasions people commented, "Though you are two people ministering, yet it seems as if just one person is communicating in a way that everything makes sense to us." This was such a great compliment to receive.

I often said, "Dad, how come?"

He said, "My son, when the love of God has been shed abroad in our hearts and we are born from above of the same Spirit of God, it is expected to happen. That's how the world will know we are one with Him and one with one another." He would look into my eyes with a contagious smile and say, "Remember, *'Even as He...'*"

I/we count it such a joy, honour and privilege to have had Mum and Dad come into our lives, making Jesus so real to us, and I must say that every word of their prayers has been answered by the Lord. They have loved both me and my family as their own flesh and blood. We all love you both and have great respect for and honour you, which will always be there till our last breath here on earth, before we too go there where Dad is, with our Lord and Saviour, Jesus Christ.

Spring and autumn were two seasons when Dad visited us. We would clean the whole house and decorate the house with blue curtains, bed sheets, bed cover, blue bowls etc. which was his favourite colour. Often he and I used to be seen in blue. The clothes he often bought for me were mostly blue in colour, which I liked so much. Now, to be honest, I/we miss him greatly, almost every day remembering and thinking of him and remembering the days spent with him. We miss you, Dad, on the two-wheeler, but I know in Spirit you are always there with me/us. Past memories flash right in front of my/our eyes and make our eyes moist, but at the same time our hope is fixed for *"that Day"*[155] – Dad often quoted *"that Day"* – when we will see you, Dad, and others once again. Words will always be inadequate to really thank you dear, dear Dad. I/we love and salute you for being '*you* you'. You were

---

[155] 2 Timothy 4:8

incredible! As I often used to say, and even now I repeat, "You are my hero."

Thanks!

With grateful hearts and gratitude to Him,

Rajesh and Usha and our four daughters.

A tribute to Fred Tomlinson
Peter Moffat

❝ I remember Fred in many ways: as a policeman, a printer, a pastor, a preacher, a person and a pioneer.

The first time I met Fred – and Sheila – was when his brother Dave first took us to a police house in Liverpool where they were living. Night shifts often took him down Devonshire Road, so he knew the area well; and not least a particular café,

Fred and Sheila Tomlinson

for his cups of coffee, which he continued to frequent on many of his trips back from Canada. He was a true Scouse!

Together we would visit some of the significant places in his journey through life. The most talked about were the many stories of his night shifts and the fun they had with their vehicles when all was quiet!

The best thing he taught me were a couple of 'holds' – painful ones – that proved very handy when dealing on occasions with my own boys!

After he left the police, he worked in the print shop of Blakes, the big Ford dealership, in Liverpool city centre, producing their office and workshop paperwork, their brochures and advertising flyers – which sometimes required him to use one of their 'posh' vehicles for a trip with the family to the country in order to get some action pictures for the brochure. He used to let me visit him in his workshop, somewhere up in the attic of the dealership; and he enabled the hiring of vans and minibuses for the Fellowship when we needed them, because he was so well respected and trusted.

He moved into Devonshire Road with the family as a pastoral elder when Norman moved over to the Wirral. It was a difficult time, with refurbishing in progress, bringing some near escapes, and also with many deep needs within the church.

For me, the most memorable aspect of that time came when Fred told me that he often used to miss the chance to preach, having got his word on a Sunday morning, as his nerves left him needing a visit to a rest room before getting up to preach, by which time someone else would have taken up the opportunity!

After moving to Canada, he kept contact with Devonshire Road, coming over sometimes twice a year to preach at conferences and special weekends. I would arrange an itinerary for him around the country which always managed to include at least one Sunday morning here towards the end of his stay – by which time he would have fully recovered from the inevitable jet-lag.

One of the things that always fascinated me about Fred's preaching was the fact that he never moved from the spot where he stood. I am a wanderer and love a wireless mic, but Fred had the ability to remain rooted. The impact of his preaching did not come from anything other than the quality of the man and the integrity of his words. Over the years, Fred's ministry input was a deep source of encouragement and blessing to us as a couple and to the church. There is so much more I could say here. Fred walked with us through our most difficult times; his presence with us was vital to our ability to continue in the work here at Devonshire Road.

Probably the best illustration of the calibre of his character came through a rather strange phone call I received one day. It was from Fred's Aunty Daisy, who was well known to us here. She was quite brief and I wasn't too sure that I had heard her right. The call went something like, "I've just heard from Canada. Fred's fallen off the roof and lost his faith." I should add that at this point we did know that Fred was 'working with the boys' in their construction outfit. So the falling off a roof was within the realm of the possible. But the other part – lost his faith? I would have had far less trouble believing that he had grown another head. Well, I hadn't heard from Canada, so the only thing to do was to call Sheila. It turned out to have been a very painful event involving a very wet day and Fred's forehead twice having an unfortunate and unintended meeting with a piece of 2x4 timber.

He had indeed fallen, but not off a roof. He bore the marks of that day for quite a while, but his faith was as robust as it ever was.

Fred has been the sort of friend who sticks with you through thick and thin. He stuck with us through some of the most trying times. When he visited the UK, he would stay with us and became part of our family – we would always drink more tea and coffee than normal, and usually we'd visit more coffee shops and cafés.

All in all, his departure will leave a huge hole in our lives, but I'd far rather have that great gap, and count it a privilege that we as a family and as a church have had so much opportunity for blessing from Fred's life and ministry.

I was reading one morning in 1 John 3:18, *"My little children, let us not love in word or tongue, but in deed and in truth."* Immediately Fred came to mind as being just that sort of person – he loved in deed and in truth.

Jesus had so impacted Fred's life that security, career, status, finances, and just about anything else you could care to mention, all had to bow before the demands of the one who had laid down his own life for Fred. The security of a lifelong career in the police with a generous pension to follow had no hold over Fred. A settled job and a nice house out in the suburbs could not keep him from the desire to follow his master. Over and over again, Fred was willing to pull up stakes and move at the behest of the one to whom he had yielded his life.

I guess that the challenge that comes to me – and to us all – from Fred's life is simple: am I – are we – willing to be pioneers for Jesus too, and to love in deed and in truth? Fred put his hand to the plough and never looked back. May we do the same.

My friend, Fred
Peter Boyle

❝ When I think of Fred Tomlinson, I will always think of him as my friend.

My wife and I met Fred at an Easter conference in a Baptist conference centre north of Toronto, Ontario. The year was 1974. We were new to the things of God; we had heard and responded to the gospel message, but in hindsight, like Apollos, we only knew the baptism of John!

That weekend conference exposed us to a man and a message that would forever make an indelible impact on our lives.

Later that year, Fred and family immigrated to Canada from the UK and settled in the town where we were living.

I have often used the account of Apollos and Priscilla and Aquila to illustrate the profound effect Fred and Sheila had on our lives. They showed unto us the Way of God more perfectly.

Over four decades have passed since that weekend conference where we heard things from the Scriptures that deeply challenged and blessed us; life-changing things that came from a man who was living the very things we were hearing. I have come to realise how rare this is. "Where are the men who know God?"

We have laboured together in the Gospel over these many decades, with Fred often saying to me, "Pete, you push and I'll steer." He always steered me to the Teacher within.

In November of 2021, my friend Fred entered into the nearer presence of the Lord.

We are so grateful to God for ever causing our paths to cross and our lives to mingle, and that we could experience the sweet friendship of a man sent from God whose name was Fred.

APPENDIX 4

UK Fellowships

A chronological list of all the UK Fellowships (including those that are no more) showing the year that they first began to meet, which was usually within a home:

1964	Queen's Road, Liverpool *
1965	Exeter Christian Fellowship
1965/66	Longcroft Christian Fellowship
1966	Auchenheath Christian Fellowship *
	Rora Christian Fellowship
1966/67	Devonshire Road
1967	Warrington Christian Fellowship
	Birmingham (Raglan Road)
1968	Worthing Christian Fellowship
	Winchmore Hill CF
	Colwyn Bay Christian Fellowship *
1968/69	Reading Christian Fellowship
1969	Otley Christian Fellowship*
	Newcastle *
1970	Lampeter Christian Fellowship
	Broadstairs Christian Fellowship
1971	Eltham Christian Fellowship
	Manchester Christian Fellowship
1972	Bryn Goleu (Llanfairfechan) *
	Leominster Christian Fellowship

1972 (cont.)	Walsall Christian Fellowship
	Wake Green CF, Molesley *
1973	Epsom Christian Fellowship
	Carlton CF, Nottingham
1973/74	Cherith Christian Fellowship, Tiverton
1974	Bramhall Christian Fellowship
	Broadstone Christian Fellowship
1975	Leamington Spa*
1976	Bracknell
	Leigh *
1977	Plymouth *
1978	Holborn Church (Leeds)
1979	Sefton Fellowship
1982	Beccles Christian Fellowship
1983	Sheffield Christian Fellowship *
	Lanark Christian Fellowship
1988	Newton Abbot CF *
2015	Cowbridge (Nr. Bridgend) *
Year unknown	Hitchin *
	Bradford *
	Bristol *
	Crystal Palace *
	Grimsby *
	Ledbury *
	Ripon *
	Whitley Bay *
	Worcester *

* no longer meeting

An alphabetical list of all the UK Fellowships with websites:

Beaconsfield Christian Fellowship (Broadstairs)	www.facebook.com/groups/45782259244
Bramhall Fellowship (Bramhall)	bramhallfellowship.org
Carlton Christian Fellowship (Nottingham)	www.carltoncf.co.uk
Chase Family Church (Enfield)	www.chasefamilychurch.com
Cherith Christian Fellowship (Tiverton)	www.cherithfellowship.org Tel: 01884 258586
Clifton Community Church (Worthing)	www.cliftoncommunitychurch.org.uk
Devonshire Road Christian Fellowship (Liverpool)	www.devyroad.com
Earley Christian Fellowship (Reading)	ecfreading.org
Eltham Green Community Church (Eltham)	www.egcc.co.uk
Emmaus Christian Fellowship (Lampeter, Wales)	www.emmaus-lampeter.org.uk
Holborn Church (Leeds)	holbornchurch.co.uk
Longcroft Church (Wirral)	www.longcroft.church
McKenzie Road Fellowship (Abbotsford, Canada)	www.mckenziefellowship.com

New Covenant Church (Bracknell)	newcovenantbracknell.com
New Life Christian Fellowship (Lanark)	www.facebook.com/NLCFL
Raglan Road Christian Fellowship (Birmingham)	www.rrcchurch.com
Rora Christian Fellowship (Devon)	www.rorahouse.org.uk
Sefton Fellowship (Sefton, Merseyside)	Contact: Mike and Jackie Howard 21 Elton Avenue, Netherton, Merseyside, L30 3SG Tel: (0151) 525 0525 E-mail: *mikeh2607@gmail.com*
Victoria Park Christian Fellowship (Manchester)	www.victoriaparkfellowship.com
Westgate Christian Fellowship (Exeter)	www.westgatecf.org.uk

There is another small group that is part of the Fellowships, which does not have a website but can be contacted by e-mail:

Beccles Fellowship: (Elder: Mike Cadman / *mcjpbds@btinternet.com*)

Social media sites

Facebook   facebook.com/GWNorthFriends
YouTube   youtube.com@GWNorth
Twitter   twitter.com/MrGWNorth
Website   gwnorth.net

Media

New Life Radio   *newliferadiofm@gmail.com*
The Biblebase   biblebase.com

APPENDIX 5

Missionary Outreach Abroad

Countries where the Fellowships have been / are working in:

1. Albania
2. Angola
3. Arctic
4. Argentina
5. Armenia
6. Australia
7. Bolivia
8. Borneo
9. Brazil
10. Cambodia
11. Cameroon
12. Canada
13. China
14. Croatia
15. Cyprus
16. Estonia
17. Falklands
18. Finland
19. France
20. Gambia
21. Germany
22. Greece
23. Greenland
24. Haiti
25. Hong Kong
26. Hungary
27. India
28. Indonesia
29. Ireland
30. Israel
31. Italy
32. Jordan
33. Kenya
34. Malawi
35. Malaysia
36. Mali
37. Mongolia
38. Montenegro
39. Mozambique
40. Myanmar
41. Nepal
42. Nigeria
43. North America
44. North Korea
45. Papua New Guinea
46. Peru
47. Philippines
48. Poland
49. Portugal
50. Romania
51. Russia
52. Saudi Arabia
53. Siberia
54. Sicily
55. Singapore
56. Solomon Isles
57. South Africa
58. South Korea
59. Spain
60. Sri Lanka
61. Sudan
62. Sweden
63. Switzerland
64. Tanzania
65. Thailand
66. Tibet
67. UEA (Abu Dhabi; Dubai)
68. Uganda
69. Ukraine
70. USA
71. Vietnam
72. Zambia
73. Zimbabwe
74. A Himalayan country

About the Author

 Gill Silver was born into a nominally Jewish home, with a father who had left his orthodox Jewish roots for radical communism and a mother who enquired into most religions except for Christianity but found no satisfaction in any.

Leaving a girls' public school at sixteen, Gill first trained privately as a nursery nurse in a Dr Barnardo Home, followed by general nurses' training, midwifery, Bible college and finally teacher training at secondary level. This led to being accepted to teach at secondary level in an independent girls' school in north London, teaching religious studies and establishing a 'Child Care and Development Course'; followed by tutoring posts in further education to student nursery nurses till her retirement, all of which she loved.

It was in her late teens that she was first really challenged about biblical truths in Scripture, but it took a further seven years before she began to understand the serious implications of living 'the normal Christian life' and the life-changing consequences of being brought into true 'new birth'. There have been many ongoing trials and not a few challenges, but through it all, she has known God's abundant grace and long-suffering patience in slowly being conformed to all that He has purposed. To have been brought into the life of the Christian Fellowships, many of which are mentioned in this book, along with personal testimonies, has been something for which she will be eternally grateful; realising that without knowing the reality of receiving a new heart and new spirit, living the Christian life would be an impossibility!

To contact the author, please write to:

Gill Silver
c/o The Longcroft
Storeton Lane
Barnston
Wirral
CH61 1BU